THE OLD LATIN TEXTS
OF
THE HEPTATEUCH

THE OLD LATIN TEXTS
OF
THE HEPTATEUCH

BY

Rev. A. V. BILLEN

M.A., D.D. (Oxford), Ph.D. (London)

HEADMASTER OF ELLESMERE COLLEGE, SHROPSHIRE
FORMERLY SCHOLAR OF UNIVERSITY
COLLEGE, OXFORD

CAMBRIDGE
AT THE UNIVERSITY PRESS
1927

CAMBRIDGE
UNIVERSITY PRESS

University Printing House, Cambridge CB2 8BS, United Kingdom

Cambridge University Press is part of the University of Cambridge.

It furthers the University's mission by disseminating knowledge in the pursuit of education, learning and research at the highest international levels of excellence.

www.cambridge.org
Information on this title: www.cambridge.org/9781316625934

© Cambridge University Press 1927

First published 1927
First paperback edition 2016

A catalogue record for this publication is available from the British Library

ISBN 978-1-316-62593-4 Paperback

CONTENTS

CHAPTER IV. *The Style of the MSS and their place in the Old Latin Version.*

INTRODUCTION

THE most complete authority for the text of the Old Latin Heptateuch is the Lyons Manuscript edited by Ulysse Robert, the first part at Paris in 1881, the second part at Lyons in 1900. This MS gives an Old Latin text of about one-third of Genesis, one-half of Exodus, three-quarters of Leviticus, and the whole of Numbers, Deuteronomy, Joshua and Judges except the last chapter and a half of Judges. More fragmentary, but equally important, are the Munich fragments of the Pentateuch, edited by L. Ziegler (Munich 1883), containing over a thousand verses, about three hundred and eighty from Exodus, a hundred and eighty from Leviticus, three hundred and thirty from Numbers, and one hundred and sixty from Deuteronomy. The Würzburg Palimpsest edited by E. Ranke (Vienna 1871) differs from both the preceding in containing portions of some of the Prophetical books, as well as fragments of the Pentateuch, but in the present work only the latter, consisting of about three hundred and sixty verses (twenty-four from Genesis, one hundred and seventy-two from Exodus, one hundred and thirty-six from Leviticus and twenty-six from Deuteronomy) are dealt with.

These three MSS (which will be denoted respectively by Lugd., Mon. and Wir.) are apparently all of the fifth or sixth century, but of course represent Latin texts which were current before the Vulgate gained general acceptance in the West, that is to say rather in the fourth or (as will be shown in the case of one of them) the third century A.D. Altogether there are about one hundred and twenty verses which are contained in both Mon. and Wir., sixty-eight from chs. xxxi, xxxix and xl of Exodus, forty from chs. xi, xix and xx of Leviticus, and fifteen from Deuteronomy xxxi. Lugd. exists in all these chapters except Leviticus xix and xx, so that we have one hundred verses represented in all three MSS, though some of them are very much mutilated in Mon. Lugd. however is missing for the twenty-four verses of Genesis and the twenty verses of Exodus xxii which are quoted in Wir., and for the long extracts from

Exodus ix to xx (nearly two hundred verses) which are contained in Mon.

The two treatises of Augustine, *Quaestionum in Heptateuchum
Libri VII* and *Locutionum in Heptateuchum Libri VII* (denoted
by *Qu.* and *Loc.*), together give a version of portions of the
Heptateuch which, though not so continuous as those in Wir.,
yet cover altogether a greater number of verses, and represent
a text of more distinctive character than that MS.

In addition to these four principal authorities, most of the
other available evidence for the text of the Old Latin Heptateuch has been collected and examined. This consists of the
quotations in the other works of Augustine (Aug.), in Ambrose
(Amb.), Cyprian (Cyp.), Hilary (Hil.), Jerome (Jer.), Lucifer
(Luc.), Novatian (Nov.), Priscillian (Prisc.), Rufinus (Ruf.),
Tertullian (Tert.), and Tyconius (Tyc.), as well as the passages
quoted in the collection of Biblical texts called the Speculum
(Spec.). One or two passages in which Cassian and Niceta have
used an Old Latin text have also been quoted for comparison;
but the works which may represent third-century texts are more
important for our purpose. Conspicuous among these is the
treatise *Aduersus Iudaeos* which was for so long associated with
the name of Tertullian; but others which are contained in the
Appendix to the Vienna edition of Cyprian, *De Laude Martyrii,
Ad Nouatianum, De Rebaptismate, Aduersus Iudaeos*, and especially *De Pascha Computus* also provide occasional readings
which are of great interest as being almost if not quite contem-
porary with Cyprian.

There are also many Old Latin readings in the *Codex Otto-
bonianus* (Ottob.) which were collected by Vercellone in his
Variae Lectiones Vulgatae (Rome 1860); these vary in length
from a few words to passages of thirty to forty verses, and altogether represent an Old Latin version of about two hundred
verses of Genesis and Exodus. Portions of chs. xii, xiii and xv
of Genesis are given by a Vienna palimpsest edited by J. Bels-
heim in 1885, and the text of Genesis xxv–xxviii used in a
Latin version of Philo's *Quaestiones* was published by F. C.
Conybeare in the *Expositor* (IV. 4); these two authorities are
quoted in this work under the titles Vindob. and Philo respectively. A few references have been made to the Biblical text of

the Latin translations of Irenaeus (Iren.) and Origen (Or.-Lat.);
and the versions of Deut. xxxii and Jud. v used in the Commentary of Verecundus (Verec.) have provided a few readings
of great interest for comparison with Lugd.

The great use which has been made of the lists of words in
the Bobbio Gospels (*k*) and in Tyconius (given in Prof. Sanday's
edition of the former, and Prof. Burkitt's edition of the latter)
showed the advisability of having word lists as complete as
possible for the chief authorities for the text. Such lists have
been made for use in the present work for each of the Old Latin
MSS, and for the Heptateuch quotations of some of the Fathers;
and on account of the extreme importance of Cyprian the list
of words in his case was made for all his Biblical quotations and
not for those from the Heptateuch only. These lists are not
reproduced here but results derived from them have been constantly used. In the examination of the vocabulary of the
Würzburg fragments the portions of the Prophets contained in
them have been entirely omitted from consideration, and wherever the usage of Augustine is referred to, his usage in the two
treatises on the Heptateuch above mentioned is meant unless
the contrary is stated. In the first chapter words are frequently
referred to as primitive without the evidence that they are so
being given. To have given the evidence there would have
interrupted the argument, but in nearly every instance these
words have been assumed to be primitive because they are used
exclusively or characteristically either in Cyprian or the Bobbio
Gospels (*k*); the grounds on which most of them have been
considered 'African' will be found set out in the list of words
which forms the concluding portion of the work. It would have
taken up much more space to make this a complete vocabulary
to the Old Latin Heptateuch, but it is hoped that all interesting
words and all those the usage of which is likely to throw any
light on the Old Latin version have been included.

Considerable use has been made of the readings of the *Codex
Sessorianus* of Cyprian's *Testimonies*, not of course as representing Cyprian's Bible, but as indicating one direction of subsequent revision. The alterations made in Cyprian's Heptateuch
text by this MS are not considerable except in one passage of
special interest (Ex. xxii. 21–24); they are most evident in

Psalms, where half the quotations are entirely reworded, and they are frequent in Proverbs and the Gospels of Matthew and Luke, but less numerous in Isaiah, though half a dozen passages in that book are quite changed. The text of this MS is here generally referred to as the A text of Cyprian, A being its designation in Hartel's edition of Cyprian.

The terms 'African,' 'Cyprianic,' and 'primitive' are used as synonymous, the state of our knowledge of the Version probably making it advisable not to attempt any distinction between these terms at present. The same applies almost as much to the terms 'late' and 'European'; it is possible indeed to see in Novatian at times traces of those characteristics which are probably correctly described as European but can obviously not be classed as late, and there is no doubt a distinction to be made between the Late African and the European types of text; but in view of the close connection between the European types of text and texts (such as the Speculum) which are perhaps correctly described as Late African, the actual points of divergence between the Late African and the European texts are matters to be discovered rather than assumed.

The abbreviations used will probably be readily understood. In addition to those mentioned above for the Latin MSS and Fathers, the abbreviations Gen., Ex., Lev., Num., Deut., Josh., and Jud. are generally used for the seven books of the Heptateuch; O.L. is often used for the Old Latin version as a whole, LXX for the Septuagint, Syro-Hex. for the Syro-Hexaplar, Symm. and Theod. for the versions of Symmachus and Theodotion, and occasionally Arm., Boh., Eth. and Sah. for the Armenian, Bohairic, Ethiopic and Sahidic versions. The MSS of the LXX are always quoted from and denoted by the letters used in the Larger Cambridge Septuagint, a work without which Chapter III at least could not possibly have been written. The number of occurrences of words in various texts is sometimes indicated by fractions; e.g. Mon. 4/6 means that the Greek word in question is represented in Mon. six times, and in four occurrences is represented by the Latin word under consideration. In the case of Augustine such fractions unless otherwise indicated refer only to occurrences in the two treatises on the Heptateuch, and in the case of Wir. only to the Pentateuch (not the Prophetic) portions of the MS. All statements about the occurrence of words in Ambrose or the Speculum refer only to occurrences in their Heptateuch quotations; but on account of the special importance of Cyprian and Novatian as early witnesses, occurrences of words from all their quotations having been collected and tabulated, statements about the usage of these two writers (and in the case of a few special words of Hilary also) refer to all their Biblical quotations.

No attempt has been made to discuss the orthography of the MSS; an adequate treatment of this would have increased the length of the work considerably, and much of the necessary material is already available in the introductions to the published editions of the MSS. The spelling which is usual in the MSS has generally been adopted without comment, and this will explain why e.g. the same prefix appears regularly as ad- in adponere, but as ap- in apparere. To judge however from one or two conspicuous examples of unusual spellings, it seems probable that some evidence could be derived from this source to strengthen the results otherwise arrived at. Thus Istrahel (with a t) is used regularly in Lugd., and its use in the A text of Cyprian, in the text of De Bened. Patr. used by Ambrose in Deut. and in the Didascalia Apostolorum furnishes additional support to the view that Lugd. is European in its text. Peculiarities of declension and conjugation and other points of accidence and syntax are also for the most part omitted; these also can be studied in the introductions to the editions of the MSS, and only a few examples which clearly indicate a primitive literal following of the Greek original are noticed in Chapter IV.

No claim is made that the conclusions arrived at in the present work will prove final, but it is hoped that they will be found incomplete rather than erroneous. As the work proceeded it became obvious that the Biblical quotations of Tertullian and Jerome are more important than might have been expected. The use of primitive Old Latin texts is clear in several of the works of Jerome, and the frequent and peculiar agreements between quotations in Tertullian and later Fathers suggest that Tertullian's text depends more often than has sometimes been supposed on an already existing Latin Version. An examination of all the Biblical quotations in Tertullian, and perhaps in those treatises of Jerome in which he used an ancient Latin Version, will probably throw back some additional light on the subject of the Heptateuch texts. Much remains also to be done on the Lyons Heptateuch, which for the present work has only been carefully and minutely examined where other Old Latin authorities exist with it. It has perhaps been too much taken for granted that the variations in the Old Latin texts correspond altogether with variation in date, but though this is clearly a great, and perhaps the greatest factor, the result of further study of the subject, and perhaps especially of further study of the Lyons MS, may be to establish the conclusion that the separate books of the Bible had from the first more individuality than it has been usual to suppose.

It will not be expected that the study of the text of the Old Latin Heptateuch will throw much light on the progress of Christian life and thought, but it is interesting to notice in the history of a few renderings hints of modification in religious ideas during the third century. The change of *donum* to *munus*, of *festus* to *solemnis*, of *ministrare* to *sacrificare*, and of *uotum* and *uouere* to *oratio* and *orare* are evidently not unrelated to the development of thought in the Christian Church, and are interesting as showing the direction of that development.

In addition to the editions of the MSS and the Larger Cambridge Septuagint, constant use has been made of the Vienna editions, and where these are not yet available, to Migne's editions of the Latin Fathers. Apart from the articles in the Encyclopaedias and Journals and a very valuable chapter in Swete's *Introduction to the Old Testament in Greek*, very little literature so far exists on the Old Latin version especially of the Old Testament. Special mention however must be made of the essay in Sanday's edition of the Bobbio Gospels, and of Prof. Burkitt's Introduction to *Tyconius* and his study on *The Old Latin and the Itala*. None of these three works deals specifically with the Old Latin Heptateuch, but it has been along the lines laid down in those books that the present work has been carried on, and it is to these two scholars, one of Oxford and one of Cambridge, that I am indebted, to the one for having set me on the path of these studies ten years ago, and to the other for the interest which he has taken in the publication of this work.

CHAPTER I

THE VOCABULARY OF THE OLD
LATIN HEPTATEUCH

(a) *The Vocabulary of the Lyons Manuscript*

A N examination of the Lyons Heptateuch soon shows that
this MS is far from homogeneous in its vocabulary and
diction. In fact each of the seven books represented in
it has its distinctive renderings and characteristic phrases, so
that it would be no exaggeration to say that the Old Latin texts
which it furnishes in Exodus and Leviticus differ from one
another as widely as do those used by Tyconius and Lucifer.
Exodus and Deuteronomy indeed have several common characteristics, and the same is true of Leviticus and Numbers, and
to some extent of Genesis and Joshua, but there are very few
words or expressions which are characteristic of the Lyons MS
as a whole, and even the books which are most closely related
show clear signs of independence in other respects.

This fact, though at first sight so unexpected, is so indis-
putably clear, and so important in the study of the MS, that it
seems worth while to set out a considerable part of the evidence
in full. The following are the most noticeable variations in
vocabulary between the different books of this MS:

For ἔτι *amplius* is never used in Lev., Num. or Jud., though found
at times in each of the other books; as between *adhuc* and *iam* Gen.,
Lev. and Jud. seldom or never use *iam*, but Ex., Deut. and Josh.
much prefer it.

Proselytus is used exclusively except in Deut. where we find *aduena*
19/20.

In Lev. *altare* is regularly used; in Ex. and Num. we have *altare*,
altarium and *ara*, but in Deut. (except that *ara* is used for βωμός)
sacrarium or *sacrificium* is used.

In most books *uisus est* is the regular translation of ὤφθη; *paruit*
and *apparuit* are found only in Ex. and Deut., and in these two books
uisus est is found only three times.

Ἔναντι and ἐνώπιον are almost uniformly rendered *ante* in Lev.
(about 65/70). *Ante* is also the usual rendering in Gen., but in Ex.
and Deut. it is seldom used, and *in conspectu* is much the commonest

rendering; the rare *palam* is also used twenty times in Ex. and Deut., but not elsewhere. In Num. *ante, coram* and *contra* each occur about thirty times.

Δόξα occurs several times in Ex. and Num., and is rendered *gloria* in the former, but *honor* in the latter (the 'African' *claritas* also occurs in Num.). *Honor* also occurs in Gen. and Josh., but *gloria* in Lev.

Delinquere and *delictum* are very rare in all books except Lev., but in that book they are nearly always used; *peccare* and *peccatum*, which are used almost without exception in other books, being correspondingly rare here.

Desertum is found in all books, *solitudo* in Deut. and Jud. only. *Eremus* is used in Ex., Lev. and Deut.; in Num. we have the form *eremia* used five times, and *eremus* does not occur.

Erythreum mare is regularly used in Num., but in Deut. *rubrum mare* is more frequent.

Dies solemnis is used always in Ex. but nowhere else, *dies festus* being the equivalent in other books.

Ἄμωμος is always rendered *immaculatus* in Ex. and Lev., but *sine uitio* in Num.

Introire prevails in Gen., Lev., Num. and Josh., but *intrare* in Ex., Deut. and Jud.

Furor (θυμός) is used a dozen times in Deut., but elsewhere is not common. *Indignatio* and *indignari* on the other hand occur several times in Num., but seldom in the other books.

Iste (for *hic*) is found nearly fifty times in Deut., and is common in Gen., Josh. and Jud. It is however rare in Lev. and Num., and is not found at all in Ex.

Iustificatio is used for δικαίωμα in Num. (5/6), elsewhere *iustitia*; in Deut. we also find *aequitas*.

Libare, libatio and *libatoria* are regularly used in Ex., but *litare* and *litatio* in Num.; both words are very rare in other books.

Commorari is frequently used in Gen., Deut. and Josh. (in Gen. generally *morari*) in place of *habitare* and *inhabitare*; it is however never found in other books.

The renderings of γενεά vary very much even in the same book, but the use of *progenies* may be considered characteristic of Ex., while *natio* is rare except in Num.

Except for one occurrence of *nequitia* in Deut., and of *nequia* in Gen., these words, with *nequiter* and *nequissimus*, are found in Num. only.

Σφόδρα is rendered by *nimis* or *nimium* always in Num. and generally in Josh., but never in Ex. or Jud., where *ualde* takes its place; the two are used equally in Gen. and Deut., but in Gen. *uehementer* (otherwise rare) is used much more than either.

Θύρα is rendered *ostium*, always in Gen. and usually in Ex. and

Num., but never in Deut. and Josh. where *ianua* is always found. *Ianua* is also usual in Lev.

Δέρμα occurs frequently in Ex. and Lev.; in the former it is rendered *pellis* (except once), in the latter always *corium*.

Consummare and *consummatio* (τελεῖν, τελειοῦν and compounds) are used in all books except Lev., where *perficere* and *perfectio* always take their place, though these are found nowhere else except twice in Num. In Num., however, *initiari* is more frequently used than either, though it does not occur in any other book.

For ἐντέλλειν and ἐντολή *mandare* and *mandatum* are usual in Num. and Deut., but *praecipere* and *praeceptum* in Gen., Lev. and Josh. For συντάσσειν and προστάσσειν on the other hand *praecipere* is usual everywhere except in Num. where *constituere* occurs frequently.

Primitiuus and *primogenitus* are both used for πρωτότοκος in Gen. and Ex.; in Deut. the latter is never used, in the other four books it is always used.

In Ex. only, but there five times, *proficisci* is used to represent πορεύεσθαι, though it occurs frequently in Num. for ἐκπορεύεσθαι or ἐξέρχεσθαι.

For ἐξιλάσκεσθαι *propitiare* is regularly used in Lev., but elsewhere only twice in Num. xxix; the usual rendering in Num. is *depraecari*, while in Ex. *exorare* is usual.

As an alternative for the common *mundare* we have *purgare* (and *purgatio*) occasionally in Lev. and Num. (καθαίρειν and καθαρίζειν), while *purificatio* and *purificare* are rather characteristic of Ex.

Quemadmodum is very rarely found in Gen., Lev. and Josh., though frequent in Ex., Num. and Jud., and above all (over forty times) in Deut. *Quasi* is very rare except in Lev. and Jud.; in Num. *tamquam* and *secundum quod* (or *quae*) are often found, while in Gen. and Josh. *sicut* is used almost to the exclusion of all its synonyms.

In Gen., Ex. and Deut. *quia* is used five or six times as much as *quoniam*, and it also prevails in Josh. especially in the later chapters; on the other hand *quoniam* is all but regularly used (25/27) in Lev., is much commoner than *quia* in Jud., and is not infrequent in Num. In Gen. *quod* is used twenty times though it seldom occurs elsewhere.

Redimere is always used for λυτροῦν (about twenty times) in Lev. and Num.; in Deut. *eruere* or *liberare* is used.

Sempiternus (αἰώνιος) is seldom used except in Ex., where it is the usual rendering. In Gen., Lev., Num. on the other hand *aeternus* is used about thirty times, but *sempiternus* only once.

In place of the usual *suauitas* which Lugd. always has in Ex. and Num., we find regularly in Lev., but never elsewhere, *suauiolentia*.

Sumere for *accipere* is never found in Lev. or Num., and very rarely in Gen., but it is very common in Ex., Deut. and Jud.

Totus is used for πᾶς a few times in most books; but *uniuersus* is found twenty-five times in Josh. though seldom or never in other books.

As a synonym for *donec* (which occurs in most books) *usquedum* is very common except in Lev. and Num. In Num. *quoadusque*, which is rare in other books, is the commonest rendering; in Lev. the shorter *quoad* is used even to the exclusion of *donec*, though it is found nowhere else in Lugd., and very seldom in the whole of the Old Latin.

Other words characteristic of Ex. are *demptio* (ἀφαίρεμα), *immolare* (θύειν), and *lenire* and *lenitio* (for *unguere* and *unctio*). In Num. may be also noticed the rare compound *concolligere* (six times), *decerptio* for both ἀφαίρεμα and ἀπαρχαί, and an unusually high number of gerundives and ablatives absolute; in Deut. *dies* is regularly used with *crastinus* and *hodiernus*, though this usage is rare in the other books.

The peculiarities of Leviticus are particularly numerous, giving the text of Lugd. in this book a character which distinguishes it not only from the other books of this MS, but also from all the recognised types of Old Latin texts. Thus we have the very rare renderings *abitus* and *uestitus* each four times for στολή, *aeternalis* in ch. vii, *abscisio* and *exceptio* for ἀφαίρεμα, *imprudenter* for ἀκουσίως, *indiligentia* and *indiligens*, *laedere*, *laesio* and *laesura* for ἀδικεῖν and ἀδικία, *mascel* for *masculus*, *peristolum* for περισκελές, *primitiuus* with or even instead of *hircus* (chs. ix and x), *quoad* for *donec*, *regia* for *atrium*, *suauiolentia* for *suauitas*, and *ueruex* for *ouis*. Other renderings which distinguish this book from the rest of Lugd. but are by no means unparalleled in the version are *cremare* used twice for *comburere*, *execratio* five times for *abominatio*, and *induere* for *uestire* (ἐνδύειν). Again *ipse* and *ille* (in place of *is*) are much rarer in Lev. than elsewhere, while only in this book of Lugd. is *seruare* more common than *custodire* for φυλάσσειν.

This list of variations has extended to a considerable length, but there are important conclusions to be drawn from it, and it seemed advisable to show that these conclusions are not drawn from insufficient data. It will be clear at once to anyone who is familiar with Cyprian's Biblical quotations that in many cases, where the usage of the books varies, Lev. and Num. preserve the 'African' or Cyprianic rendering, and that these two books rarely reveal the use of distinctively late forms; as conspicuous examples we may select *altare, cremare, delinquere, delictum, induere, perficere, quasi, quoniam,* and *seruare* in Lev., *indignari, iustificatio, natio, nequiter, nequissimus, nimis* and *sine uitio* in Num., and *introire, purgare* and *purgatio* in both these books; there is also the absence or rareness of *quemadmodum* and *mandare* in Lev., of *sumere, usquedum* and of *dies* with *crastinus* in both Lev. and Num., and probably the use of the Greek words *erythreum* in Num. and *proselytus* in Lev. and Num. In Ex. and Deut. on the other hand later words repeatedly prevail, and there is hardly a single 'Africanism.' As examples we may mention the use of *amplius, intrare* and *usquedum* in both books, of *demptio, immolare, lenire, proficisci, solemnis* and *sumere* in Ex. and of *aduena, appropiare, appropinquare, furor* and *sacrarium* in Deut.

We must not however omit to notice the exceptions to these general statements though they are very few. *Ostium* is evidently earlier than *ianua* but Ex. has a decided preference for *ostium* (12/17) while Lev. prefers *ianua* (20/24). Num. however as well as Gen. nearly always uses the earlier *ostium*, while Deut. regularly has *ianua*. *Iste* for *hic* is also certainly 'African,' but in Lugd. it occurs frequently in Deut. and Josh. (forty to fifty times in each); Gen. and Jud. have it less than twenty times each, Lev. and Num. (where we might have expected it most) only half a dozen times each; it does not however occur at all in Ex. Apart from this frequency of *ostium* in Ex. and of *iste* in Deut. the characteristics of these two books—and perhaps especially of Ex.—seem uniformly late and European.

It would however be a mistake to describe the text of Lugd. as Cyprianic either in Lev. or Num. As will be seen later when the text of this MS is compared with a true 'African' text, it possesses in these books as elsewhere many of the marks of a late text; and even without the aid of direct comparison it is clear that while some later words are almost or entirely absent from the Lugd. text of these two books, there are others which are used almost regularly in Lev. or Num. or both. We have just referred to the frequency of the late *ianua* in Lev.; the rendering of ἄμωμος provides another example, for though in Num. we always find the earlier *sine uitio*, yet in Lev., as in Ex., the late *immaculatus* is always used. These are the most conspicuous examples of late words in Lev. because they are so often repeated, but others will be found when we come to compare the Munich text of Lev. In the Lugd. text of Num. there are also several obviously later usages; *custodire* is generally used for φυλάσσειν (11/14); *deseruire* is the usual rendering of λειτουργεῖν, the Cyprianic *ministrare* being found only once; *mandare* is generally used for ἐντέλλειν (seventeen times), the earlier *praecipere*, which is usual in Lev., being used only twice; and *uestire* is used for ἐνδύειν (2/2) though *induere*, which is used generally in Lev., is evidently the earlier rendering; yet in spite of these later usages the Lugd. text of Num. seems clearly to belong to an earlier stage of the O.L. than any book except Lev.

When the usage of Lugd. varies from book to book, it will be found in nearly every case for which other evidence is available that the form used in Lev. and Num. is earlier than that found in Ex. or Deut. This opens up a new method of verifying possible 'Africanisms,' which may lead to new light on the subject. We may here anticipate by saying that several words which we shall have reason to regard as primitive from the evidence of the Munich MS are found in Lugd. in Lev. and Num. rather than in Ex. and Deut.; examples of such words which, in spite of the absence or uncertainty of evidence from Cyprian, may be regarded as 'African,' are *corium* for *pellis*, *uideri* for *apparere* and *fusile* for *conflatile*.

Against all this evidence of diversity in the various books there are only a few signs of a common vocabulary to suggest the unity of the text of the Lyons MS. Apart from points of orthography (as *e.g.* the constant use of *Istrahel*) which are due to the conditions under which the actual MS was written rather than the character of the text from which the MS was derived, the most conspicuous links between various books are the use of the rare *augere* (or *adaugere*) in Gen., in Lev. (five times) and in Deut. (five times) instead of *adponere* or *adicere*, the use of *honor* instead of *claritas* or *gloria*, almost regularly in Gen., Num. and Josh., of *instanter* and *instantia* for ἐνδελεχῶς and ἐνδελεχισμός both in Ex. and Num., of *maritus* for ἀνήρ in Num. and Deut., and of *saeuus* for πονηρός in Gen. and in Deut., though each of these words is rare and Aug. differs in every case for which his text can be quoted. The preference for *adponere*, *manducare* and *munus* rather than *adicere*, *edere* and *donum*, which is seen throughout, is less noticeable because it is characteristic of all later texts; in view of the general lateness of the MS we may perhaps attach more weight to the fact that *plorare* is used twenty-five times in the MS and *flere* only seven, for *plorare* is evidently the earlier word and it predominates in all books of Lugd. The occurrence of the somewhat rare *morari* and *commorari* in Gen., Deut. and Josh. has been already mentioned; it is not however found at all in the other four books of the Heptateuch, and it is certainly true that the numerous peculiarities of the text of the MS are in the great majority of instances confined to a single one of the seven books.

In fact it is clear that not only the MS as a whole, but even two of the separate books (Lev. and Deut.) cannot be regarded as homogeneous throughout. The MS has a considerable gap towards the end of Lev. (xviii. 30–xxv. 16) and the two and a half chapters which follow this gap show several differences from the eighteen which precede it; *e.g.* all the five occurrences of *(ad)augere* which are found in Lev. are in chs. xxvi and xxvii; *custodire* appears here for φυλάσσειν on each occasion though *seruare* is used everywhere in the first eighteen chapters; *ille* is used instead of *is* over forty times in these two chapters though scarcely more than a dozen times in the rest of the book (the rarity of *ille* in chs. i–xviii is remarkable considering that the MS as a whole shows an exceptional fondness for it); paraphrastic phrases like *qui habitat circa* for τοῦ παρά (Lev. xxv. 47) though common in Ex. are seldom or never found in the earlier chapters of Lev. (contrast vi. 22 where *qui pro* represents the same Greek phrase). These and a few other similar facts seem to indicate that the concluding chapters of Lev. are derived from a different text from the rest of the book. This conclusion, though at first sight unlikely, will not appear so strange when we remember the evidence adduced by Dr Sanday to show that in a MS of the Old Latin Gospels (*e*), which generally has an 'African' text, there is a passage in Matt. xiii which has a decidedly European appearance.

The evidence for the composite character of the Lyons Deut. is even clearer. Dividing the book into two unequal parts to-

wards the end of ch. xii, we have the following clear differences
between the two parts. In the first part *sumere* and *accipere* are
used almost equally (about fifteen times each), in the second
sumere hardly occurs at all though *accipere* is found twenty-five
times; in the first part ἐξολεθρεύειν is rendered *extirpare* (sixteen
times), in the latter *exterminare* (ten times). In the first part
ambulare is generally used for πορεύεσθαι (ten times—elsewhere
only two or three times in Lugd.), in the latter part *ire* is used
practically always; in the earlier part κληρονομεῖν, which occurs
more than sixty times in Deut., is generally represented by
possidere hereditatem, but after ch. xvi *hereditatem* is omitted
and *possidere* is the usual rendering; *is* is unusually rare all
through Deut., but whereas in the early chapters *ille* constantly
takes its place (about one hundred and fifty times) and *ipse* is
rare, in the latter *ille* is rare and *ipse* is used over one hundred
times. In the earlier part *amplius* is used for ἔτι, but in the
latter part *adhuc* or, more frequently, *iam*; *ualde* and *nimis* each
occur seven times in Deut., but while most of the occurrences
of *ualde* are early, all those of *nimis* are after ch. xvii; *plebs*
(λαός) is found in Deut. over forty times in place of the more
usual *populus*, but none of these occurrences are early; *quoniam*
in place of *quia* is not common in Deut. but most of the twenty
occurrences of it are early; in the early part *praecipere* and
praeceptum are the usual renderings of ἐντέλλεσθαι and ἐντολή,
but in the latter part *mandare* and *mandatum* are six times as
frequent; lastly in the first part φυλάσσειν is (except very rarely)
represented by *seruare* and *obseruare*, while in the latter part
custodire is used almost regularly. In each of the cases just
given the evidence is so clear and uniform that taken together
they leave no doubt that there is a decided change in the character of the text as we pass from the early to the late chapters
of the book. It will be noticed that of the words distinctive of
the early chapters *seruare* (with *obseruare*), *ambulare* and *quoniam*
point to an earlier type of text, as does the absence of *plebs*,
mandare and *mandatum*; on the other hand the avoidance of
sumere, the preference for *nimis* rather than *ualde*, and for *iam*
and *adhuc* rather than *amplius* seem to show that in some
respects the latter part of Deut. has more affinity with the
earlier types of text. As a matter of fact no part of the Lyons

Deut. can be regarded as early; the Cyprianic characteristics are few, and the general character of the book is in all parts decidedly European.

It is more difficult to attach a definite character to the text found in Gen., Josh. and Jud., because in each of these books we have a more confusing mixture of early and late forms. Certainly none of these three books has so many or such clear primitive marks as the Lugd. text of Lev. and Num., while each of them has more than Ex. or Deut. In Gen. the early characteristics seem more numerous than the later, while in Josh. and Jud. the later words are more noticeable. Thus in Gen. the regular use of *adhuc* and *ne forte*, the frequency of *totus* and *iste*, and the rarity or absence of *sumere* and *mandare* are early, though the use of *custodire*, *furor* and *uniuersus* points as clearly in the opposite direction. The prevalence of *nimis*, the frequency of *iste*, and the almost entire absence of *mandare* in Josh. and the frequency of *quoniam* and *adhuc* in Jud. are the chief early signs in these two books, but there are many more regular or prevailing usages which seem distinctly late.

A few unusual renderings are found in these three books. We have already noticed the frequent use of the somewhat rare words *morari* (and *commorari*) in Gen., Josh. and Deut. (forty to fifty times in all) and *honor* in Gen., Josh. and Num.; *uniuersus* is another word which is characteristic of Josh., occurring there twenty-five times, though elsewhere in the MS only five times, three of which are in Gen. *Capere* is used a dozen times in Josh. and Jud., practically always in the perfect tenses; this word also is very rare in the Old Latin, the compound *accipere* or (in some later texts) *sumere* being the usual rendering of λαμβάνειν. Another characteristic rendering of Gen. is *uehementer* (σφόδρα) in place of the early *nimis* or the later *ualde*; this word is also rare in the O.L., though found again in Lugd. once in Ex. and once in Josh. Uncommon words, however, are equally conspicuous in the other books of Lugd.; e.g. *laedere*, *laesio*, *quoad* and *suauiolentia* (Lev.), *initiari* (τελεῖσθαι) and *eremia* (Num.), *inchoare* and *sacrarium* (Deut.), are seldom or never found outside one particular book in which they are frequently used, so that the general impression received in passing from one book of this MS to another is that the difference in the texts is as great as that which exists between any two of the Old Latin authorities.

(b) The Vocabulary of Augustine's Treatises "Quaestiones et Locutiones in Heptateuchum"

Our next most extensive authority for this part of the Old Latin Bible is the Munich MS, but before proceeding to the examination of its vocabulary we may consider the vocabulary of two treatises of Augustine—*Quaestionum in Heptateuchum Libri VII* and *Locutionum in Heptateuchum Libri VII*—which together give us a Latin version of several hundred verses of the Heptateuch. These two treatises were written about the same time, and evidently represent the same type of text. It is well known that Augustine used texts of very different kinds, and the variations between quotations found in earlier and later works of his are often very great, but the common quotations in *Qu.* and *Loc.* not only agree with each other, but nearly always agree against quotations of the same passage in other works of Augustine where such exist. A tabulation of the words found in each of the two treatises showed the same phenomena present in each, and we can therefore take the evidence of the two treatises together as representing one of the texts used by Augustine. The quotations in these two works are fairly well distributed over the Heptateuch, and provide sufficient data to trace any variations there may be in the characteristic vocabulary of the seven books; the quotations in Augustine's other books are confined on the whole to a rather limited number of often-quoted passages—especially of Gen.—and in the present section their evidence is omitted altogether.

When, therefore, the words used in these two works of Augustine are collected and examined, it is again found that there are obvious differences of rendering in the various books of the Heptateuch. Thus *adponere* and *adicere* are found with equal frequency in Gen., Lev. and Jud.; but in Ex. and Deut. the former is used and in Num. the latter, in each case to the exclusion of the other. Δῶρον is rendered *donum* in Lev. (six times) but *munus* in Gen., both words being used in Num. In several books both *eremus* and *desertum* are found, but in Num. the former is always used (three times) and in Deut. always the latter (also three times). *Cibus* and *esca* are each used twice in Lev., but only the former is used in Num. and only the latter in Gen. *Iste* is frequently used for *hic* in Num. (twelve times) and in Lev. (nine times); it occurs half a dozen times in Deut. and about the same number in Josh., but is almost entirely absent from Gen., Ex. and Jud. Λειτουργεῖν is rendered by *ministrare* regularly in both Num. and Deut., but on the only occasion on which it is represented in Ex. *deseruire* is used. For ἐντέλλεσθαι and ἐντολή we have *praecipere* and *praeceptum* in Lev. (6/8) and in Ex. (3/3), but *mandare* and *mandatum* in Deut. (9/9) and Jud. (4/5); in the other books the occurrences of the two are nearly equal. Καθαρίζειν and καθαρισμός are represented six times in Lev., three in Num. and two in Ex.; in Lev. *purgare* and *purgatio* are always used, in Num. *mundare* or *emundare*, and in Ex. *purificare* and *purificatio*. In Ex. and Deut. the European *uniuersus* as well as the common *omnis* is used, but not the 'African' *totus*; in Num. *totus* is found, but not *uniuersus*. Several other examples, some of which are more striking than these, will be given shortly, but those already mentioned will be sufficient to indicate a change in the manner of representing the same Greek word in passing from one book to another.

When the words distinctive of each of the seven books of the Heptateuch are collected, it will be found that in Lev. and Num. the characteristic words are in nearly every case 'African.' From each of these two books fourteen to sixteen examples could be given, while on the other hand very few words indeed which are late or European are prevalent in either book. In Gen., Ex. and Deut. on the contrary the early forms are few compared with the later ones; while in Josh. and Jud. 'African' and late characteristics seem to be present in about equal numbers.

It will not have escaped notice that Augustine seems to agree with Lugd. in having a more 'African' type of vocabulary in Lev. and Num., and a later one in Ex. and Deut. They agree further in having a more mixed vocabulary in Josh. and Jud., though with this difference, that while in Lugd. the later type prevails in these books, in Augustine early and late forms are found with equal frequency. They differ also in Gen., which in Augustine is as late in vocabulary as Ex. or Deut., whereas

in Lugd. it is rather the earlier characteristics which are conspicuous. The general similarity of our results for Augustine
and Lugd., however, naturally leads on to the enquiry whether
the two agree in their actual variations in rendering the same
Greek word. To some extent at least they do; both use *aduena*
in Deut. (Aug. 3/3, Lugd. 19/20) but *proselytus* in Lev. and
Num. (Aug. 4/4, Lugd. 20/20)—a truly remarkable agreement.
In both *apparere* (or *parere*) is used more frequently than *uideri*
in Ex. and Deut., though it never occurs in Lev. and Num.;
we notice however that in Gen. Augustine always uses *apparere*
but Lugd. always *uideri*. Augustine always uses *demptio* in Ex.
and *ablatio* in Lev. for ἀφαίρεμα; Lugd. has these and other
renderings also, but agrees in that *demptio* is used in Ex. only
and *ablatio* in Lev. and Num. only. Yet more noticeable is
dies festus, because this (evidently the more primitive form) is
used by both, not only in Num. but also in Deut., where primitive forms are seldom found in either; while *dies solemnis* is used
by both in Ex., and by Augustine in Lev. in a chapter which is
missing in Lugd. In both *ne quando* prevails in Ex., but the
earlier *ne forte* in Gen.—one of the few 'Africanisms' in Augustine's Gen. Augustine and Lugd. regularly use *sine uitio* in
Num., elsewhere however Augustine uses *sine macula* but Lugd.
immaculatus. In both *introire* prevails in Lev. and Num. (Aug.
10/12, Lugd. 43/56) but *intrare* in Ex. and Deut. (Aug. 14/16,
Lugd. 60/72); in Gen. however Augustine uses *intrare* (9/10),
while in Lugd. *introire* is twice as common as *intrare*. *Sumere*
is used by each more frequently than *accipere* in Ex., occasionally in Deut. and Jud., but never in Lev. and Num.; the usage
in Gen. again provides a clear contrast, for in that book Lugd.
uses *sumere* only twice (*accipere* occurring more than fifty times)
while in Augustine *sumere* is about twice as common as *accipere*
(10/16). As between *quoniam* and *quia* both show a decided
preference for *quoniam* in Lev. and Jud., this word being in
each case at least seven times as frequent as *quia*. This is especially significant because in other books *quoniam* is comparatively
rare in Lugd.; the only other book in which it is at all common
is Num. (twenty-four times), and this is another book in which
Augustine shows a decided preference for it. It is also noticeable that *quod* is used in Gen. by Augustine in place of these

words four times, and that in that book it is used nearly twenty times by Lugd.; yet it is found nowhere else in Augustine and only two or three times elsewhere in Lugd. It is perhaps not a mere coincidence that some other Latin authorities also (such as Speculum, Tertullian and Wir.) use *quod* occasionally in Gen., but seldom or not at all in other books of the Heptateuch.

There are one or two interesting peculiarities in the text of Josh. and Jud. which may be noticed here. Augustine has *commorari* three times in Josh. (and not elsewhere); we have already mentioned that this word is used forty times in Lugd., and it happens that half of these occurrences are in Josh.; the word is found in other Old Latin texts (not Cyprian), but only rarely. We have already noticed that *capere* (or rather the perfect *cepisse*) is used a dozen times by Lugd. in Josh. and Jud. in place of the usual *accipere* or the late *sumere*; it is used also a few times in these same books by Augustine, a remarkable connection seeing that the simple verb is found nowhere else in the O.L. Heptateuch. In Josh. ii and vi Augustine and Lugd. both use *meretrix* for πόρνη but in Jud. xi both use *fornicaria*; both these words are quite common, but the coincidence, if it is only a coincidence, is rather remarkable.

This list of coincidences, however, striking as it undoubtedly is, must not be taken as implying an identity of vocabulary in Lugd. and Augustine, even in the books where they are most alike; we shall see in the next section that in Lev. Augustine constantly agrees with the Munich MS against Lugd.; and against the above list of coincidences we should have to place many differences of usage. Augustine *e.g.* generally uses *edere* in Lev. and Num., but Lugd. prefers *manducare* everywhere. The distribution of synonyms for *ante* and for *sicut* will also show differences between the two as well as agreements. Lugd. and Augustine agree in a prevailing use of *ante* in Gen. and Lev. They agree too in Ex. not only in using *in conspectu* more than any of its equivalents, but also in a frequent use of *palam* —a word which Augustine uses in no other book though it is also conspicuous in Lugd. Deut. In Num. the two agree in using *contra* frequently, but differ in that *in conspectu* is common in Augustine but rare in Lugd., while *coram*, though very frequent in Lugd., does not occur in Augustine in this book.

Augustine's clear preference for *coram* in Deut. and Josh. is also not shared by Lugd. So with regard to synonyms of *sicut*; Augustine uses *quomodo* frequently in Lev. but only seldom elsewhere, whereas in Lugd. *quomodo* is common only in Jud.; *quemadmodum* is very rare in Augustine except in Gen. and Deut., but in Lugd. it is very common especially in Ex. and Deut. Augustine and Lugd. however have a remarkable agreement in using *secundum quae* in Num. but not elsewhere.

But, though the differences of usage in Augustine and Lugd. are considerable, the agreements pointed out above are remarkable enough to demand some explanation. Even in Gen., where the divergence of vocabulary is most clearly marked on account of the lateness of Augustine's text, we have the use of *quod* in both in place of *quia* or *quoniam*; and the contrast which each presents between an earlier type of text in Lev. and Num. and a later one in Ex. and Deut. is so conspicuous that there must be some explanation of it. It is most unlikely that the agreement is merely accidental—that in the same two books both Augustine and Lugd. happened to select MSS of a later type, and in two others used MSS with an earlier type of text, but this becomes a possible explanation if the revision of Ex. and Deut. preceded that of the other books, so that a revised Ex. and Deut. were in common use at the same time as an earlier 'edition' of Lev. and Num. A reference to the index of quotations in Cyprian, Lucifer and Speculum will show at once that Lev. and Num. were little used in comparison with Ex. and Deut., and for this reason they may have remained unrevised for a longer time. This may seem rather an unnatural explanation but perhaps it is more likely than any other. The alternative would be to suppose that most or all of these differences between the four books which appear in both Augustine and Lugd. were characteristic of the original translations of the respective books, and have thus survived in both their texts; in this case however we should expect them to be reproduced to some extent throughout the whole of the Old Latin version, and to be especially conspicuous in the earliest forms of the version; and it is a fatal objection to such a theory that most of the common characteristics of Augustine and Lugd. in Ex. are quite clearly not primitive, and that many of the early words

characteristic of their Lev. and Num. certainly found a place
in the earlier texts of Ex. also. Such words as *demptio, intrare,
solemnis* and *sumere* (to take four clear examples from the words
which are characteristic of Ex. both in Augustine and Lugd.)
cannot come down from the primitive Old Latin Ex., for they
are conspicuously absent from the Exodus texts of Cyprian and
the Munich MS (which will be shown in the next section to
have a primitive text) though their 'African' equivalents are
frequently found; and words which we should have to regard
as characteristic of the primitive Lev. or Num., such as *altare,
cremare, delictum* and *sine uitio*, are used in the earlier Cyprian
or Mon. not only in these two books but in others also. In fact,
as will be seen later, the Würzburg MS in the latter part of Ex.
shows a curious mixture of the two types of vocabulary, and
early and late equivalents of the same original used in close
proximity seem to show the O.L. text in a transitional stage
between the earlier form of Cyprian and Mon. and the later
form which is seen in Augustine and Lugd. It seems therefore
that the differences found in both Augustine and Lugd. in
respect of vocabulary when Ex. and Deut. are compared with
Lev. and Num. are not to be explained by assuming these
differences to have been a feature of the O.L. version from the
beginning, but rather by the supposition that both use a partially revised text of Lev. and Num., and a more thoroughly
revised Ex. and Deut. The use of *quod* in Gen. by Augustine,
Lugd. and Speculum may seem more like the survival of a
primitive feature of the translation of that book; even this
however is uncertain for Cyprian never uses *quod* in Gen.,
having *quoniam* even in xlviii. 17, one of the places where Lugd.
has *quod.*

It would be interesting to examine the quotations from the
Heptateuch in the other Latin Fathers with a view to tracing
any change in the character of their text as they pass from one
book to another. In no case however is the evidence sufficiently
extensive to allow a conclusion to be drawn with security. In
the Speculum *e.g.* early features appear occasionally in each
book mixed with what seems on the whole to be a late and degenerate text, but a few results of an examination of the Speculum usage may suggest a conclusion though only tentatively.

Sumere is as common as or more common than *accipere* in each book except Lev., where *accipere* only is used (4/4); the early *indignatio* is found once in Num. (for θυμός) but not elsewhere in the Heptateuch; *donum* is used in Lev. but *munus* in Ex. and Deut.; *ostium* in Lev. and Gen., but *ianua* in Deut.; *introire* in Lev. (and once in Deut.) but *intrare* in other books; *totus* is found in Num. and Deut., *uniuersus* in Gen.; *adicere* in Lev. and Deut. but *adponere* in Ex. On the other hand *aduena* is found not only regularly in Ex. and Deut. (eight times) but generally in Lev. also (3/4), *proselytus* being found in Num. and once in Lev. Some of these usages may be accidental, and in most cases the occurrences are limited to one or two in each book, but as far as they go they seem to point to the survival of more primitive elements in Lev. than in other books. From the above examples it might appear that the Deut. text of Speculum contains numerous early marks; especially as, in addition to the above, we can quote *cremare, egens, eicere, grandis, ministrare* and perhaps a few others; but on the other hand a longer list of distinctly European or late words could be quoted from Deut. than from any other book (of the Heptateuch) in the Speculum. A count of distinctly early and late words in Speculum would indicate that the early O.L. text survives most in Lev., Num. and Jud. and least in Ex. and Josh. It must however be remembered that the evidence from which these conclusions are drawn is very limited in amount.

The evidence of Ambrose, though even more scanty, is, as far as it goes, in the same direction. His quotations from Lev. are indeed altogether too few and fragmentary for any conclusion, but his quotations from Num. are more numerous. In the next chapter we shall see that the resemblance of some of the texts he used to Lugd. is quite as clear in Num. as in any other book, and if the words used by Ambrose which have any appearance of being 'African' are collected the majority of those used in the Heptateuch will be found in the book of Numbers. It is for example in Num. that Ambrose uses *donum* for *munus*, *ministrare* (λειτουργεῖν), *natio* for *gens*, *obseruare* for *custodire*, *promouere* (ἐξαίρειν and ἀπαίρειν), and *quoadusque* for *usquedum*. In most cases the later equivalents of these words can be most easily quoted from Gen., but this is because Num. and

Gen. provide most of Ambrose's quotations from these early books of the Bible. From Gen. however we can quote a frequent use of the earlier *adhuc*, and for the later *amplius* we have to go to Deut. where it is regularly used. We may notice also that the late *plebs* (for *populus*) is found only in Ex. It will be shown later that the Würzburg MS in Lev. seems to have a similar text to that which it has in Ex., but with this exception all our authorities, in which the evidence is sufficient to allow any conclusions to be made, seem to retain more features of the primitive Old Latin in Lev. and Num. than elsewhere.

It may be remarked in concluding this section that the definite and distinct character of Augustine's version in the various books of the Heptateuch shows that his Latin text in *Quaestiones* and *Locutiones* does on the whole represent a genuine form of the Old Latin version. Working doubtless with the Greek text before him it might be thought that he frequently gives his own rendering of the original; this may occasionally be so in *Loc.* not only when he definitely contrasts the literal rendering with the rendering found in Latin MSS, but also in other places where he is not so explicit; but unless the Latin text used were on the whole that of a definite MS before him, we should certainly have found a greater uniformity in his manner of translating the same original throughout the seven books of the Heptateuch than is found either in *Qu.* or *Loc.*

(c) The Vocabulary of the Munich Manuscript

The results of an examination of the Munich fragments of the Pentateuch (which will be denoted by Mon.) will be made clearer if we consider the MS in three sections instead of as a whole. The section which will be considered first, and which comprises nearly half the MS, consists of the latter part of Exodus (ch. xxxi to the end), Leviticus, and the latter part of Deut. (ch. xxii to the end). The second section consists of the surviving parts of Num. and a passage in the earlier part of Deut. (chs. viii to x); the third is formed by what survives of the earlier part of Ex. (chs. ix to xx). Of these three sections the whole of the second and the greater part of the first (except Lev. xviii. 30 to xx. 3) are represented in Lugd.; but no part of the third section is in that MS. It will be found that each of these three sections has its distinct characteristics.

(1)

The first section is remarkable for the almost uniformly primitive character of its vocabulary. From Ex. xxxi to the end of Lev. we have scarcely a dozen words (in three hundred verses) which have any appearance of being late or European. This primitive character is well preserved in Deut. xxii and xxiii, but in Deut. xxx to xxxii we get a more noticeable admixture of late elements, nearly a dozen European words being used in the last sixty verses of Mon. Even here however the general primitive character of the text is clear.

A comparison of the text of this first section with Lugd. shows that where there are alternative renderings in use in the O.L. version it is the exception rather than the rule for the two MSS to agree. It is impossible to give here all the variations in vocabulary between the two MSS since they would amount to several hundreds; perhaps the texts of the two MSS in all these chapters are as different from one another as any two texts of any part of the Old Latin Bible. The interesting point about these variations is that in the great majority of cases Mon. gives the primitive equivalent and Lugd. the later equivalent of the original; and this is so not only in Ex. and Deut. but also in Lev. where as has been already shown Lugd. is on the whole decidedly earlier in vocabulary than in the other books now under consideration.

The following list gives some of the words in Mon. which are characteristic of Cyprian or of *k*[1]; and can therefore with confidence be pronounced 'African'—in each case the later equivalent is added as given in Lugd.:—*accipere* for *sumere* (often), *alere* for *nutrire*, *altare* for *ara* (often), *ambulare* (πορεύεσθαι) for *incedere* (often), *coniux* for *uxor* (five times), *cremare* for *comburere* (twice), *curare* for *sanare* (twice), *delinquere* and *delictum* for *peccare* and *peccatum* (in Ex. and Deut.), *edere* for *manducare* (often), *eicere* for *educere* (six times), *festus* for *solemnis*, *finis* for *consummatio*, *fortitudo* for *uirtus*, *grandis* for

---

[1] *Codex Bobbiensis*, the most primitive Old Latin Gospel MS, edited in 'Old Latin Biblical Texts' by Wordsworth and Sanday.

magnus, illic and *illoc* for *ibi, imperare* (συντάσσειν) for *praecipere*
(twice), *induere* for *uestire, introire* for *intrare* (often), *iste* for *hic*
(often), *ministrare* for *deseruire, nequam* for *malus, nouellare* for
plantare, obseruare for *custodire* (often), *ostium* and *porta* for
ianua, perimere for *occidere, plangere* for *lugere, populus* for *plebs,*
praecipere and *praeceptum* (ἐντέλλεσθαι and ἐντολή) for *mandare*
and *mandatum* (often), *quoadusque* for *usquedum* (four times),
quoniam for *quia* (often), *sacrificare* for *immolare, sermo* for
uerbum, totus for *omnis* (often), *unguere* and *unctio* for *lenire* and
lenitio.

In contrast with these numerous examples of 'Africanisms'
in Mon. which are replaced by their later equivalents in Lugd.,
the number of places in which Lugd. contains an earlier word
than Mon. is very small, so small in fact that a complete list of
them can be given here. In Ex. there is but one example, Lugd.
having *potare* where Mon. has *dare bibere* (xxxii. 20). Even in
Lev. where Lugd. contains several 'Africanisms' there are only
two or three places where Mon. has a later equivalent for a word
in Lugd.; indeed in view of the fact that Lugd. here has so
many marks of an early date, the almost consistent priority of
Mon. forces us to regard it as belonging to the very earliest form
of the Latin version. The early *delinquere* and *delictum* are usual
in the Lugd. Lev., even in chs. iii and iv where Mon. has
peccatum and *peccare* as frequently as their 'African' equivalents; Lugd. also in Lev. avoids almost entirely the later *man-*
dare and *mandatum*, but in Lev. iv. 13 *mandatum* is found in
Mon.; this however is quite exceptional, for in other books Mon.
frequently has *praecipere* and *praeceptum* where Lugd. has
mandare and *mandatum*. It is also possible that *moratio* of Mon.
(Lev. iii. 17) is later than *habitatio* which is there used by Lugd.;
moratio does not occur in any other early text, but is rather a
rare word and it is not perhaps certain that it is distinctly late.
Towards the end of Deut. we again meet with a few examples
of early renderings preserved in Lugd. but not in Mon. Thus
we have in Lugd. *iste* (twice), *natio, iam* and *exire* where *hic,*
generatio, ultra and *egredi* are found in Mon.; these however are
quite contrary to the usual practice of the MSS, for Mon. uses
iste frequently and *natio* twice where Lugd. has later equivalents; *ultra* is found only in this one place in Mon. (Deut.

xxxi. 2), *adhuc* being the usual equivalent; while the use of *egredi* by Mon. in Deut. xxviii. 25 is parallel to its use by Cyprian in Deut. xxiii. 23 where Lugd. again has *exire*. The half-dozen cases therefore in which Mon. has a later word than Lugd. are quite exceptional, being altogether contrary to the usual practice of the MSS. The conclusion thus reached is supported by the vocabulary of Mon. in Lev. xix where Lugd. does not exist, and where, in addition to further occurrences of some of the 'Africanisms' mentioned above, we have also *in crastinum, egens, insidiose, odio habere, perficere* and *profanare*, but not a single word which can be called distinctively late.

The list of 'Africanisms' in Mon. which was given above seems to be such a long and clear one, and the words pointing to the opposite conclusion are comparatively so few and uncertain, that we have a very strong presumption that where Mon. and Lugd. differ Mon. has the earlier and Lugd. the later equivalent. We may feel doubtful in the case of words used only towards the end of Deut., for Mon. evidently has a later admixture there; but in the case of the following words we are probably justified in regarding their use by Mon. as establishing their primitive character with practical certainty, though it would be rather doubtful judged only by the usage of Cyprian and *k* because either the evidence of these authorities is scanty or their usage varies. Some of the words now to be given have already been tentatively classed as 'African' by earlier investigators, and might therefore have been put in the previous list, but they are included here since the new evidence provided by their occurrence in Mon. is especially valuable and practically decisive as to their 'African' character:—*aes* for *aeramentum, animus* and *animatio* for *ira* (θυμός), *aulaea* for *atrium* (αὐλαία), *donum* for *munus, esse* for *fieri, eximere* (ἐξαιρεῖν), *iter* for *uia* (often), *pergere* for *uadere, purgare* and *purgatio* for *mundare* and *mundatio, serpens* for *repens* and *reptile* (often), *superesse* (κατα-λείπεσθαι), *uelut* or *quomodo* for *sicut, sine uitio* for *immaculatus, uociferari* for *clamare* and *uolucer* for *uolatile*.

There are yet other words which we may, from their use in Mon., regard as probable 'Africanisms' even though support from Cyprian and *k* is lacking; such words would be *collectio* for *congregatio, condicere* for *praecipere, corium* for *pellis, foedare* for *humiliare, fucatus* (κίβδηλος) for *monstruosus, in gyrum* and *in gyro* for *in circuitu, importare* (ἐπάγειν), *oblatio* for *demptio*, *placatus* and *placatorium* for *propitiatus* and *propitiatorium*, *residuus* for *reliquus, sancire* for *sanctificare, trahere* (ῥεῖν) for *fluere, uarietas* and *uarius* for *lepra* and *leprosus*, and *uitiligo* for *lepra*; and to these might be added some of the unusual words for σφάζειν, *iugulare, laniare* and *mactare*, and perhaps *secundum quae* for *sicut*.

In the case of one or two of these words there is some evidence supporting the view that they are 'African' though they do not occur in Cyprian or *k*; e.g. *residuus* is used in *De Pasc. Comp.*, *uarietas* and *uarius* by Tertullian and in the Epistle *Ad Nouatianum*; it is however likely that some of these words are peculiarities of Mon. rather than ordinary 'Africanisms.' Mon. certainly has a few unusual words such as *aeuum, alites, inuolare* and *proles* which do not appear to be primitive, and it is possible that some of the words just given (including perhaps *in gyrum* and *sancire*) ought rather to be classed with these as rare, but not clearly early, words.

It is interesting to notice that many of these words, the 'African' character of which is confirmed or suggested by their use in Mon., are also used by Lugd. and Augustine in Lev. and Num., the two books in which they are often 'African' in vocabulary; among such words are *corium, donum, fusilia, purgare, quomodo, residuus, secundum quae, sine uitio, superesse, uelut* and *uolucer*. The double line of evidence increases the probability that these words really are 'African,' and in the case of the other words in the above list the evidence from this further source is non-existent rather than contradictory.

The wide divergence between the vocabularies of Mon. and Lugd. has already been noticed; we see clearly how great the divergence really is when we begin to collect coincidences in vocabulary where coincidence has any real significance. Except towards the end of Deut., where Mon. has a later element in its text, such agreements are not at all common. We happen however to have four close together in Ex. xxxii, viz. *crastina die, uirtus, ne quando* and *sempiternus*; these are all late or European words, and therefore quite opposed to the usual practice of Mon., the 'African' equivalents of all four being found elsewhere in that MS. As they all occur within the space of a few verses (5–13) it seems likely that Mon. has been influenced just here by a later text, though there are many 'Africanisms' which survive in the immediate neighbourhood. Towards the end of Deut. we have more connections between the two MSS.; in the thirtieth and following chapters we have *adhuc*, *natio* and *quomodo* which are all rather 'African' and therefore rare in the Lugd. text of Deut., but we have a longer list of words common to the two MSS (*congerere*, *consummare*, *esca*, *furor*, *intrare*, *plebs* and *quemadmodum*) which are late or European. Of these *congerere*, *esca*, *plebs* and *quemadmodum* are solitary examples of late forms for which elsewhere Mon. regularly uses the earlier equivalents; the use of *intrare*, though repeated here in Mon., contrasts with a clear preference for *introire* elsewhere; *furor* also is repeated in this section, but it contrasts with the use of *animus* and *animatio* by Mon. in Ex. xxxii; nearly all these words, though distinctly opposed to the general usage of Mon., are used here in accordance with the regular practice of Lugd.; and they show that the primitive character of Mon. has been obscured towards the end of Deut. by the incorporation of later elements similar to those which are found throughout Lugd. That these European elements, however, are insertions from another text not altogether harmonising with that into which they have been incorporated is illustrated by the fact that, in the very first verse of Deut. xxx represented in Mon., that MS has four clear 'Africanisms' remaining in its text which are not reproduced in Lugd.

Elsewhere also Mon. is occasionally found agreeing with Lugd. in a rendering which seems late. Examples of this however are so few that each can be mentioned separately. *Appropinquare* (Ex. xxxii. 19), *mox* (Ex. xxxi. 18) and *ianua* (Lev. iv. 4) are late words of which the early equivalents are used frequently by Mon.; *ostium* e.g. is used over a dozen times, but *ianua* in this place only. *Consummare* and *sempiternus* are rather different, each being used three or four times, while the Cyprianic equivalents *perficere* and *aeternus* are used but once each. The use of *excelsus* by Mon., four times in all, is noticeable, for *altus* is used by Cyprian in Gen. xxii. 2 and in Tyconius' Isaiah, and in those places at least is evidently the primitive rendering.

There are two other words in which Mon. will have to be regarded as late if the evidence of Cyprian is taken as the infallible standard of primitive usage. Cyprian uses *collum* twice but *ceruix* not at all; and though his evidence is not available as between *fusile* and *conflatile*, he uses *conflare* twice and *fundere* not at all. The use of *fusile* regularly by Tertullian and by Lugd. and Augustine in Num. (neither word is used by either in Lev.) suggests that this may be the earlier, and since there are clear cases (which will be mentioned at the end of this chapter) in which the primitive Old Latin rendering of the same Greek original varied from book to book, it may quite well be that the use of *ceruix* (Deut. xxxi. 27) and, with even more probability, of *fundere* (Ex. xxxviii) and *fusiles* (Lev. xix. 4) by Mon. represents the primitive form of the version in each place. The case of *dedit bibere*, already mentioned, is perhaps not quite of the same kind, because the evidence for the primitive character of *potare* (Cyprian, *k*, Tyconius and Novatian) is unusually strong and varied.

Before leaving this first section of Mon. it may be interesting to notice the varying manner in which Augustine's vocabulary compares with that of the MSS. It agrees with the view already set forth that Augustine and Lugd. are both late, and Mon. is early in Ex. and Deut., when we find that Augustine and Lugd. on the whole agree against Mon. in vocabulary in these books. An examination of the passages quoted by all three from these books will show that agreements of Augustine and Lugd. against Mon. are at least three times as numerous as agreements of Augustine and Mon. against Lugd. Moreover where Augustine and Lugd. agree it is frequently in places where Mon. has a clearly primitive rendering (*e.g.* they have *educere, magnus, intrare* and *uxor* where Mon. has *eicere, grandis, introire* and *coniux*); but where Augustine and Mon. agree against Lugd. (as in *cultus, spargere* and *adulescentula* for *ornatus, seminare* and *iuuencula*) it is in no case possible to say with certainty which of the alternatives, if either, is earlier than the other.

In Lev., on the other hand, where both Augustine and Lugd. have an earlier vocabulary than in Ex. and Deut., this close agreement between Augustine and Lugd. against Mon. disappears. In fact agreements of Augustine and Mon. in this book are just about as frequent and conspicuous as Augustine's agreements with Lugd. in the other two books. Augustine however has some agreements with Lugd. in Lev. especially in places where Mon. seems to retain unusually primitive words; for example in a long passage quoted by all three from Lev. xii.–xiii, though Augustine repeatedly agrees with Mon. against Lugd., he yet agrees with Lugd. in using the common *lepra* instead of the unusual *uarietas*. A close examination of the three authorities in Lev. makes it clear that though Lugd. has a text which seems 'African' when compared with the Lugd. text in other parts, yet even in Lev. it is decidedly late when compared, not only with Mon., but even with Augustine.

The comparison of the MSS with Augustine also emphasises the wide divergence between the MSS throughout; for whether in Ex., Lev. or Deut. the agreements of the MSS against Augustine are remarkably few in number, and insignificant in character compared with the agreements of Augustine with either. It would probably be impossible to collect more than a dozen such agreements altogether, and half of these would be in the latter part of Deut. where the connection between the MSS is closer than elsewhere.

(2)

Mon. preserves about three hundred and thirty verses from Numbers, and comparing these with Lugd. and Augustine, it at once becomes clear that an entirely different relation between the three exists in this book. The same renderings are found in the two MSS, even for words which both render differently elsewhere; both for example use *adampliare* in xxxiii. 54, *causa* (ἕνεκεν) in xii. 1, and *tribulare* (κακοῦν) in xxix. 7, though none of these renderings occurs again in Mon., and only one, and that rarely, in Lugd. But while Lugd. and Mon. are almost identical, Augustine seldom agrees with either against the other, though in other books agreements of Augustine and one MS against the other are continually found. Almost any verse of Num. contained in the three will illustrate this; in the following list of words in which Mon. and Lugd. agree against Augustine, only those are given which seem to indicate the relative ages of the MSS and Augustine. Augustine would seem earlier in using *adicere* for *adponere* regularly, *aut* for *siue* (xxx. 3), *edere* for *manducare* (xi. 21), *iste* for *hic* (xxxii. 5), *occidere* for *interficere* (xi. 22) and *uouere uotum* for *orare orationem* (xxx. 3); in xii. 7 and 8 Augustine uses *quomodo* for *sicut*, and *claritas* for *honor*, but these are in a quotation from *De Gen. ad Litt.*, in which he uses an earlier type of text than usual. On the other hand the rendering of the MSS seems earlier in *causa* for *ut* (τοῦ and inf. xxxi. 16), *colligere* and *concolligere* for *congregare* (xi. 22), *natio* for *generatio* (xxxii. 13), *nimis* (xi. 33 and xxxii. 1) and *nimium* (xii. 3) for *ualde*, *quoadusque* for *donec* (xxxii. 13) and *tamquam* for *sicut* (xii. 10). Even if the evidence for one or two of these words is not so clear as could be desired, both lists contain some undoubted 'Africanisms,' and suggest that the text of the MSS combines earlier and later elements.

This conclusion is supported by the general character of the MSS where direct comparison with other texts is impossible. Thus we find early words such as *indignari*, *ostium*, *plorare*, *quasi*, *quoniam*, *totus* and *sine uitio* as well as *in crastino* and *in crastinum* without *dies*, and to these might be added the Greek words *erythreum*, *bolides* and *ortygometra*, all three of which are translated in other parts of the MSS. On the other hand we have several later words: *furor*, *uirtus* (not *fortitudo*), *mandare* and *mandatum*, *sanare* (not *curare*), *adponere* (not *adicere*), *quemadmodum* (six times), *custodire* (not *obseruare*) and *mundare* (not *purgare*). This list shows that Mon. has a very different character in this book from that which it has in Ex. or Lev. For some words we have early renderings in one passage and later in another, the MSS agreeing on each occasion; thus in addition to the common *exire* we find *proficisci* used four times; the Cyprianic *iustificatio* is used in xxxi. 21, but the later *iustitia* in xxxvi. 13; *intrare* is used twice though *introire* is much more common; and *praecipere* and *constituere* are used with equal frequency for συν- and προστάσσειν. Ἀποσκευή is rendered twice by *apparatus*, once by *praeparatura*, and twice by *impedimenta* (the form used by Augustine), the two MSS agreeing with each other in every case. The rough and literal *diem festum agetis diem festum* for ἑορτάσατε ἑορτήν (xxix. 12) contrasts with and hardly seems due to the same translator as the periphrastic *ad pascenda pecora utile* for κτηνοτρόφος in xxxii. 4, or *aptus* in xxxii. 1.

Mon. and Lugd. have scarcely a dozen differences in vocabulary in the whole book; in Num. iii. 46 and 49 Lugd. has *redemptio* for *eliberia*, in iv. 6 *pellis* for *corium* and *anaphoros* for *balteos*, several times in ch. iv *litare* and derivatives for *libare*, etc. (in ch. xxix both MSS have *litatio*), in iv. 31 *ianua* for *ostium*, in iv. 39 *intrare* for *introire*, in iv. 49 *praecipere* for *constituere* (συντάσσειν), in v. 2 *leprosus* for *uarius*, in xxxii. 9 *sensus* for *cor*, and in xxxii. 15 *quod* for *quoniam*. This list, which contains all the significant differences between the two, is interesting because Mon. has the more primitive rendering in several instances (*corium, ostium, introire, uarius* and *quoniam*),while Lugd. has it only once (*redemptio*). Mon. however is not by any means Cyprianic in this book.

As great a similarity between Mon. and Lugd. is seen in the forty verses quoted from Deut. viii–x. We have as in Num. unusual words (such as *conuentus* ix. 10, and *ceruicosus* ix. 6 and 13) used by both MSS here, but nowhere else in either; the common renderings selected for mention here however show rather the combination of early and late forms in these chapters. *Istinc* (ix. 12) certainly seems early, and so does the perfect *fuistis* in ix. 22, while *edere* and *praecipere* (twice each) are more common in early than late texts. The words however which point to a later date are rather more numerous; we have *sumere*, *ualde, intrare* and *quia* (the last two several times) where we should expect *accipere, nimis, introire* and *quoniam* in a primitive text. The accusative of duration (ix. 9) and *eruere* for λυτροῦν (ix. 26) are also later, and *quemadmodum* is found in x. 3 though *sicut* is used just before and after.

Where Mon. and Lugd. differ, the indications of priority seem equally divided. Lugd. has *fuerunt* for *erant* (ix. 15), *quoniam* (ix. 16) and *iste* (ix. 19), but Mon. uses *promouere* (three times) for ἀπαίρειν, and has *accipere* and an ablative of duration where Lugd. has the later *sumere* (ix. 17) and accusative (ix. 18).

On comparing the MSS with Augustine's quotations we find much the same result as in Num. Augustine has not a single agreement with Lugd. against Mon., and only two or three with Mon. against Lugd., such as *quanta* (Lugd. *quaecumque*) and *increduli* (Lugd. *diffidentes*) in ix. 7; while in nearly thirty places the MSS agree against Augustine. Here again it is not clear whether Augustine or the MSS represent the earlier form of the version, the evidence being scanty and conflicting.

The similar connections between the three authorities in this passage and in Num. might make it appear as if a common text extended through the two MSS from Num. into Deut., but we have already shown that Lugd. in Num. and Deut. represents two different texts each with its distinct peculiarities; and in the passage now under consideration we have a few striking examples of peculiarities in the MS text of this early part of Deut. *Heres esse* (κληρονομεῖν) is used by Mon. six times in this section but nowhere else, and in Lugd. apart from nine occurrences in Deut. between chs. ix and xvi it is only found twice in Jud., *possidere* or *hereditare* being usual in both MSS. *Heres esse* in fact is quite rare in the Old Latin, and as it is not found at all in Cyprian (though he uses *possidere* and *hereditare* each a few times) it may be a later form. Both MSS again use *extirpare* four times in Deut. ix and x, though elsewhere they agree in using *exterminare*.

It seems strange indeed that these two MSS should have a common text in Num. and a common text of a different character in Deut. viii–x, seeing that in other parts they are so dissimilar, but the fact seems to be so, and suggests that one of the two MSS in these books was transcribed, if not from the other, yet at least from a MS not far removed from the other.

Before leaving the subject of the relation between the vocabularies of Mon. and Lugd. there is one more fact to be illustrated which will be of very great importance when we come to consider the question of the unity of the version as a whole, namely the striking similarities in vocabulary between the two MSS in places where the difference between them appears fundamental.

In Ex. xxxii. 13, a chapter in which Mon. and Lugd. are almost as different as any two Old Latin texts anywhere, we have in both the expression *memoratus famulorum tuorum*. In a similar phrase in Deut. ix. 27 they agree in using *seruus*. Since the Greek has οἰκέτης in the first place and θεράπων in the second, the agreement between the renderings of the nouns does not seem remarkable until we discover that both renderings are

rather exceptional in Lugd. where *famulus* generally represents
θεράπων and *seruus* οἰκέτης. *Memoratus* is also a noticeable
agreement, for in Deut. ix. 7 (Mon. is mutilated in *v.* 27) both
MSS have *in mente habere*. In the same chapter of Ex. *prae-
uaricare* is used in both MSS for παραβαίνειν, an uncommon
rendering.

Again in Lev. xviii, another chapter in which Mon. is very
primitive, and differs widely from Lugd., Mon. uses *execratio*
three times; Lugd. agrees each time, though it uses this word
only five times in all (all in Lev.), the usual rendering being
abominatio. In Deut. xxxii. 23,. Mon. and Lugd. both have
congerere, a word used only very rarely by Lugd., and not at all
again by Mon.; for except in Num. xi, where both MSS have
three times the rare compound *concolligere*, Mon. everywhere
uses *colligere*. Numerous examples of this kind could be quoted
from Num., but they would not show, as these do, the real
connection between the two MSS in places where at first sight
they seem to be entirely unrelated.

(3)

The third and last section of Mon. to be considered consists
of about eight chapters between Ex. ix. 15 and Ex. xx. 5.
Throughout these chapters Lugd. is missing, and there is little
material for direct comparison with Mon., but it is clear that
we have a type of text differing widely from that which Mon.
represents in the later portion of Ex. and in Lev.

Many words occur in these chapters which are evidently
'European.' Thus we have *intrare* (not *introire*), *dies solemnis*
(not *festus*), *custodire* (with Lucifer, xix. 5), *mandare, interficere,
egredi, proficisci, aduena* and *uia* (xiii. 21, Cyp. *iter*). *Peccatum*
is used even where, as in x. 17, Augustine has the 'African'
delictum; the earlier *quoniam* is found only three times, *quia*
very often; the late *sumere* (or its compounds) appears six times,
including two where Augustine keeps the earlier *accipere*; *co-
turnix* (so also Ambrose) would probably be later than the Greek
ortygometra, used by Mon. in Num. and by Tertullian; *dies* is
generally used with *crastinus* and *hodiernus*, though its omission
is usual in the early texts; and the later *amplius* is more frequent
in these chapters than the earlier *adhuc*. In the great majority

of the instances just given, the practice of Mon. is exactly the opposite of what it is elsewhere; but we still find a few of the characteristics of an early text, such as the frequent use of *totus*, *nimis* and the perfect tense of *esse*. The mixture of early and late forms in this part of Mon. is probably to be seen also in *eremus* and *desertum*, which are both frequently used, and in *mare rubrum* (x. 19) compared with *eritreum mare* in xiii. 18.

We have rare but not apparently early words in *in aeuum* (xix. 9), *ne casu* (xiii. 17 and xix. 24), *demonstrare* (xiii. 21), and the frequent use of *palam*.

(d) The Vocabulary of the Würzburg Fragments

In its vocabulary the Würzburg MS (Wir.) clearly occupies a position between Mon. and Lugd. In all places where Wir. and Mon. are both extant Mon. has the more primitive text, while generally Wir. is not so late as Lugd.

Perhaps Ex. xxxix and xl best illustrate the intermediate position of Wir., for while Mon. and Wir. have numerous agreements against Lugd., and Wir. and Lugd. quite as many (and perhaps rather more) against Mon., there are no agreements in vocabulary between Mon. and Lugd. against Wir., though there are a few significant agreements between all three MSS. Even more instructive however are half a dozen words, in rendering which Mon. and Lugd. differ, and for which Wir. uses sometimes the form found in Mon., and sometimes that found in Lugd. Thus Wir. uses *altare* several times with Mon., but as often uses *ara* with Lugd.; in one verse it uses *ministrare* with Mon. and in the very next verse represents the same Greek word by *deseruire* with Lugd.—yet another rendering, *sacrificare*, being used by Wir. in Ex. xxxv; so Wir. uses at times *unguere* and *unctio*, *ostium* and *secundum quae* with Mon., but at other times *lenire* and *lenitio*, *ianua* and *quemadmodum* with Lugd. In every place where the three MSS coexist there are examples of this combination of early words from Mon. with later ones from Lugd. to be found in Wir., but nowhere are they so clear as in these last two chapters of Ex.

In Lev. xi and in the greater part of Ex. xxxii, Wir. is closer to and only slightly more primitive than Lugd., and its agreements with Mon. are correspondingly less numerous. On the

other hand in Lev. iv. 23–25 and Lev. xviii. 18–21, where the
three MSS coexist only over a few verses because one breaks off
just after another begins, Mon. and Wir. have a remarkable
number of agreements and Wir. and Lugd. practically none.
There is also a short passage in Ex. xxxii. 26–29 in which Wir.
has more resemblance to Mon. than to Lugd.; but though sometimes nearer Mon. and sometimes nearer Lugd., Wir. maintains
throughout its place between them, for from all these chapters
it is not easy to quote a single significant agreement of Mon. and
Lugd. against Wir. The nearest approach to such an agreement
is found in their use of *imponere* in Lev. iv where Wir. has
superponere, and of *unusquisque* in Ex. xxxii where Wir. has the
somewhat rare *singuli*. Even when Mon. is missing and our
materials for comparison are not so plentiful, it is clear that
Wir. varies in the character of its text in different places, for
though in Lev. xx–xxii it has several primitive elements, and
in many places in Ex. xxxiii and xxxv seems decidedly earlier
than Lugd., yet in Lev. vii and viii it sometimes appears to be
later in its vocabulary than Lugd.

When the vocabulary of Augustine is compared with that of the
MSS, the most conspicuous result is that while in Lev. Augustine
and Wir. agree in the great majority of instances against Lugd.,
in Ex. the two MSS for the most part agree against Augustine.
Since however we have already shown that both Augustine
and Lugd. change the character of their texts in passing from
Ex. to Lev., it may be that Wir. is the most constant of the
three; it is at any rate difficult to trace any change in the
character of Wir., as it is throughout characterised by an unusual
combination of early and late forms. This combination has been
illustrated above from Ex. xxxix and xl; a few more examples
are added here from chapters of Ex. in which Mon. is missing.
Δόξα is rendered *gloria* by Lugd. and Wir. in Ex. xxxiii. 22, but
in *vv.* 18 and 19 Wir. uses the earlier *claritas*; ἀφαίρεμα in Ex.
xxxv. 24 and 29 appears as *demptio* in both MSS but in *vv.* 21
and 22 Wir. has the earlier *adlatio*; both MSS render χρίσις by
lenitio in xxxv. 28, but in *v.* 19 Wir. has the earlier *unctio* (which
Lugd. has in *v.* 14); both MSS have *redimere* for λυτροῦν in
xxxiv. 20, but in the same and following verses Wir. also uses
liberare; in Ex. xxv. 37 Wir. first has *lucernae* and then *luminaria*,

Lugd. and Ottob. having the former each time. In Ex. xxii for κακοῦν Cyprian has *uexare* and Speculum *nocere*; Lugd. is here missing but Wir. quite characteristically has first one rendering and then the other in consecutive verses. In Lev. Wir. shows the same variety in rendering Greek words; we have for example both the earlier *donum* and the later *munus* for δῶρον; we have the earlier *uolucer* and the rarer *auis* used, though in ch. xi, where Mon. has *uolucer*, Wir. regularly uses *uolatile* with Lugd.; in ch. xi again, where Mon. has *serpens* and Lugd. *repens* eight times each, Wir. not only uses each of these words in turn but has also a third equivalent *reptile*; in Lev. xx Wir. has *sine filiis* in *v.* 20 with Augustine and Speculum, but in the next verse *sine liberis* with Tertullian. These variations are quite different from those which are found in Lugd., where the different renderings are characteristic of different books of the Heptateuch; it would perhaps be impossible to find any other Old Latin MS which showed so many variations in such close proximity as Wir.

The twenty-six verses of Deut. which are contained in Wir. do not present any special features. Where Lugd. and Wir. differ, the latter is generally the more primitive. We have already had occasion to recognise an admixture of later words in Mon. towards the end of Deut., so that we are not surprised to find that Wir. has the common *ira* and (twice) the earlier *iste* where Mon. as well as Lugd. has the later *furor* and the common *hic*; these however are contrary to the usual practice of Mon. and to the prevailing relations between the MSS even in Deut.

We have in an earlier section noticed the use of the Cyprianic *potare* by Wir. and Lugd. in Ex. xxxii, where Mon. has *dare bibere*; perhaps the only other example of an 'African' word in Wir. which is not found in Mon. is *claritas* in Ex. xxxii. 18 and 19. Lugd. here has *gloria*; Mon. is missing, but uses *honor* and *gloria* elsewhere. In some places Wir. seems to have altered the wording, irrespective of the Greek original. Thus in all forms of the version *abominare* is the usual equivalent of βδελύσσειν, but twice (Lev. xi. 43 and xx. 25) Wir. uses *coinquinare*, which elsewhere seems always to represent μιαίνειν; so ἔθνος which is regularly rendered *gens*, or in primitive texts *natio*, is represented by *populus* in Lev. xxi. 2, though *populus* is the usual equivalent of λαός; *exterminare* is used in Lev. xx. 3 for ἀπολλύναι, a word which is regularly rendered *perdere*; *mundus* is used for ἀγαθός in Deut. xxviii. 47, though *bonus* is the usual equivalent and is given by Lugd. here, *mundus* being the equivalent of καθαρός; *mandatum* is used for πρόσταγμα in Lev. xviii. 5 and xix. 37, though it seems elsewhere to be used only for ἐντολή. These look like alterations made unsystematically and without any reference to the original text; such arbitrary alterations are often found in Speculum, but do not seem common elsewhere, though Mon. has at least one example, *plebs* for ἔθνος in Ex. xxxii. 10.

The connection of Wir. in vocabulary now with Mon. and now with Lugd. provides another argument for the unity of the versions represented by the three MSS. More direct evidence of this can be provided by quoting a few of the most striking instances in which Wir. makes the same variations as the other MSS in rendering the same original in different places; a few examples from Mon. and Lugd. have been given already.

In Ex. xxxii. 30 all three MSS render ἐξιλάσκεσθαι by *depraecari*; this Greek word is frequently represented in each MS, but neither Mon. nor Wir. uses *depraecari* elsewhere; nor does Lugd. in Ex., though *depraecari* is its usual rendering in Num. Again for compounds of τρίβειν Wir. has four different renderings, Mon. has six and Lugd. nine; in those places where only two of the MSS exist they do not indeed always agree, but strangely enough, in the only two places where the three are extant, they all use the same words, *comminuere* in Ex. xxxii. 19 and *confringere* in Lev. xi. 33; Augustine in the latter place differs, using *conterere*, but the agreement between the MSS can hardly be accidental. These agreements too are specially remarkable because of the extensive divergence between Mon. and the other MSS in Ex. xxxii, and between all three MSS in Lev. xi.

Two more examples which introduce Speculum readings also may be added; for καθαιρεῖν Wir., Lugd. and Speculum use *destruere* in Ex. xxxiv. 13, but the two MSS agree in using *demolire* in Deut. xxviii. In the same chapter of Exodus, Wir., Lugd. and Speculum have *inuitare* for καλεῖν, though all three use *appellare* or *uocare* everywhere else in the Heptateuch. These common usages provide a strong argument for the unity of the version; they show that even where our Old Latin authorities differ most widely they can hardly represent independent versions of the Septuagint.

We may conclude this chapter by pointing out that there are signs that even in the time of Cyprian the vocabulary of the Old Latin version was not altogether homogeneous throughout, so that apparently there were variations in the way of rendering the same Greek word in different books even in the original translation.

The rendering of ἁμαρτία is a good illustration of this; this word and the corresponding verb are represented by *delictum* and *delinquere* seventeen times in Cyprian and generally in Mon.; these words are also used by Lugd. almost regularly in Lev. but rarely elsewhere, and are generally, and no doubt correctly, described as 'African,' since several times when they are found in Cyprian they are removed in the A text or Speculum. When however the distribution of their occurrences in Cyprian is examined we find that these words are never used by him in Isaiah, a book in which his text is in many respects unusually primitive, but in which *peccatum* and *peccare* are used as many as sixteen times. From Cyprian's Apocalypse, it seems indeed that some of the primitive marks had been already removed, but Isaiah is in most respects one of the most primitive books in his Bible; it therefore appears improbable that this 'Africanism' had been already removed from his Isaiah, and we are probably justified in supposing that these words did not have a place in the original African Isaiah—in other words that the original Old Latin was not uniform in its manner of translating these two words. *Delinquere* and *delictum* appear only occasionally in Augustine, Lucifer, Ambrose and Speculum; it would be interesting to know how the occurrences are distributed in their quotations.

The entire absence of *facinus* and *scelus* and their derivatives from Mon. is noticeable, if Mon. represents as early a text as has been claimed; but these words also appear to be characteristic of certain books of the Bible; Cyprian uses *scelus* (and derivatives) only in Isaiah and Ezekiel, *facinus* very rarely outside Psalms, Matthew and Isaiah; the latter is especially common in Isaiah, in which book indeed Cyprian uses neither *iniquus* nor *iniquitas*. In Tyconius too these words are confined to very much the same books. Some other points of the same kind will emerge when the style of the MSS is discussed; such are the remarkable agreement of all authorities in the use of *quodsi* in the early part of Exodus and of *si autem* practically everywhere else; the prevalence of *quoniam* rather than *quia* in the same books in such remote authorities as Cyprian and Lucifer, and the signs of agreement in various authorities in the use of certain synonyms of *ante* in special books. Another example is furnished by the rendering of ἀπαρχαί, which both Speculum and Ambrose represent by *initia* in Ex., but by *primitiae* in Num. (Lugd. also agreeing in Ex. but using both words in Num.). There is also a curious difference between Cyprian's rendering of ὁδός in Ex. and in Psalms. In Ex. he uses *iter* (2/2) and since Mon. also uses *iter* four times, and in each case the later authorities (Augustine, Ambrose and Lugd.) use *uia*, *iter* has every appearance of being 'African.' Yet in two places in the Psalms (xlix. 23 and lxvii. 5) Cyprian uses *uia*, and this is replaced in the A text (and in xlix. 23 in Speculum also) by *iter*. Cyprian's Psalms and his Exodus are certainly both very primitive and it looks as if the different usage in the two books goes right back to the earliest days of the version; it is however very remarkable that the original renderings should be modified in exactly opposite directions in the two books by the later authorities. The example of *iter* and *uia* makes us wonder whether perhaps after all *ceruix* may not be primitive in Mon. Deut., since Wir. and Lugd. use *collum*, although in Is. lviii. 5 *collum* is evidently the primitive rendering, being used by Cyprian and replaced by *ceruix* in Lucifer and Speculum. Whether this be so or not the foregoing instances will warn us that we may find the primitive Old Latin version inconsistent with itself in its rendering of the same Greek word in different books.

CHAPTER II

THE RELATIONS OF THE MSS TO THE QUOTATIONS IN THE FATHERS

I T will be possible to check and extend the results of the previous chapter by comparing the text of the MSS with the quotations of each of the Latin Fathers in turn. In this way we shall be able to see whether the variation in the character of the texts of Lugd. and Mon., which has been indicated by the changes in their vocabulary from one book to another, corresponds to a change in the writers with which the MSS show the most agreement in different parts. In this chapter account will be taken not only of agreements or disagreements in actual vocabulary, but also of particles and pronouns, insertions and omissions, those however being postponed for the most part which involve the use of different Greek texts.

(a) Cyprian

The four verses quoted by Cyprian from Ex. xxxii (1 and 31–33) are of unusual interest and importance, because they are the only verses found in all three of the MSS of which we possess Cyprian's text; v. 1 is not indeed actually in Wir., but v. 23, which is practically a repetition of it, is; vv. 31–33 are quoted three times in Cyprian with practically no variations; vv. 1, 31 and 32 are found in Augustine, v. 32 in Ambrose, v. 33 in Ambrosiaster, and v. 1 (or 23) in the treatise *Aduersus Iudaeos* which is certainly early African. The greater part is also quoted by Cassian, whose text, though of course very late, provides at least one point of interest. Such an array of Old Latin witnesses to a continuous passage extending over three verses is seldom met with, at least in the Heptateuch.

We notice at once that the four verses as quoted by Cyprian are almost identical with Mon.; not only do the two agree in the use of several 'Africanisms' such as *delinquere, delictum, grandis* and *eicere*, but also in the omission of *et* before *fecerunt* against all other authorities, the use of *si qui* for *si quis*, and of *ante* and *deleam* where Lugd. and Wir. have *coram* and *delebo*.

The text of *Adu. Iud.* is the one which is in closest agreement with Mon. and Cyprian. It only contains *v.* 23, but these three alone have *eicere* and *accidere* where Wir., Lugd. and Augustine have *educere* and *factum esse*, and these three alone put *scimus* last in the sentence. *Accidere* is clearly primitive in this place though Cyprian uses the other equivalents also. The differences between Cyprian and Mon. are insignificant and where these two do differ the connections of each with other authorities seem accidental and variable.

The agreement between Wir., Lugd. and Augustine (and Ambrose in *v.* 32) is scarcely less remarkable than that between Cyprian and Mon., but Lugd. is rather further removed from Cyprian and Mon. than the other two. Thus Wir. and Augustine (*Loc.*) use *praecedant* (*v.* 23) as Cyprian and Mon., but Lugd. has *praeeant*; this last word is used by Augustine in *Tract. Ioan.* 3, and though the quotations in this work are very free, the correspondence with Lugd. suggests that the word was used in a text known to Augustine; the use of *sin alias* for *sin autem* by Lugd. and Cassian also indicates that we have in Lugd. a somewhat later stage of development of the Old Latin than that represented in Wir. and Augustine and even Ambrose.

The quotations of *vv.* 32 and 33 in Ambrose and Ambrosiaster are interesting. Ambrose follows the earlier texts in using *dimittere* (not *remittere*) and in the omission of *eorum*, but differs from them in substituting *peccatum* for the 'African' *delictum*. In this way he gets a text exactly agreeing with that used by Augustine everywhere (at least five times) except in *Qu.* The appearance of the later *remittere* and *illorum* in *Qu.* agrees with the usual assumption that in his casual quotations the text of Augustine is often more primitive than in the formal *Qu.* We seemed to have an exception in the use of *praeeant* in *Tract. Ioan.*; but this might be accounted for by the fact that this is certainly one of his later works. Ambrosiaster too has *ante* and *deleam* with Cyprian and Mon. but he also has *peccatum*, and hence shows (like Ambrose and Augustine) a text intermediate between those of the early Cyprian and Mon. and the late Wir. and Lugd.

Lugd. contains both *vv.* 1 and 23 and the words common to both verses are quoted (with one exception) in exactly the same form; Mon. also contains both verses but shows five points of difference between the two verses. It is very remarkable that in all the five variations the form adopted by Mon. in *v.* 1 is almost exactly reproduced each time in Cyprian's quotation of *v.* 1, while the form adopted by Mon. in *v.* 23 is in several respects reproduced in the quotation of that verse in Wir. For example in Mon. *v.* 1 the words *quod ei acciderit* come before *nescimus*, but in *v.* 23 they are placed after it; Cyprian (*v.* 1) has the former and Wir. (*v.* 23) the latter order; again Mon. and Cyprian have *uir* in *v.* 1, but in *v.* 23 Mon. with Wir. has *homo*. It would seem that the differences between *vv.* 1 and 23 in Mon. go back to the primitive form of the version, and that the two verses have been assimilated to one another considerably in Lugd. The alternative view that the variations in Mon. are due to subsequent alteration of one verse is unlikely; thus in the case of the first point just mentioned *quod ei acciderit* is placed after *nescimus* in Wir., Lugd. and Augustine as well as Mon. in *v.* 23, and since this agrees with the Greek order it has every claim to be regarded as original there: but the other order which is adopted by Mon. in *v.* 1 cannot be a late modification because of the very early testimony to it in Cyprian, so that we are led to suppose that the two forms both occurred in the original version, one in each verse exactly as we have it in Mon.

There is no other passage in the parts of Mon. which we have found reason to regard as primitive in which direct comparison with Cyprian is helpful, the few words quoted by both from Lev. xix providing material too slight for any useful comparison. From Num., a book in which Mon. is remarkably like Lugd., Cyprian quotes only six words which can be compared with Mon. (xii. 3), but three of the six have points of interest. Augustine retains *lenis* but changes *nimis* to the later *ualde*, Lugd. and Mon. retain *nimis* (in the form *nimium*) but change *lenis* to *mansuetus*, a word which Jerome uses in all three of his quotations of this passage though it does not appear in the Vulgate. Lugd. and Mon. also change the 'African' *fuit* to *erat*; Augustine quotes the words without a verb which he says is to be understood, apparently showing that the text on which he is here commenting (*Loc.*) is the Greek and not the Old Latin.

The conclusion that the Mon. version of the earlier half of Ex. differs considerably from that found in the later chapters is borne out by direct comparison with Cyprian, for instead of the close likeness between the two which was found in ch. xxxii, we have a very considerable amount of difference wherever such comparison is possible here. In xii. 46 Mon. has *efferre*, Cyprian *eicere*; in xiii. 21 Mon. has *demonstrare* and *uia*, Cyprian *ostendere* and *iter*; in xvii. 9 Mon. has *super* and *crastina die*, Cyprian *in* and *in crastinum*; in xvii. 12 and xix. 10 Mon. has participles as in the Greek, Cyprian having in the former an ablative absolute and in the latter a clause; in xx. 3 Mon. has *praeter*, Cyprian *absque*. In most of these places Mon. evidently represents a later type of text than Cyprian; even the restoration of the participles will be classed among late signs if it be true, as has been asserted, that the avoidance of present participles is 'African.'

The same result is suggested by Ex. xix. 10 and 11, where Aug. (*Qu.*) has four distinct agreements with Mon. against Cyprian, while Cyprian and Mon. have nothing striking in common. It is interesting to compare with this xix. 22, where Augustine agrees in two obvious respects with Cyprian against Mon. The explanation of the change is probably to be found in the fact that in xix. 22 Augustine is quoting the words from Parmenian (*Con. Ep. Parm.* ii. 7) in a passage where there are quoted together three separate texts of Ex. and Lev. which Cyprian also frequently quotes together. It is clear from the juxtaposition of these three texts in each that either Parmenian derived them from Cyprian, or both got them from the same source. In Ex. xiii. 21 and 22 Cyprian and Mon. each have resemblances to Augustine and Ambrose, but they have not a single significant point of resemblance to each other. In their quotations of xvii. 9–14 however, and there alone in these early chapters of Ex., Cyprian and Mon. have noticeable agreements both in readings and renderings. Among the latter we notice the avoidance of the Greek participle in *v.* 9, *ut sit* used for εἰς in *v.* 14, and *sustentare* and *stabiles* used by each in *v.* 12 for στηρίζειν and its perfect participle respectively.

Exodus xxii. 22–24 is quoted by Cyprian and in the Speculum; here Mon. and Lugd. are both missing but the passage provides our best opportunity (after the one given from Ex.

xxxii) for comparing Wir. directly with Cyprian. This is one of those passages which have been considerably changed in one MS of Cyprian (*Cod. Sess.* or A) so that we have practically four authorities for these verses. We at once notice three clear agreements between Wir., Speculum and the A text of Cyprian, *occidam, uxores* and *filii* for the true Cyprian's *perimam, coniuges* and *pueri*, though *perimam* and *coniuges* are retained in the fifth-century treatise *De Vita Christiana* (Migne's Augustine, vol. 6). It was noticed in the first chapter that Wir. for κακοῦν first uses *nocere* with Speculum and then *uexare* with Cyprian (and *De Vita Chr.*). Wir. has another point of similarity with Cyprian in *exclamationes* (Spec. *clamorem*) which is all the more striking because the Greek has a singular whether we read φωνῆς with AB or βοῆς with FM. It is possible that here *De Vita Chr.* in reading *uociferationem* has preserved the primitive Old Latin even better than Cyprian[1]. However this may be it is clear that Wir. comes between Cyprian and Speculum in the development of the version, but is more closely akin to Speculum and the A text of Cyprian than to Cyprian himself.

A few words must be added on *vv.* 20 and 28. Cyprian, Augustine and Speculum quote *v.* 20 in exactly the same form, *sacrificans diis eradicabitur nisi domino soli.* Wir. is only partly legible but differed remarkably (*et qui immolauerit diis ali... praeter...*). We may suppose that the form in Cyprian became stereotyped by frequent use (Cyprian himself uses it four times) and hence survives in Speculum and Augustine, though, as we have just seen, Speculum adopts most of the alterations in the Cyprianic text of this chapter which are found in Wir. *Immolare* in Wir. is a later equivalent of *sacrificare*, but the insertion of *alienis* shows emendation from a Greek text which is preserved only in a minority of MSS. Possibly a somewhat similar explanation is to be given of *v.* 28. Wir. breaks off in the middle of this verse, reading *deos alienos non maledicetis et principe.... Alienos* is only represented in two Greek cursives (*km*), and that it was not read by Augustine is clear from his discussion of the application of *deos*. Cyprian and Speculum, though not exactly agreeing with one another, omit *deos* as well as *alienos*, beginning their quotation with *non maledices*; they may have been

---

[1] J. Rendel Harris concludes that *uociferantes* for *clamantes* is probably primitive (*Codex Sangallensis*, pp. 28 and 42); see also p. 221.

influenced by Acts xxiii. 5, for both quote this verse in isolation from its context. That the rendering of Wir. in spite of its scanty support is not merely an eccentric reading of this MS is shown by Filastrius, who quotes *diis alienis non maledicetis*, agreeing with Wir. not only in representing *alienis* but in the plural verb which has no other support whatever.

A passage which is represented in Lugd. alone of the Old Latin MSS but quoted by nearly all the Latin Fathers is Gen. xlix. 8–11. Hilary and Irenaeus share some of Cyprian's primitive readings, *e.g.* Cyprian and Hilary alone have *frutice* (others *germine* or *germinatione*) and Cyprian and Irenaeus alone have *spes* and the 'African' *quoadusque* for *expectatio* and *donec*, but it is Augustine's quotations (*De Ciu. Dei*, xvi. 41 and *Con. Faust*. xii. 42) which have the most interesting resemblance to Cyprian; some other Latin texts besides Augustine retain Cyprian's *amictum* and *cilicium*, but Augustine and Cyprian alone among the Latins retain what is doubtless the correct reading in *v*. 10 (*quoadusque ueniant deposita illi* or as Augustine quotes it *donec ueniant quae reposita sunt ei*). The other Latin Fathers including Ambrose, Hilary, Novatian, Irenaeus and Jerome as well as Lugd. and Ottob. have *donec* (Iren. *quoadusque*) *ueniat cui* (Nov. *is cui*) *repositum est* (Nov. *repromissum est*, Lugd. *reposita sunt*), obviously a subsequent modification made to connect the verse more clearly with the coming of Christ. Rufinus knew both readings and so evidently did Augustine, for though his two formal quotations as noticed above agree with Cyprian, he refers to the other rendering in *De Ciu. Dei*, xviii. 45, *Con. Faust*. xxii. 85, and *Enarr. in Ps. lxxv*. 1. Among Greek MSS this modification is found only in a few cursives (*ejlntvb₂*), and the evidence of Cyprian shows that the original Old Latin was free from it; but it was evidently both early and widespread as it is found not only in most of the Latin authorities from Novatian onwards, but also in Justin and Hippolytus as well as in Origen and the Armenian Version.

Other passages contained in Cyprian and Lugd. emphasise the divergence between these two texts and show the lateness of Lugd. In Ex. iii. 2–6 and iv. 11–12 we find frequent agreements of Lugd. and Augustine against Cyprian. In their quotations from Josh., Augustine and Lugd. agree against Cyprian almost as regularly as Lucifer and Lugd. do; for each clear agreement of Cyprian and Augustine against Lugd. or of Cyprian and Lugd. against Augustine we have a dozen of Augustine and Lugd. against Cyprian. In Num. on the other hand, though the divergence between Cyprian and Lugd. is as clear as elsewhere, Augustine, instead of agreeing regularly with Lugd., agrees frequently with Cyprian, so that he occupies a place rather between them. In spite of the wide difference between Cyprian and Lugd. however they do not seem to be unrelated; for example both have *imponere* in Num. xx. 25, though it is not here the natural rendering of ἀναβιβάζειν, and in Num. xix. 22 the plurals which both have (*omnia quaecumque...immunda erunt*) are supported by no Greek MS at all; so in Gen. xxvii. 28 Lugd. and Cyprian add *et olei* with no Greek support whatever. In neither of these last two places does Augustine agree with them, which may seem to indicate that he used a text which had been corrected from the Greek. Num. xxiv. 7–9 is not quoted by Augustine, but we have Priscillian's text as well as those of Cyprian and Lugd., and here Lugd. and Priscillian are almost identical, having over a dozen clear agreements against Cyprian; among these we notice what is evidently a primitive blunder (*cubitos* for τὰ πάχη) which is corrected in Cyprian. Evidently unless we suppose Cyprian's is a different translation, some primitive mistakes had already been corrected by his time, though they survived until a much later period in some texts. Other signs of Lugd. being closer to the Greek than Cyprian are occasionally found, *e.g.* in Gen. xlviii, where *super* (*v.* 17) and *patri* (*v.* 18) more literally follow the original than do Cyprian's renderings.

(b) Lucifer

In Lucifer, as in Cyprian, we have just one passage of some considerable length, also in Ex. xxxii, which is represented in all three of our MSS (*vv.* 26–29); and here Lucifer's text bears the same remarkable likeness to Lugd. as Cyprian's did to Mon. in *vv.* 31–33. Augustine (*Loc.*) also gives a few words from *v.* 26, while Ambrose (*Ep.* 66) quotes parts of *vv.* 26 and 27; Augustine, Ambrose and Tertullian all refer to an interesting point in *v.* 28.

In these four verses there are thirteen clear agreements of Lucifer and Lugd. against Mon.; and of these thirteen readings, in each of the seven for which we possess the readings of Ambrose he agrees with Lucifer and Lugd. The European character of Lugd. as compared with Mon. seems indisputable. The connecting link between these two types of text is here provided by Wir. which agrees with Mon. in seven, and with Lugd. and Lucifer in five, of the thirteen places just mentioned, differing from all in the last. Augustine shows something of the same intermediate position as Wir., for while in *v.* 26 he differs from Mon. and Wir. in reading *quis* for *si qui* (or *si quis*) and *ueniat* for *pergat*, he agrees with them in *v.* 28 in having *XXIII* for *quasi tria*.

There are solitary examples of other connections between the various Latin authorities, but they contrast very clearly with the thirteen-fold agreement of Lucifer and Lugd. and the seven-fold agreement of Lucifer, Lugd. and Ambrose against Mon. Lucifer once agrees with Mon. in using *proximum* for *adfinem*, and once with Mon. and Wir. in having *usque ad* for *in*. In four places where there are variations in the texts Mon. and Lugd. agree. They omit *in* before *illa die* (Lucifer and Wir. insert it); they have *uirorum* with Wir. (Luc. *hominum*); they have *unusquisque* with Lucifer (Wir. *singuli*) and they insert *paratus* with Lucifer and Ambrose (Wir. and Augustine omit it).

The possible 'Africanisms' in this passage are *pergat* (Mon. and Wir.), *singuli* (Wir.), *secundum quae* (Mon.) and *proximum* for *adfinem* (Mon. and Lucifer). Even if some of these are uncertain it is natural to conclude from the already ascertained character of Mon. in the verses immediately following (31–33) that here also Mon. represents an early form of the version, and Lugd. (agreeing so closely with Lucifer and Ambrose) a distinctly European form. The intermediate position of Wir. and Augustine is clearer in the present passage than it was in *vv.* 31–33. The addition of *paratus est* in *v.* 26 in Ambrose, Lucifer, Lugd. and Mon. is noticeable, for the words have an equivalent in no Greek text at all. The primitive character of Mon., which is so conspicuous in this chapter, is against the words being regarded as a local European gloss, and we more probably have in it an indication that the European text was derived from the early 'African' version represented by Mon. The removal of

the word by Wir. and Augustine (*Loc.*) would seem to be an alteration made subsequently to conform the reading to the Greek;
such alterations are often found in Augustine's treatises on the
Heptateuch, and we have already noticed some in Wir., though
most of the latter have been transmitted to Lugd. also. The
occurrence of *XXIII milia* in *v.* 28 is remarkable because of
St Paul's use of this number in 1 Cor. x. 8. He is referring to
Num. xxv where the number is given as 'twenty-four thousand'
in all authorities, but it seems likely that the authorities which
have 'twenty-three thousand' in the present verse (Cyril, the
cursive *r*, the Bohairic, and Mon., Wir. and Augustine among
the Latins) derived it from St Paul's use of it in the Epistle.
Its appearance in Mon. and Wir. suggests that it may have been
the original Old Latin reading (other connections with the
cursive *r* will be noticed later) in which case *quasi tria* of Lugd.,
Lucifer, Ambrose and Optatus will be a European correction.
Tertullian however also has 'three thousand,' and it might be
argued that he preserves the original Old Latin, and that Mon.
and Wir. have here suffered a corruption of text. Such a corruption however would have to be considered both early and
widespread, for Augustine also has it though in Ex. he has no
specially close connection with Mon.; perhaps it is more likely
that Tertullian derived his reading from a Greek MS. We have
a very similar case in *v.* 27, except that Tertullian and Augustine
cannot here be quoted. If Mon. and Wir. (*gladios uestros in
femoribus uestris*) represent the original Old Latin, then Lugd.,
Lucifer and Ambrose (*gladium suum in femore suo*) offer another
example of a European correction, but again it is just possible
that Mon. and Wir. show the effect of an early but not original
Latin departure from the Septuagint. In the same verse we
have the words *usque ad portam*, not only in Mon. and Wir.
but also in Lucifer: the Greek MSS have ἐπί or εἰς but it is
probable that the Latin depends on a reading ἕως though no
such Greek reading is quoted. The reading of Lugd. (*in portam*)
seems much more like a correction than the original reading,
for it is not at all likely that the same alteration in the Latin
would appear in three texts so dissimilar as Mon., Wir. and
Lucifer. Perhaps this last example makes it more credible that
in the two passages given just before, Mon. and Wir. may

preserve the original Old Latin in spite of the weakness or absence of Greek support.

Lucifer also quotes Ex. xxxiii. 5–7; Wir. is missing but again Lucifer agrees almost exactly with Lugd., while Mon. has a dozen striking differences from them. Augustine agrees with Mon. in using *cultum* for *ornatum* but otherwise is decidedly on the side of Lugd. and Lucifer, his text being especially like that of Lucifer. The MSS have two agreements against Lucifer, and there are four clear connections between the three texts in *v.* 5 (the introduction of a participle, the singular *gloriae* or *honoris* for the Greek plural, the omission of the first *tibi* and the change of the second to *uobis*) which strongly support the view that Mon. in spite of its differences is not independent of the other two authorities.

As we might expect, Lucifer has many more resemblances to Mon. in Ex. xix. 3–6 than in Ex. xxxii and xxxiii. Here the somewhat uncommon *quanta, prae* for ἀπό, the singular *aquila* for the Greek plural, and above all *regnum sacratissimum* for βασίλειον ἱεράτευμα, all of which are found in both Mon. and Lucifer, show that even if not identical, their texts are much more closely related. We may also notice that in Ex. xx. 4 (= Deut. v. 8), though the Latin authorities vary between *omnem* (Lugd., Lucifer, Irenaeus, Jerome) and *ullam* (Mon., Augustine *Qu.*, Ambrosiaster, Priscillian and most MSS of Speculum), all of these agree in representing πᾶν; but nearly all the Greek MSS in both places have παντός which is represented by *cuiusquam* of Cyprian, Speculum (*Cod. Sess.*) and Augustine (*Cons. Euang.* and *Ser.*). Here again Mon. is evidently with the later or European group of texts.

The remarkable likeness between Lugd. and Lucifer in Josh. and Jud. has been recognised from the first; here long passages in the two are practically identical, showing that an even closer relation exists between them in these books than in Ex. It has not however been as clearly recognised that in Deut. Lucifer has a different relation to the MSS. In quoting Deut. xxviii. 12–20 Lucifer has almost as much in common with Mon. as with Lugd., his vocabulary coming between and sharing the character of the early Mon. and the late Lugd. As we approach the end of Deut. Mon. shows more resemblance to both Lucifer and Lugd., while the two latter draw apart from one another. Thus in Deut. xxxi. 9–11 Lugd. and Lucifer have fewer agreements with one another than Mon. has with either, and in Deut. xxxii. 15–18 the likeness between Mon. and Lucifer becomes even more marked, Lugd. diverging very much from both. It is clear that the relation between Lugd. and Lucifer is quite different here from what it is in Ex., Josh. and Jud.

The relations between Lucifer, Lugd. and Wir. also show variation from book to book. It so happens that we have one good passage for the comparison of these three from each of the books Ex., Lev. and Deut. In Ex. we have seen that Lucifer and Lugd. are the closest of the three; in Deut. (xxxi. 11–13) the MSS are the closest pair (though Lucifer and Lugd. again show more resemblance than do Lucifer and Wir.); in Lev. (xviii. 2–5) Lucifer and Wir. are decidedly closer to one another than Lugd. is to either. Considering that Mon., though it has a mixture of later elements towards the end of Deut., is uniformly 'African' in Lev. we are not surprised to find that Lucifer's resemblance to Mon., which was noticed at the end of Deut., is not evident in Lev. xix. It appears then that in Ex. Lucifer is most like Lugd. and least like Mon.; in Deut. (at least towards the end) he is most like Mon. and least like Wir., but in Lev. he is most like Wir. and least like Mon. Such variations in Lucifer's relation to the three MSS are remarkable but a tabulation of all the agreements and differences can lead to no other conclusion. Lucifer has only two quotations from Num., and in both he has a very peculiar text; in the longer one especially (xxv. 10–13) he has many differences from the other existing texts though these are all European.

A direct comparison of Lugd. and Lucifer in those numerous passages of Deut. where Mon. is not available will bring out not only the divergence between Lucifer and Lugd. in this book, but also the fact suggested by the affinity of Lucifer with Mon., that Lucifer represents on the whole a rather earlier text of Deut. than Lugd. In ch. xvii for example Lucifer seems earlier in *postremo* and *totus* (*v.* 7), *obseruare* (*v.* 10), *quomodo* (*v.* 14), *quoniam* (*v.* 15), *iustificatio* and *iste* (*v.* 19) and *praeceptum* (*v.* 20); and in *vv.* 12 and 13 his text is much nearer to Cyprian than Lugd. is. This priority of Lucifer to Lugd. is seen in ch. i as well, where not only has Lucifer a dozen earlier words in his vocabulary, but Lugd. is later in style and polish, besides conflating the readings of Augustine and Lucifer in *v.* 30. It is only occasionally (as in xix. 13) that Lugd. is more literal than Lucifer or has primitive marks which are removed by him. The divergence between Lucifer and Lugd. in this book however must not be exaggerated; in several places where Augustine also exists (*e.g.* in parts of xiii. 1–4) they agree against him considerably, though in other places (as in parts of ch. xvii) agreements of Augustine and Lugd. are more conspicuous. Augustine and Lucifer on the other hand seldom have conspicuous agreements against Lugd.

(c) Ambrose

Taking first the quotations in Ambrose which can be compared with Wir. only of the three MSS, we may begin with Ex. xxii. 25–27 which is quoted not only by Ambrose (*De Tobia*, 14), but also in Speculum. Verse 26 is given also in Augustine (*Loc.*), and a comparison of the four texts of this verse reveals an interesting phenomenon. In every one of the eight variations in this verse three authorities agree against one, and every time the MS is one of the three, Augustine departing from the others three times, Ambrose three times and Speculum twice. In other words Wir. has the support of two of the three for every word in the verse, and every departure from the text of Wir. is an unsupported peculiarity. The verse is probably unique in this respect, but it seems to illustrate the superiority of MSS to quotations, and shows that here Wir. represents the normal Old Latin text of an age not far removed from that of Augustine and Ambrose. In *vv.* 25 and 27 the departures of one text from the combined readings of the other two seem due to various causes. The reading *exiges ab eo* of Speculum may well be an example of the numerous arbitrary alterations found in that work, but if the combination of Wir. and Speculum may be taken to represent the true Old Latin, it appears that Ambrose by restoring *itaque* and transposing *solum* (or *tantum*) is being influenced by a knowledge of the Greek text. So the omission of *tui* by Augustine in *v.* 26 seems to be a deliberate correction to agree with the Greek, for its appearance in Wir.,

Speculum and Ambrose shows that it really had a place in the Old Latin version.

In Gen. xl Ambrose (*De Ioseph.*) provides a certain amount of material which can be compared with Wir., and in spite of Ambrose's freedom in quoting, there are indications that here also his version had much in common with Wir. Their use of *officium* and *pristinum* in *v.* 13 and addition of *mali* in *v.* 15, as well as their common modification of the phrase *Pharaoni in manu eius* (*v.* 13) where Augustine (*Loc.*) literally follows the Greek, show that they are closely akin.

In the latter part of Ex. where Lugd. is extant Ambrose continues to show some noticeable agreements with Wir., but he has even more in common with Lugd. In xxxiii. 19, for example, Lugd. and Ambrose (*Spir. Sanc.* i. 13) have *antecedam te, uocabo* and *in conspectu tuo*, but Wir. *praecedam prior te, uocabor* and *coram te*. The use of *omnis artis* by Ambrose (*Ps. cxviii*) in xxxv. 32 is a clear connection with Lugd. for Mon., Augustine and Wir. all use such words as *architectonizare* or *architectio*, but Lugd. always *omne arte facere* or *omnis artis scius*. Ex. xxxiii. 22 is twice quoted by Ambrose; in *Ps. xliii* he gives a form (*operiam te manu mea*) which is more like Wir., but in *Spir. Sanc.* iii. 5 one (*protegam manum meum super te*) which more resembles Lugd. The latter follows the Greek more closely, and perhaps represents the text used by Ambrose twenty years before he wrote on *Ps. xliii*. If we could generalise from a single quotation from Deut. (xxviii. 43 and 44 in *De Tobia*, 19) Ambrose in that book also had less connection with Wir. than either of them had with Lugd.

In contrast with this considerable amount of agreement between Ambrose, Lugd. and Wir., we find a great diversity between Ambrose and Mon. in the latter part of Ex. wherever they can be compared. In xxxii. 2 we have three points of agreement between Ambrose (*Ep.* 66) and Lugd. against Mon., but the insertion of *anulos et* before *inaures* in all three, with no other support whatever, shows that Mon. is not altogether unrelated to the European authorities in these chapters. The decidedly closer connection between Mon. and Ambrose in Ex. xii and xiii gives us yet another indication of the European affinities of Mon. in the early part of Ex. This is well seen in

Ambrose's quotation of xii. 29–33 in *Ep.* 23; the quotation of xiii. 21 and 22 in *Ps. cxviii* agrees most closely with Augustine (*De Trin.* ii. 14) but Mon. agrees with these two much more than with Cyprian.

In Deut. ix we have two verses (4 and 5) quoted by Ambrose (*De Cain et Abel*, i. 7) which are contained in Mon. and Lugd. These same two verses are also quoted in the *De Praedestinatione et Gratia* (Migne, Aug. vol. 10), and though this treatise is not by Augustine it can with reasonable safety be taken as giving his text because Augustine's quotation of *v.* 4 in *Loc.* agrees exactly with it though Mon., Lugd. and Ambrose have numerous and considerable differences. There are two striking connections between Ambrose and the MSS which are not shared by Augustine—the insertion of *coeperit* and the (Hexaplaric) omission of *bonam.* However Augustine also has agreements with the MSS against Ambrose, while in other respects Augustine and Ambrose agree against the MSS.

In view of the differences between the earlier and later parts of Deut. in both Mon. and Lugd. we do not expect the same relations to hold in the quotations from the latter part of Deut. In ch. xxii Ambrose (*Ps. xliii*) has many resemblances to Lugd. and Augustine, and in ch. xxviii as many to Lugd. and Lucifer, but in each chapter there is very little resemblance to Mon.; in ch. xxxii, on the other hand, Lugd., Mon. and Ambrose are all close (e.g. *v.* 11 in Amb. *Hex.*), and in *v.* 21 Ambrose (*Ps. xxxvi*) is more like Mon. and Tertullian than Lugd. All this agrees with our previous conclusion that though in ch. xxviii there are signs of Mon. and Lucifer drawing together, yet it is only in chs. xxxi and xxxii that the European element in Mon. becomes at all conspicuous. In ch. xxii, as in ch. ix, we find in Ambrose and Augustine connections which are not shared by Lugd. or Mon.; *e.g.* they have *per omne tempus* in *v.* 29 (Lugd. *omni,* Mon. *toto, tempore*), *uim faciens v.* 28 (Mon. *per uim,* Lugd. corrupt); the similarity between Ambrose and Augustine however is not of the closest kind either in the earlier or later parts of Deut.

Altogether there is a considerable amount of material from Ambrose available for comparison with Lugd., and though except in the parts already dealt with neither of the other MSS is extant, yet we frequently have Augustine's evidence; the closeness of the texts of Ambrose and Lugd. varies somewhat in different books of the Heptateuch, and in different works of Ambrose, but on the whole the relation between them is an exceedingly close one.

Taking Ex. first, in this book four passages seem deserving of separate notice. Ambrose quotes parts of Ex. iv. 10–12 frequently (*e.g.* in *Abr.* ii. 10, *Ep.* 8, *Hex.* i. 2); here we notice especially the phrase common to Augustine, Lugd. and Ambrose (*Ep.* 8) *gracili uoce et tardiore lingua*, and the use by all three of *debeas* for μέλλεις. Augustine indeed uses *locuturus es* in *Qu.*, but there he seems to be translating from the Greek for himself, for he uses *debeas* in quoting the verse elsewhere. In the second passage (Ex. vi. 5–8) there occurs another noticeable connection between the three, the relative ὅν being represented in Lugd. and Augustine by *quemadmodum*, and in Ambrose (*De Cain*, ii. 3) by *quomodo*. Of the many distinctive agreements of Ambrose and Lugd. in these verses however, one at least seems unknown to Augustine, for he quotes *adfligunt* as the Latin rendering remarking that *in seruitutem redigunt* would better represent the Greek; Ambrose and Lugd. actually have *in seruitutem deprimunt*. In Ex. xxviii. 42–43 Lugd. and Ambrose (*De Off.*) are very close; they have e.g. *tegatur* (*v.* 42) in place of the active, and in *v.* 43 they have seven agreements against Cyprian, four of which (*super, ara, sacrificare* and *peccatum*) seem to be European modifications. It is noticeable that both Jerome and Augustine in this verse follow Cyprian closely; Jerome however is in several of his works (of which *Con. Lucif.* is a good example) very primitive in his Old Latin version, and with regard to Augustine, the divergence from Lugd. and Ambrose is explained by the fact that Augustine is here (*Con. Ep. Parm.* ii. 7) quoting Parmenian; we have already noticed the primitive character of Ex. xix. 22 when quoted by Augustine under the same circumstances. In Ex. xxx. 12–16 Ambrose (*Ep.* 7) again has several noticeable agreements with Lugd., e.g. *quodquod* for ὅσοι, *cum coeperint* for ἐν τῷ, παραπορεύεσθαι represented as if it were εἰσπορεύεσθαι in *v.* 14 but correctly in *v.* 13, ὑμῶν rendered by *suis* in *v.* 15 but by *uestris* in *v.* 16. Augustine also quotes *v.* 12, and there we notice an agreement between Augustine and

Ambrose against Lugd. (*computatio* for *collectio*) as well as two or three clear agreements between all three.

In Lev. the relation between Ambrose and Lugd. is rather less close. Sometimes as in Lev. xxv. 37 we have noticeable connections between them, but in the quotation of Lev. x. 17–20 (Amb. *Ep.* 67) Augustine has as many connections with each as they have with one another. Here the agreements of Ambrose and Lugd. are, in most cases, 'European' modifications of the 'African' text of Augustine; they have e.g. *manducare* (four times) for *edere* or *comedere*, and *sicut* for *quomodo*.

In spite of the 'African' element in the Lugd. text of Num., its relation to Ambrose seems as close as in Ex. It is unnecessary to quote in detail the numerous coincidences which are found in *De Off.* 50 (Num. i. 50 and 51), *De Exc. Fr. Sat.* 2 (Num. x. 1–10), *De Cain* ii (Num. xv. 18–19), *Ep.* 63 (Num. xvi. 3–11), *Ps. cxviii* (Num. xxv. 11–13) and *De Fuga Saec.* 2 (Num. xxxv. 11–14). The quotation from Num. xxv is specially noticeable for the clear and repeated agreements of Lugd. and Ambrose against Lucifer, that from Num. xxxv for the equally clear agreements against Augustine. It is also significant that in Num. Ambrose, like Lugd., has signs of an earlier type of vocabulary than in other books.

In Deut. the connection between Ambrose and Lugd. is again very close. In *Ps. cxviii* Ambrose quotes Deut. xii. 19 in the very same words as Lugd., and his quotations from xxi. 10–17 in *Ep.* 33 and *De Cain*, i. 4 have evidently a very close connection with Lugd.—the parts in *Ps. xliii* are rather less like Lugd. In Deut. viii. 17–18 Lugd. and Ambrose (*De Cain*) have several clear agreements against Augustine, but other quotations (as that from xxiv. 6) indicate that all three belong to the same version. Deut. viii. 11–14 is quoted in *De Cain*, i. 7 and in *Hex.* vi. 8, and though the latter is rather free, it evidently has much less connection with Lugd. than the former, where we notice e.g. *repletus*, *completus* and *plenus* used in turn for the same Greek verb, and σοι ἔσται represented by *coeperis possidere* exactly as in Lugd. Possibly however the quotations from Deut. xxxiii in *De Bened. Patr.* have the closest and most numerous connections with Lugd. This is all the more remarkable because, as we shall see shortly, the text of Gen. used in this work

differs very widely from Lugd.; and we may therefore enume-
rate a few of the most remarkable agreements in Deut. xxxiii.
Both have, besides such uncommon words as *cursus, conuenientibus* and *satietas*, several unusual or incorrect renderings of
the original such as *finibus* v. 13 (most Greek MSS ὡρῶν), *factam*
v. 14 (γενημάτων), *ab initio* v. 21 (ἀπαρχήν), the active *acci-
pientium* or *excipientium* for δεκτῶν in v. 23 (though both have
acceptus in v. 24), *magnus et decens* v. 26 (μεγαλοπρεπής) and
cum nebula roris v. 28 (συννεφὴς δρόσῳ).

In Jud. too there are many coincidences between Ambrose
and Lugd., *e.g.* in ch. xiv Ambrose (*Ep.* 19) uses *quaestio* in
v. 12 but *parabola* in v. 18 for πρόβλημα, and Lugd. has exactly
the same variation. In Jud. vi. 36 *sqq.*, however, Lugd. has
eleven agreements, some of them very significant, with Augustine against Ambrose (*De Spir. Sanc.*); but the passage from
Augustine which shows this remarkable connection with Lugd.
is from the treatise *De Unit. Eccl.* (ch. v), and this evidently
has an exceptionally close relation to Lugd., agreeing with it
even against Aug. *Qu.* and all the Greek texts. That the relation
between Lugd. and Ambrose is not so close as usual in this
book is however suggested by xi. 39–40, where though Lugd.
has some noticeable connections with Amb. *De Off.*, especially
the unusual *decretum*, it has more with Aug. *Qu.*

In Gen. xlviii and xlix we find a wide divergence between
Lugd. and Ambrose's quotations in *De Bened. Patr.*, a divergence which is the more remarkable both because of the extraordinary agreements with Lugd. shown by the Deut. quotations
in the same treatise, and because the Genesis quotations in most
other treatises of Ambrose show his usual closeness to Lugd.
A few examples will make this clear:

Gen. xlviii. 22 Amb. (*Iob*), Lugd., Ottob. *magnificam*: Amb. (*Patr.*,
Abr.), Aug., Jer. *praecipuam.*

Gen. xlviii. 22 Amb. (*Iob*), Lugd., Jer. *sagitta*: Amb. (*Patr.*), Aug.,
Ottob. *arcus.*

Gen. xlix. 17 Amb. (*Ps. xl*), Lugd. insert *sicut*: Amb. (*Patr.*),
Ottob., Ruf., Jer. omit.

Gen. xlix. 22 Amb. (*Ps. xliii*), Lugd., Ottob. *iunior*: Amb. (*Patr.*),
Ruf. *adulescentior.*

Gen. xlix. 23 Amb. (*Ps. xliii*), Lugd., Ottob. *insidiari*: Amb. (*Patr.*),
Ruf. *intendere.*

Gen. xlix. 23 Amb. (*Ps. xliii*), Lugd., Ottob. *sagitta*: Amb. (*Patr.*), Ruf. *arcus*.

Gen. xlix. 25 Amb. (*Ob. Theod.*), Lugd. *mamillarum*: Amb. (*Patr.*), Ruf., Ottob. *uberum*.

This table clearly indicates a division of the texts into two groups, Amb. *De Bened. Patr.* (and perhaps *De Abr.*) with Rufinus and Augustine on one side, and on the other the other works of Ambrose with Lugd.—Ottob. changing from one group to the other but being rather with Lugd. than against it. Amb. *De Abr.* is here put in the group which opposes Lugd., though only one example occurs in the above list, because in Gen. xvii. 9–14, where we can compare Amb. *De Abr.*, Amb. *Ep.* 72, Aug. *De Ciu. Dei* and Lugd., though all four are evidently related, yet Amb. *Ep.* 72 and Lugd. go frequently together in opposition to Amb. *De Abr.* and Augustine. We have also in places where Lugd. is not extant significant connections between Amb. *De Abr.* and Augustine (*e.g.* in xii. 4, xiii. 9 and xxiv. 6–8) which suggest that in this treatise as in *De Bened. Patr.* Ambrose uses a text which is not quite as close as usual to Lugd. The other works of Ambrose have many significant connections with Lugd. in Gen., e.g. *De Iacob* (Gen. xxxi. 32), *De Ob. Theod.* (xxxii. 2 and l. 3), *De Ioseph* (repeatedly in chs. xxxvii and xliii), *Hex.* (xlvi. 27) and *De Off.* (xlvii. 25). The looser connection of *De Abr.* and *De Bened. Patr.* with Lugd. cannot be due to their date, for both belong rather to the middle period of Ambrose's literary career, and in *De Bened. Patr.*, where the difference is most conspicuous, the Deut. quotations agree so remarkably with Lugd. Evidently more than one type of text was used by Ambrose, just as more than one type of text is represented by Lugd. in the different books of the Heptateuch.

(d) The Speculum

Having now established the European character of Lugd. by showing its unusual resemblance to Lucifer and Ambrose and its wide dissimilarity from Cyprian, we may proceed to an examination of the Speculum quotations.

It is clear that the Speculum nowhere has any decided connection with Mon. except such as is shared by other Old Latin authorities. In Lev. xix Augustine, chiefly because he often retains an 'African' vocabulary, has several agreements with Mon., and he has more with Speculum, but Speculum differs very much from Mon., perhaps just about as much as Lucifer does. Mon. and Lugd. are, of course, unusually close in Num. and in Deut. viii and ix, but where they do diverge, as in Num. xii. 7 and Deut. viii. 19–20, Speculum follows Lugd., except for one agreement of Speculum and Mon. (Deut. viii. 19) which is due to Lugd. having made an accidental or Hexaplaric omission. In Deut. xxxii the MSS diverge widely, and Speculum has a very close relation to Lugd. while Mon., as already mentioned, has some clear agreements with Lucifer (e.g. *v.* 18 Mon. and Luc. *alentem*, Spec. and Lugd. *qui nutriuit*). Nor has Mon. any close connection with Speculum in Ex. xix, in spite of the MS having here a different type of text which frequently brings it into agreement with Augustine.

There is decidedly more connection between Speculum and Wir. This is well seen in Ex. xxii. 22–27 where these two have much in common with Ambrose and the A text of Cyprian, while the true text of Cyprian stands alone; Speculum however is not so close to Wir. as Ambrose is. In Ex. xxxiv where we have a considerable passage (*vv.* 12–17) in Speculum, Wir. and Lugd., the two MSS are very closely connected and several times agree against Speculum, the connections of Speculum with either MS against the other being trivial or uncertain. There are signs of a closer connection between Speculum and Wir. again in Lev. xix to xxii, where Lugd. is missing. Here Wir. has several alterations of an arbitrary nature unsupported by any Greek authority which remind us of the similar alterations in Speculum. Two of these (the change to the plural and the insertion of a pronoun after *quia* in xix. 34) are indeed common to the two, which just here are remarkably similar.

When Speculum is compared with Lugd. we find a remarkably close agreement between their texts. This is especially true in Deut., where Speculum and Lugd. are as closely related as any pair of texts with the single exception of Lucifer and Lugd. in Josh. and Jud. Conspicuous examples of an agreement which is found almost everywhere may be cited from Deut. iv. 6 (insertion of *tam*), Deut. vi. 8 (*mobilia*), Deut. viii. 2 and 3 (*omnia experire*), Deut. xxiv. 11, Num. x. 35 (*in milia Israhel*), Ex. xxi. 19 and Gen. xxviii. 22 (*dederit dominus* for *dederis*); in Gen. xxxii. 24–30, though Augustine, Ambrose and Novatian also exist in parts, Lugd. and Speculum are very much the closest of all.

The most interesting passages are of course those for which we have other Old Latin texts in addition to these two. We commence with some passages from Deut. and Num., not only because the relation between Lugd. and Speculum is most consistently preserved here, but also because the quotations from these books cover more than half the material from the Heptateuch common to Lugd. and Speculum. Where Speculum, Lugd. and Ambrose coexist there is evidently a very close connection between them all, but Speculum and Lugd. are the closest of the three; this is well seen in Deut. xxiv. 10–13, Num. xv. 20 and xxiii. 21, and perhaps Speculum and Ambrose have no passage in the Heptateuch in which they are so alike as in Lam. iii. 24–32. In view of a suggested Gallic or Spanish origin of Speculum it is noteworthy that Speculum has no special connection with Hilary except (as will be noticed later) occasionally in Gen.; on the whole as in Deut. xxxii. 2 Speculum, Lugd. and Ambrose agree against Hilary, and in Deut. x. 12–13 Ambrose is the one of the three which is inclined to agree with Hilary against the others.

Where Augustine exists he sometimes agrees with Lugd. or Speculum against the other, but Speculum and Lugd. agree very much more against Augustine (as in Deut. viii. 2, Num. xii. 6–9 and xv. 30–31). Where Ambrose also can be quoted we find that the three agree against Augustine, except in Deut. xxiv. 10–13, where Ambrose has almost as much resemblance to Augustine as to Lugd. and Speculum. Considering the greater divergence between Lugd. and Lucifer in Deut., we are not surprised to find that Speculum and Lugd. repeatedly agree against Lucifer (*e.g.* Deut. xix. 15 and xxvii. 19), while coincidences between Lucifer and either of them against the other, though sometimes unmistakable, are fewer. There are also connections between all three (as in Deut. i. 17 and xxv. 15) striking enough to show their underlying unity. Where Cyprian can be quoted we find clear traces of a relation between Cyprian and Speculum (Num. xvi. 26, Deut. xvii. 12–13, xxiii. 19–23), but for the most part Speculum, Lugd. and Ambrose all agree together against Cyprian, even in the passages just enumerated.

In Lev. the relation between Speculum and Lugd. is less close than in any other book; in x. 1–2 Speculum is closer to Ambrose, and in viii. 35 closer to Augustine than to Lugd., while the remarkable coincidences between Speculum and Lugd. are all at the end of the book (*e.g.* xxv. 46 and xxvii. 30–31). We have already noticed that there are differences in the vocabulary of Lugd. before and after the gap which extends from the end of ch. xviii to the middle of ch. xxv, and we have here another indication that these last chapters in Lugd. are not homogeneous with the earlier chapters. We have also already noticed the slighter connection between Lugd. and Ambrose and between Lugd. and Lucifer in Lev., all of which emphasises the conclusion arrived at from the examination of its vocabulary that Lugd. in Lev. has a peculiar element which is not European. In Lev. xiv. 43–45 Speculum, Lugd. and Mon. all differ very considerably from one another; in the middle of a long quotation from Lev. xix Speculum inserts two clauses into *v.* 19 which are found in Pelagius (*Ep. ad Dam.*) but in no other authority.

In Ex. Lugd. and Speculum are again more closely related, though not only Lugd. and Wir. (ch. xxxiv) but also Lugd. and Ambrose (*e.g.* xxviii. 42) have an even closer relation with each other. In xxi. 22–25 Speculum often agrees with Augustine against Lugd. and Lucifer, and with Lugd. against Augustine and Lucifer, but never with Lucifer unless supported by Lugd. also. This divergence between Speculum and Lucifer is again seen in xxiii. 1–3 where they never agree against Augustine, though each agrees with Augustine against the other. In Ex. xii Speculum occupies an intermediate position between the African Cyprian and the European Niceta and Jerome, and in Ex. xix it has coincidences with Cyprian against Augustine and Mon.

In Gen. Speculum and Lugd. agree very closely against Novatian (xxxi. 11–13 and xxxii. 24–30) and Augustine (xxxii. 24–30, *Con. Max.* ii. 26) and even at times against Ambrose. Speculum again shows contact with Cyprian in xii. 1–3 (against Aug. *De Ciu. Dei* and Ambrose) and in xix. 24, but in xxxv. 1

departs widely from Cyprian as well as from Augustine and Ambrose and is much like Hilary.

In Josh. and Jud. Lugd. and Speculum are again very close; in addition to several coincidences in the Greek text implied, which will be noticed later, they both have the rare *uehementer*, both render ἐκκλίνειν by *egredi* in Josh. xxiii. 6, and in Josh. xxiv. 23 agree three times against Augustine, though Augustine has no agreement with either against the other. In Jud. the agreement is even closer than in Josh. (see especially xv. 5 *igni lampades* and xix. 21 *misit cibum*).

The similarity of Speculum to the late European group formed by Lugd., Ambrose and Lucifer shows that it must be regarded as representing a distinctly late type of Old Latin text. It has recently been suggested that there may have been a somewhat close connection between the late African and the Italian texts, and if Speculum can be taken as representing the late African type, such a connection is indisputable.

When we try to decide whether Speculum or Lugd. represents the earlier form of the version, we shall find the evidence conflicting. A dozen or more 'Africanisms' could be found in various places in Lugd. where Speculum evidently represents a later text, but there are at least as many places where the opposite is true. In Deut. xxiii. 15 the reading of Speculum (*qui confugit ad uos*) seems to show the influence of the Vulgate; but though in addition to this Speculum has many corruptions, paraphrases and arbitrary alterations not found in Lugd. which are also doubtless to be taken as indicating a late and degenerate text, yet the frequent agreements of Speculum with Cyprian against Lugd. in Num. and Deut., which have already been referred to, are significant on the other side. Our conclusion is that Speculum and Lugd. rather represent parallel developments of the Old Latin than that either is derived directly from the other.

Before leaving the Speculum some of the readings of *Codex Sessorianus* ('S') must be noticed in those numerous places where it differs from the readings of all or most of the other five MSS of Speculum.

An examination of the readings of the different MSS will make it clear that in the majority of cases *Cod. Sess.* agrees with Lugd. in a reading which is earlier than that of the other MSS. In the following places *Cod. Sess.* and Lugd. evidently preserve the better reading (which is given first):

Gen. xvi. 9 *humilia te* with Hil., Amb.: other MSS *humiliare* with Vulg.

Gen. xxviii. 22 *decimabo* with Amb.: other MSS *offeram* with Vulg.

Gen. xxxii. 26 *oriens*: other MSS *aurora* with Aug. and Vulg.

Gen. xxxii. 29 omit *quod est* with Aug.: other MSS fill out the text.

Gen. l. 17 *sume* with Ottob. (Lugd. *tolle*): other MSS *obliuiscere* (paraphrasing).

Ex. xxi. 19 *cessationes* (Lugd. *quod cessabit*): other MSS *operas* with Vulg.

Num. xii. 9 *ira indignationis* (Mon. Lugd. *ira animi*, Aug. *ira animationis*): other MSS *indignatio* only (simplifying).

Num. xvi. 26 *eis* with Cyp., Aug.: other MSS *in eis*.

Num. xvi. 26 *peccato* with Cyp., Jer.: other MSS *peccatis* with Aug. and Vulg.

Deut. viii. 3 *exierit*: other MSS *egreditur* with Vulg.

Deut. viii. 3 repeat *uiuit homo* as Greek: other MSS omit the second time with N.T.

Deut. xiii. 4 *hunc* with Tert.: other MSS *ipsum* with Luc. and Vulg.

Deut. xvi. 19 *sapientium*: other MSS *uidentium* as in Ex. xxiii. 8.

Deut. xix. 15 *in ore duorum testium et in ore trium*: other MSS assimilate to N.T. with Luc. and Aug.

Deut. xxiii. 9 *et* as in Greek: other MSS omit (simplifying).

In several other passages, especially Jud. xv. 4 and 5, Lugd. agrees with *Cod. Sess.* against the other MSS, but their readings, though probably superior, are not obviously so. *Cod. Sess.* also seems to preserve the better reading in the following places where Lugd. is missing or (in Ex. xxxiv. 14) differs from both Speculum readings:

Gen. vi. 2 *angeli* with Aug.: other MSS *filii* with Tert. and Vulg. (from the Hex. and known to Aug.).

Ex. xx. 12 *longinqui temporis*: other MSS *longaeuus* with Aug., Amb. and Vulg.

Ex. xxiii. 4 *boui* with Aug. and Greek: other MSS *ouem* (a likely correction).

Ex. xxxiv. 14 *deo alio*: other MSS *deum alienum* with Vulg.

Lev. xix. 9 *tui* with Greek: other MSS *uestri* (an improvement)— Aug. knows both.

Lev. xix. 16 *facies aggressuram* (with BAN*hnya*$_2$ and Mon.): other MSS *eris consentaneus* (with other Greek MSS and Luc.).

Lev. xix. 18 omit *ipsum* with Mon.: other MSS insert it with Luc. and Vulg.

Only in two places does it seem at all likely that the reading of *Cod. Sess.* and Lugd. is later than that of the other MSS of Speculum. In Gen. xxviii. 20 *Cod. Sess.*, Lugd. and Ambrose have *manducare* but the other MSS *ad edendum*, and though Jerome and the Vulgate use the gerundive (*ad manducandum* and *ad uescendum*) yet *edere* certainly seems 'African' as compared with *manducare*. In Deut. i. 17 *Cod. Sess.* and Lugd. have *sumes personam*, while the other MSS of Speculum with Lucifer have *accipies*. *Accipere* is on the whole earlier than *sumere*, but here the Vulgate has *accipere* and perhaps in this phrase there was a tendency to use *accipere* in later times. In the second half of the verse all the MSS of Speculum with Lugd. and Lucifer have *sumere*.

There are fewer places in which Lugd. agrees with the other MSS of Speculum, and in each of the four in which it is possible to decide between the two readings *Cod. Sess.* seems to have the earlier one:

> Ex. xx. 4 'S' has *cuiusquam* with Cyp.: other MSS *ullam* with Mon., Prisc. (Aug. uses each of these, Lugd., Luc., Iren. and Vulg. *omnem*).
>
> Ex. xxi. 19 'S' has *innocuus*: other MSS and Lugd. *innocens* as Vulg.
>
> Ex. xxxiv. 14 'S' has *zelo nomen* (perhaps a primitive error); other MSS with Wir. and Aug. *zelans* (Lugd. *zelabile*).
>
> Deut. viii. 2 'S' has *quam* with Aug. and Greek; other MSS *per quam* with Lugd. and Vulg. (an obvious emendation).

In fact besides Gen. xxviii. 20 and Deut. i. 17 mentioned above, the only place in which *Cod. Sess.* seems inferior to the other MSS is Gen. vi. 3, where *carnales* which is found also in Ambrose and Jerome may seem European; even this however is not certain for the reading of the other MSS (*caro*) may be from the Vulgate, though it is also the usual Old Latin rendering found in Augustine, Tertullian, Hilary and generally in Ambrose. One other interesting variant may be noticed. In Deut. xxv. 16 *Cod. Sess.* has *iniusta* and the other MSS *ista*. Lugd. and Lucifer following the Greek (and Hebrew) have *qui facit haec, qui facit iniqua* (Lugd. *iniustitiam*). *Ista* and *iniusta* however are more primitive than *haec* and *iniqua*, so that Speculum in each clause seems to preserve the earlier rendering, but *Cod. Sess.* has dropped out one clause and the other MSS the other. This seems more likely than that *ista* is a corruption of *iniusta*.

(e) Augustine

The general relation between the three MSS and the text used by Augustine in *Qu.* and *Loc.* has already been touched on in the first chapter; the results of a comparison between these four authorities may be briefly stated as follows. In Ex. Wir. and Lugd. are much the closest of the four; Augustine has some clear points of contact with Mon., but very many more with the common text of Wir. and Lugd.; Mon. seldom combines with the other MSS against Augustine, but in one or two places Mon., Wir. and Augustine combine against Lugd. In Lev. Augustine has much less connection with Lugd. than with either of the other MSS. His connections with Mon. are specially noticeable, not being confined to vocabulary, but extending to other details as well. As between Mon. and Wir., Augustine has some agreements with Wir. against Mon. such as (*ex*)*horrere* for προσοχθίζειν and *morticinum*, but rather more with Mon. against Wir., as *nolens* (ἀκουσίως), *obseruare* and *profanare* (βεβηλοῦν) as well as a more frequent use of *donum*, *inquinare* and *proselitus* rather than their later equivalents. That the changed relation between Augustine and Lugd. in passing from Ex. to Lev. is not due solely to the change in Lugd. is clear from the fact that while in Ex. xxii Augustine agrees with a later group (Wir., Ambrose and the A text of Cyprian) against Cyprian, in Lev. xix he rather agrees with the earlier Mon. and Cyprian against the later Wir., Speculum and Lucifer. In Num. and Deut. viii–x Lugd. and Mon. agree almost without exception against Augustine. In the later chapters of Deut. we find that Augustine agrees with Mon. and Lugd. in turn, with Lugd. on the whole in vocabulary but with Mon. frequently in other ways; *e.g.* in xxii. 17 Mon. and Augustine have *ecce* where Lugd. and the Greek MSS have *haec*; in xxii. 8 Mon. and Augustine have *si cadat qui cecidit*, but Lugd. *si ceciderit cadens*, though in the same verse Augustine and Lugd. agree in *aedificare* and *corona* where Mon. has *instruere* and *balteus*. This example shows the avoidance of participles and of the future perfect tense both of which are conspicuous in these chapters in Mon. as compared with Lugd. In both respects Augustine sometimes follows Lugd., though in this verse he agrees with Mon. In Ex. ix–xx there is a much closer connection between Mon. and Augustine than in the later part of Ex., so that whereas in ch. xxxii Mon. and Cyprian agreed against Augustine, in ch. xix Mon. and Augustine agree against Cyprian. The agreements between Augustine and Mon. here sometimes indicate not merely the use by each of a later version but also the use of nearly related versions: each *e.g.* has *commodare* (χρᾶσθαι) xii. 36, *demonstrare* (σημαίνειν) xviii. 20, *monere* (συμβιβάζειν) xviii. 16, and in xvi. 33 each replaces εἰς διατήρησιν by a verb *ut* (Mon. and Ottob. *et*) *seruetur.*

There can be no doubt that apart from the primitive Cyprian and the earlier parts of Mon., Augustine's is the Old Latin text which differs most widely from Lugd. We may therefore collect here some of the most striking agreements between Augustine and Lugd.: Gen. xxxii. 8 *in salutem* (εἰς τὸ σώζεσθαι), xxxii. 11 and xxxvii. 21 *ferire* for πατάσσειν (usually *percutere*); Ex. ii. 25 and xxx. 36 *innotescere* (used by neither again), iii. 22 *inquilina,* though as Augustine remarks this does not correctly represent the Greek, vi. 9 *defectio animi,* xxi. 35 *partiri* and then *dispartiri* for διαιρεῖν (generally *diuidere*), xxviii. 31 *fungi sacerdotio* (here only for λειτουργεῖν though often for ἱερατεύειν), xxix. 30 *qui successerit ei* for ὁ ἀντ᾽ αὐτοῦ (cf. Lugd. *qui pro eo* Lev. vi. 22); Lev. xxvi. 33 *perambulans gladius,* xxvi. 36 *uolantis* (φερομένου); Num. xvi. 33 *praeesse* (κατάρχειν), xxii. 22 *ut non transmitteret* (Aug. *permitteret*) *eum* (ἐνδιαβάλλειν), xxii. 32 *dilatio* (διαβολή); Deut. xvi. 10 *prout* and then *secundum quod* (both rare in Deut.), xxix. 5 *adduxit* (unsuitably for ἤγαγεν); Josh. iii. 4 *longum interuallum* (μακράν) and *ire* followed by *abire* (both for πορεύεσθαι), vi. 1 *prodire* (rare in both), vi. 28 *resaluare,* viii. 12 *erant ciuitati* (τῆς πόλεως); Jud. i. 1 *defunctus est* (for noun), ii. 1 *clauth montem* (κλαυθμῶνα—Lugd. *ploratio* in *v.* 5), ii. 10 *eius quae* (ὅ), viii. 26 *torques* for two different words, xi. 3 *latrones* (whether for κενοί or λιτοί) and xiii. 23 *sed nec.* Such intimate connections as these show that, whatever divergence there may be in other respects, the most dissimilar of the Old Latin texts must ultimately come from the same source.

So far the quotations from Augustine which have been used have been taken from *Qu.* and *Loc.,* but in Genesis at least we have a considerable amount of material from other works of Augustine for comparison. The whole question of Augustine's different texts is one of special complexity; each of his works seems to give us a different text, so that we often get as much variety in Augustine's different works as in all the other representatives of the version; and except in such works as *De Ciu. Dei, De Trin., De Gen. ad Litt.* and *De Gen. con. Man.* we have to rely on a few detached quotations which are not sufficient to generalise from. In the case of these four works however it is possible to put forward a few conclusions which seem sufficiently well founded. We will commence with a few passages for which other authors can be quoted, and which are long enough to show that we have more than a casual reference to deal with.

Num. xii. 6–9 is quoted in *De Gen. ad Litt.* xii. 27, and we have also the texts of Speculum, Mon. and Lugd. The last three are all very closely related, Mon. and Lugd. also having a few special agreements not shared by Speculum and Speculum and Lugd. a few not shared by Mon. Augustine on the other hand differs considerably from the others, his text having a decidedly more primitive character than theirs; he uses *e.g. claritas* and *quomodo* which are both early words, and the literal genitive *audite uerborum* is very unlike his usual practice. Lugd., Speculum and the Latin Origen in *v.* 7 have *non sicut famulo meo Moysi qui* but Augustine and Mon. follow all the Greek authorities in having a nominative *famulus meus* and omitting *qui*. The former seems like a later modification of the text. Tertullian's two quotations from this passage are not very helpful, being so free and contracted that his use of *ad Moysen* cannot be taken as evidence that he read the dative; at the most we can say that the turn he gives to the sentence suggests the manner in which the paraphrase arose which is found in Lugd., Speculum and Or.-Lat.

Parts of Ex. xxxiii are quoted in *Qu., De Trin.* and *De Gen. ad Litt.* In *Qu.* Augustine uses *gloria* for δόξα as Lugd.; Wir. first uses *claritas* (*vv.* 18 and 19) and then *gloria* (*v.* 22). In *De Gen. ad Litt.* Augustine uses *claritas* (*v.* 18) and *maiestas* (*v.* 22), but in *De Trin.* he uses *maiestas* in both verses. The last word is rare but *claritas* gives an 'African' appearance to *De Gen. ad Litt.* In *v.* 23 *De Gen. ad Litt.* and *De Trin.* agree twice again against *Qu.*, Lugd. and Wir.

In the much quoted verse Gen. xix. 17 there are two clearly distinguished renderings. Lugd., Speculum and Aug. *De Trin.* agree in numerous points, while the quotations in Jerome and in Aug. *Qu., De Ciu. Dei* and *Con. Max.* agree very closely together in a very different text. The former group have *neque stes in hac uniuersa regione, in montem uade et ibi saluaberis,* but Jer. and Augustine in *De Ciu. Dei* and *Con. Max.* give *nec steteris in tota regione, in monte saluum te fac;* and the five-fold agreement of *Qu.* with the latter in the following verses against Lugd. and *De Trin.* shows that *Qu.* must here be classed with *De Ciu. Dei* and *Con. Max.* The use of *hac* for the article and *saluare* are 'African,' but on the other hand *uniuersus* is generally considered European. In the immediate neighbourhood of this verse, however, we notice the 'African' *eicere* in Speculum, and *ne forte* and *quoniam* in *De Trin.* and Lugd., where the other group has *educere, ne quando* and *quia,* so that with the exception of *uniuersus* all points to the form in Lugd., Speculum and *De Trin.* being the earlier. On the whole therefore we may say that the evidence of the three passages considered suggests that *De Trin.* and *De Gen. ad Litt.* have an earlier type of text, and *Qu., De Ciu. Dei* and *Con. Max.* have a later one. An examination of the Genesis quotations in *De Ciu. Dei* supports the opinion that in that book Augustine has a later type of text than usual. *Sumere* is very often used there, and this is a distinctly late word; in Gen. xxviii. 10 we find *proficisci* used in *De Ciu. Dei* where Lugd. has *ire,* and in Gen. xxii. 12 *scire* where Cyprian, Hilary, Speculum and Aug. *Qu.* and *De Trin.* use *cognoscere.* On the other hand the peculiarities of the *De Trin.* quotations seem early; in Ex. iii. 2–6 although the Cyprianic *cremare* and *grandis* are removed the early *iste* and *clamare* are retained. If we could be sure that *uideri* is 'African' we should have another clear indication of the same thing, for *De Trin.* has it frequently (*e.g.* Gen. xii. 7, xvii. 1 and xxii. 14) where *De Ciu. Dei, Qu.* and Ambrose have *apparere.*

With regard to the other works of Augustine the smaller amount of material makes a division of their texts into early and late precarious; but with *De Trin.* and *De Gen. ad Litt.* we may suspect as representing an early type of text *De Grat. et Lib. Arb.* (*e.g.* in Ex. viii. 32 and Deut. viii. 18), *Con. Iul.*

Impf. (Deut. xxiv. 14 and 17—both quoted from Julian), *Sermones* (Ex. xv. and xx. 4), *De Doct. Chr.* (Num. xiii. 20) and *Con. Adu. Leg. et Pro.* (Deut. xxviii. 56). Among the later texts with *De Ciu. Dei* we should place *De Unit. Eccl.* (Jud. vi. 36–39), *De Perf. Iust. Hom.* (Deut. xxx. 10–11) and perhaps *Con. Max.*

Lugd. has some close agreements with many of the treatises of Augustine, but sometimes it differs in one place from a text with which it has clear agreements in others. In Gen. xxviii. 13–14 Lugd. and Aug. *Con. Ep. Parm.* have several clear agreements against *De Ciu. Dei* and *De Unit. Eccl.*, but Lugd. has a striking similarity to *De Unit. Eccl.* in Jud. vi. 36–40, agreeing with it clearly several times against *Qu.* as well as Ambrose (*Spir. Sanc.*); again though Lugd. opposes *Qu.* in Gen. xix. 17, yet in Num. xxv. 4 and in Deut. xxviii. 54 and 56 it agrees with *Qu.* or *Loc.* against *Con. Adu. Leg. et Pro.*, and in Ex. xxxiii. 19 with *Qu.* against all Augustine's other quotations in having *misericordiam praestitero* for *misericors fuero*. A striking agreement with Lugd. is found in *De Perf. Iust. Hom.* 9, for *consummatus* of Lugd. and *inconsummatus* of Augustine (Deut. xxiii. 17) evidently rest on the same misunderstanding of the Greek; so also in quoting Gen. xxx. 15 in *Con. Faust.* xxii Augustine has *uis accipere* for λήμψῃ with Lugd. Ambrose frequently shows a considerable amount of agreement with various treatises of Augustine; in addition to several instances already mentioned we may notice the agreements with *Loc.* in Gen. xxiii. 3 and xxiv. 6–8 (especially *reuocare* and *uenire* in the latter), and with *De Trin.* in Gen. xxii. 2 and Ex. xxiv. 17.

The first three chapters of Genesis are quoted almost complete in *De Gen. con. Man.* and *De Gen. ad Litt.* and most of the first in *De Gen. Impf. Lib.* Considerable portions of these chapters are also found in Ambrose, Lucifer and Tertullian, and we have two other early quotations of value, Gen. iii. 14–19 in Cyprian, and Gen. i. 14–16 in *De Pasc. Comp.* Cyprian is remarkable for his close agreement with *De Gen. con. Man.*; we notice especially *omni pecore, omni genere bestiarum, pectore, tunc dixit Deus, tristitia* and *gemitu*. Cyprian and *De Gen. con. Man.* each have some peculiarities, and perhaps it is only when *De Gen. con. Man.* is thus eccentric that *De Gen. ad Litt.* has any noteworthy agreements with Cyprian. *De Pasc. Comp.* also agrees much with *De Gen. con. Man.* against *De Gen. ad Litt.*, but has an even closer resemblance to *De Gen. Impf. Lib.*; these two *e.g.* have *initium diei v.* 16 and ablatives *in signis* and *in temporibus v.* 15 (*De Gen. con. Man.* and *De Gen. ad Litt.* have *inchoationem* and accusatives); the three agree against *De Gen. ad Litt.* in omitting a clause in *v.* 14.

When Ambrose is compared with Augustine's various texts in these three chapters, we find that he has more resemblance to *De Gen. ad Litt.* than to *De Gen. con. Man.* or *De Gen. Impf. Lib.*, and in ch. iii Lucifer as well as Ambrose is less eccentric than either of the texts of Augustine. Lucifer has certain connections with Ambrose (e.g. *indicare* iii. 11) and some with *De Gen. con. Man.* (*sed neque* iii. 3, *domine* iii. 10) but fewer with *De Gen. ad Litt.*

It remains to notice an apparent inconsistency in the nature of the text of *De Gen. ad Litt.* In discussing Num. xii. 6–9 and Ex. xxxiii. 18 this treatise was found to exhibit an early type of text, but in the first three chapters of Gen. it seems to have a later one. It is however easy to account for this. The quotations from Ex. and Num. would probably be given, if not from memory, at least from a well-known and old-established text, but for the actual chapters of Gen. on which the treatise is written a corrected and revised Latin text seems to have been used; perhaps also a Greek MS was before the writer for in many places in these chapters it seems possible to trace the influence of the Greek text on the rendering given. We have already noticed in the substitution of *locuturus es* for *debeas loqui* in Ex. iv. 12 an example of a similar correction of the current Latin text from a Greek MS in *Qu.* On the other hand there can be no doubt that *Qu.* does preserve many genuine Old Latin renderings, apart from those instances in which Augustine states that he is quoting from the Latin version. For example Ex. xxxiii. 13 is twice quoted in *Qu.*, once *in loco* and once in Deut.; the two quotations differ in several respects, but probably both are from genuine Old Latin texts for one agrees with the quotation in *De Gen. ad Litt.* and the other with that in *De Ciu. Dei.*

(f) The Ottobonian MS

The Old Latin fragments contained in the Ottobonian MS are evidently closely related to the other MSS, all the more obviously perhaps because the parts which can be compared with Mon. are from the chapters in which Mon. has a later type of text than elsewhere.

The close relation between Ottob. and Mon. in Ex. xvi and xvii is clear from such agreements as *in tabernaculis* (xvi. 16 σὺν τοῖς συσκηνίοις), *domicilio* (xvi. 29), *terra habitationis* (xvi. 35), *uenerunt* (xvii. 1 παρενέβαλον), the insertion of *coepit* (xvii. 2), *quid* followed by *quare* (xvii. 2, both for τί) and *palam* (xvii. 6). If we enquire which of the two here represents the earlier form of the version we shall find the evidence inconclusive; Ottob. would seem later in *manducare, proficisci, quemadmodum* and *usquedum*, but earlier in *exire, maiores natu, promouere* and *sermo*. In view of the comparatively late type of text in each we are not surprised to find that they agree considerably against Cyprian in Ex. xvii. 9.

A similar result follows from the comparison of Ottob. and Lugd. in Genesis. That the two are closely connected is shown by such common readings as *introire* for πορεύεσθαι (xxxvii. 20), *ex Iacob* (xlvi. 15), *ut esset* and *applicare* (xlviii. 13), *ecce* (xlviii. 22), common omissions in xxxvii. 30 and xlviii. 20, and insertions in xxxviii. 6 and xlix. 32, as well as by the twenty agreements of the two MSS against Ambrose and Rufinus in Gen. xlix to be noticed shortly; and if Ottob. seems later than Lugd. in *Ismahelitae* (xxxvii. 28), *nominare* (l. 11), *consolari* (l. 21) and the avoidance of *iste* in xlix. 28 and l. 24, it seems earlier in *cognoscere* for *scire* (xxxviii. 9), *pessimus* (xxxviii. 7 and 10), *quoniam* (xlvi. 30) and *totus* (l. 8) and in the primitive mistake *singularium* for μονίμων in xlix. 26, which is corrected in Lugd., as well as in Ambrose and Rufinus, to *manentium*.

Ottob., Lugd. and Wir. are evidently all related to one another in Ex. (*e.g.* in xxvi. 2, 10 and 11), but the connection between Ottob. and Lugd. is not so close as in Gen. Not only are Lugd. and Wir. much closer than Ottob. is to either, but where Ottob., Lugd. and Augustine coexist, the most noticeable agreements (as in xxvi. 10) are generally between Ottob.

and Augustine. This close connection between Ottob. and
Augustine is also seen in Ex. xxiii and xxiv where Lugd. is
missing, but these two have such common readings as *amentem
faciam* (xxiii. 27), *per partes* for κατὰ μικρόν (xxiii. 30) and
partem reliquam for ἥμισυ (xxiv. 6); they are also very similar
in xxiii. 20 and 21 where Tertullian and Cyprian differ considerably. Such clear coincidences between these two are much
rarer in Genesis, and in Ex. xvi and xvii they seldom agree
against Mon., though Mon. agrees with each in turn. Ottob.
and Ambrose are also evidently akin. In Gen. xli both use
uaccae though this word is very rare, and Wir. and Augustine
use the common *boues*; in l. 20 both have *in hodiernum* where
Lugd. and Speculum following the Greek have *sicut hodie*; in
Ex. xvi. 17 both have superlatives where Mon., Irenaeus and
the Greek have positives; in quoting Ex. xxiv. 17 Ottob.,
Ambrose and Augustine (*De Trin.*) are identical.

In Gen. xlix, where we have many verses quoted by Lugd.,
Ottob., Rufinus and Ambrose (*De Bened. Patr.*), Lugd. and
Ottob. are very much together, and Ambrose and Rufinus
almost as much. Over twenty times we find clear agreements
of the first pair against the second, while connections of other
pairs are comparatively rare; we have Lugd. and Ambrose together five times, Lugd. and Rufinus three times, Ottob. and
Ambrose three times, Rufinus and Ottob. once. The three
other texts seldom agree against Ottob. and even more rarely
against Ambrose, but Rufinus has ten clear differences from the
combined readings of the other three. Some of these are due
to the freedom with which he uses his text, perhaps also to his
use of a Greek MS, but sometimes they are due to peculiar connections between Lugd., Ambrose and Ottob., as in *v*. 21 where
these three render ἐπιδιδόναι by the rare *porrigere*. Lugd. also
has many divergences from readings common to the other three,
but it has already been remarked that when Ambrose quotes
from this chapter in other works, Lugd. agrees with such quotations against *De Bened. Patr.*; in *v*. 17 *e.g.* Ambrose in *De
Bened. Patr.* gives *factus est Dan ipsi*, but in *Ps. xl* has *fiat Dan
sicut* exactly as Lugd. though *sicut* is represented in no other
text Latin or Greek. Very little of Augustine and Cyprian
exists for comparison in this chapter but Augustine is closest to

Cyprian in *v.* 10, and sometimes (as in *dentes candidiores v.* 12) agrees with Ambrose against all other authorities.

On the whole distinctive 'Africanisms' are not very numerous in Ottob., though perhaps they are more conspicuous than we should have expected in a text which is so evidently late; we have *adhuc* regularly, *colligere* and *collectio* frequently (*congregare* twice), *eremus* twice, *ne forte, nequitia, pessimus* (superlative for positive), *plorare* (*flere* only once), *praecipere* often (*mandare* only once), *seruare, obseruare* and *conseruare* (not *custodire*), and *totus* five times (*uniuersus* twice). Later words however are more conspicuous; we find for example *aduena, consummatio, esca* (not *cibus*), *furor* (twice), *immolare* and *immolatio, intrare* five times (*introire* twice), *manducare* often (*edere* only once), *parere* often (*uideri* once), *pellis, plebs, proficisci, solemnis* frequently (*festus* once), *sumere* a dozen times (even when Augustine has *accipere*), *ualde* (not *nimis*) and *usquedum* (twice); we have also the accusative and infinitive construction and several conflations, while *iste* and *quoniam* occur only once each.

Ottob. is frequently free in its renderings *e.g.* in Ex. x. 15 and often in Gen. xli; it has also many eccentric readings and mistakes. One conflation may be noticed particularly; in Ex. xxvi. 13 Ottob. repeats a part of *v.* 12, but in words which are much more like Lugd. and Wir., his earlier form being like Augustine's; thus we have the second time *dimidiam partem* for *dimidium, abscondere* for *subtegere*, and *hinc* and *illinc* for *ex hoc* and *ex illo*.

(*g*) Other Old Latin Texts

THE VIENNA FRAGMENTS. The text of the Vienna Palimpsest Fragments of Genesis xii, xiii and xv is evidently European. It contains no 'Africanisms,' but several words which are clearly late; it is much like the text used by Augustine in *De Ciu. Dei*, and even more like Ambrose's text in *De Abraham* (the only work of Ambrose which quotes these chapters considerably). In ch. xii Ambrose and Vindob. have *dixisti* in *v.* 18 though this word is rare for ἀπαγγέλλειν (Aug. *adnuntiare*); both have *sed* for ἵνα τί (*v.* 19) and the rare *saeuissimus* (*v.* 17); both insert *mihi* and *hinc* in *v.* 19 and use first *sumere* and *uxor* and then just afterwards *accipere* and *mulier* for the same Greek words.

The two also agree in being more polished than the primitive Old Latin and even at times paraphrastic. In ch. xv the coincidences with Aug. *De Ciu. Dei* are especially noticeable; each has e.g. *dominator v.* 8 and *contra faciem alterum alteri v.* 10, while in *v.* 12 the same word is rendered first *inruere* and then *incidere* in each; in xiii. 9 we have *uel* inserted with no Greek authority by Vindob., Augustine and Ambrose. It is interesting to notice that we have already observed a closer connection between *De Ciu. Dei* and *De Abr.* than is usual in Augustine and Ambrose.

THE LATIN VERSION OF PHILO. The text of Gen. xxv–xxviii used in the Latin version of Philo is also European in character. Words which have an earlier appearance are not altogether wanting, for we find *ne forte* (xxvii. 12), *illic* (xxvi. 8 and 25), *iste* (xxvi. 4), *iustificatio* (xxvi. 5) and *quasi* (xxvii. 23), but the direct coincidences with Lugd. and Ambrose show that the text is on the whole of a late type. It seems probable that the text used does not altogether follow any particular Latin MS, but is in part directly translated from the Greek. An indication of this is to be seen in the very frequent use of *pergere* in place of *uadere* and *abire*. *Pergere* is a rare word in all forms of the version and perhaps is rather 'African,' but it is used in Philo far more than in any other Latin text, and was probably introduced by the translator himself. The text is not remarkably like Cyprian, though the influence of the Old Latin version used by Cyprian is discernible; in xxvi. 3–5 we notice clear resemblances to Tyconius and to Aug. *De Ciu. Dei*, though there is more divergence from Augustine's other texts. The resemblance to Ambrose and Lugd. however is most conspicuous. It has been stated that Lugd. shows the closest resemblance of all to Philo, but this seems to be a mistake; Philo and Ambrose have four coincidences against Lugd. which are clearer than any coincidences of Philo and Lugd. against Ambrose. Philo and Ambrose alone have *abundantia* in xxvii. 28 (others *multitudo*), and they (with Hilary) by stopping the clause at this word connect it with the preceding rather than with the following words; they also have *fuge* in xxvii. 43 where Lugd. has *proficiscere*, and in xxviii. 2 have a participle (with *De Ciu. Dei* and the Greek) where Lugd. has a verb.

TERTULLIAN. The whole question of the text of Tertullian

is a difficult one, owing to our uncertainty as to the extent to which he used a Latin version, and how far he translated for himself from a Greek MS. It is possible that a careful comparison of all his quotations with the other surviving witnesses to the Old Latin text would suggest that he used a Latin version much more than has sometimes been admitted. In the Heptateuch at least his text frequently agrees remarkably with later authorities which show no signs of the direct influence of his works.

In Gen. i we do not find such a close agreement as we might expect between Tertullian and Augustine's earlier treatises. There are some agreements with *De Gen. Impf. Lib.*, more with the common text of this work and *De Gen. con. Man.*, but practically none with *De Gen. con. Man.* alone, and there are some conspicuous agreements with *De Gen. ad Litt.* against both. Some of the agreements with Augustine's earlier treatises against *De Gen. ad Litt.* seem due to Augustine having conformed the latter to a current Greek text. This is probably the explanation of the appearance of *super terram* in *De Gen. ad Litt.* at the end of *v.* 11 where the words are omitted in Tertullian and the other works of Augustine and apparently in Ambrose, and therefore presumably in the Old Latin version. Gen. i. 12 is quoted by Ambrose in two forms: in *Hex.* he has *produxit terra herbam foeni* as Tertullian, but in *De Noe* has *eiecit terra herbam pabuli* with Augustine. Tertullian has some other noticeable agreements with Ambrose such as those against Lugd. in Deut. xxxii. 21 (*in natione insipiente*) and xxxiii. 17 (*uentilare* for *incornuare*). Agreements between Tertullian and Augustine against Lugd. are, as we might expect, more frequent: we have for example *quam terribilis* in Gen. xxviii. 17 (Lugd. *sicut uerendus*), *auertes* and *fenus fenerabis* in Deut. xv. 7 and 8 (Lugd. *prohibebis* and *mutuum dabis*), *pallium* or *uestimentum* in Deut. xxiv. 13 (Lugd., Speculum, Ambrose *pignus*—the difference here involving a difference in the Greek text), *transfretabit* in Deut. xxx. 13 (Lugd. *transibit*). In the verse last quoted however, Tertullian also has a clear agreement with Lugd. against Augustine, involving a difference in the Greek text (*auditum* for *audientes*).

Tertullian makes considerable use of Lev. xiii. and xiv in

De Pud., and his vocabulary here is decidedly akin to that of Mon. and Augustine, and differs much from that of Lugd.; in Deut. xxxii. 15 Tertullian is with Mon. and Lucifer rather than Lugd.

An extraordinary connection between Tertullian (*Scorp.*) and Lucifer is seen in Deut. xiii. 6–10; in the preceding verses of this chapter there are traces of it (e.g. *et dixerit v.* 2), though on the whole in *vv.* 1–4 Lugd. and Lucifer agree against Tertullian (three or four times very clearly); but in these later verses Tertullian and Lucifer have quite a dozen clear agreements, in half of which Cyprian and Lugd. agree against them, though nowhere else are coincidences between Cyprian and Lugd. at all clear. Cyprian agrees with Tertullian and Lucifer several times, but Lugd. seldom does so, and after Tertullian and Lucifer stop at the end of *v.* 10, Cyprian and Lugd. seem to draw further apart. The reappearance of his text in Lucifer seems to show that Tertullian here represents an actual Latin version of this passage, and is not translating for himself; if however this is so the difference between Tertullian and Cyprian is greater than we should have expected.

In Ex. xxiii. 20 and 21 we have three early authorities existing, Cyprian, Tertullian and the treatise *Adu. Iud.*, as well as Augustine and Ottob. Tertullian and *Adu. Iud.* are much alike, sometimes with no other support, once clearly with Cyprian, but once with Augustine and Ottob. Where Tertullian differs from *Adu. Iud.* he rather agrees with Augustine and Ottob., while *Adu. Iud.* goes with Cyprian. Augustine and Ottob. are much alike.

In spite of the fact that Tertullian and Lugd. are so far apart in the version, such a passage as Num. xxv. 1–3 (*Scorp.* 3) indicates that the two belong to the same version; here they agree in *diuertere, abire* (in place of βεβηλοῦσθαι) and *initiari*; sometimes however Tertullian's rendering is more independent of the other members of the Latin version. In Gen. ix. 5 he seems to know a text agreeing with the Hebrew and a few Hexaplaric MSS of the Septuagint, but not found in Ambrose or Augustine or the majority of Greek MSS. In this passage and a few which will be noticed in the next chapter he may have used Greek MSS of a different kind from those used in the Latin version, but the peculiar connections with Mon. and Augustine, and in some places with Ambrose and Lucifer, seem to show that he was already acquainted with a Latin version akin to the version which they afterwards used.

JEROME. Jerome was of course acquainted with many types of text, and evidently used Old Latin MSS of various characters. Perhaps the most remarkable thing about Jerome's Heptateuch quotations is the frequency with which they agree with Tertullian's. This agreement is seen for example in Gen. ix. 5, Ex. iii. 8 (*manare* for *fluere*), Num. xi. 4–6 (*uesci, uenerunt in mentem* and *at*) and Deut. xxvii. 15: in the first and last of these the agreement extends to the use of a Greek text different from that followed by the rest of the Latins. In several passages Jerome's text has a distinctly primitive appearance; in Gen. l. 9–10 (*Ep.* 39) for example *grandis, fortis* and *nimis* all seem 'African,' and frequently in certain treatises (*De Perp. Uirg. Mar., Con. Lucif.* and *Adu. Pelag.*) we find such words as *delictum, fortitudo, iste* and *quasi* which are characteristic of the earlier texts.

Jerome also shows a certain amount of resemblance to Mon. in quoting Deut. xxviii. 25 (on Isaiah). Besides agreeing in the use of *dispersio* for *disseminatio*, they both have *una uia* (Jer. *uia una*) *egredieris...et per septem...* where Lugd. has *in una uia exibis...et in septem.* However the agreements of Jerome and Lugd. are almost as noticeable (Jerome indeed agrees with each more than they do with one another), for though Jerome uses *dispersio* his rendering *eris in dispersione* is similar to Lugd. (*eris in disseminatione*) while Mon. has *erit dispersio tui.*

Naturally however Jerome frequently has a close connection with the European group of authorities, Lugd., Ambrose and Lucifer; agreements with Augustine are seldom remarkable, though we notice that Jerome (*Con. Lucif.*) is with Cyprian and Speculum rather than with Lugd. in Num. xvi. 26, and with Cyprian and Parmenian (*apud* Aug.) rather than with Lugd. and Ambrose in Ex. xxviii. 43.

NOVATIAN. It is not easy to draw definite conclusions from the Heptateuch quotations in Novatian. His longest one (Gen. xxxii. 24–31) shows a closer relation to Augustine (*Con. Max.*) than to any of the other texts, and a remarkable divergence from

Lugd., while with Speculum and Ambrose he has both agreements and differences. Such close relation with Augustine is
not found elsewhere; but the wide difference between Novatian
and Lugd. is seen everywhere, except in Gen. xxxi. 11–13,
where Novatian agrees with Lugd. and Speculum against Augustine and Cyprian, as *e.g.* in the use of *lapis stans* for στήλη,
which, except in Lugd. Gen., is nearly always rendered *titulus*.
Ambrose shows some similarity to Novatian again in Gen. xlviii.
15–16, but Jerome has more resemblance to him than any other
Old Latin text (see *e.g.* Gen. viii. 21, xi. 7, Ex. iv. 13, Deut.
xxxii. 8). Very little material for comparison with Cyprian
exists in Novatian, but what there is offers no suggestion of a
very close connection. Hilary too shows more differences from
than agreements with Novatian. The relation between Novatian
and the other Old Latin texts is therefore uncertain and obscure;
differences from them are generally more conspicuous than remarkable agreements, but this may be due to Novatian's freedom
in quoting for, in spite of his wide divergence from Lugd. and
Hilary, his agreements with Ambrose and Speculum, with
Augustine in one passage, and with Jerome everywhere seem to
indicate that his text is linked up with the others, and does not
represent a separate tradition.

The Heptateuch quotations alone however cannot settle the
question of Novatian's version, and an examination of Is. xxxv.
3 and 4 and lxvi. 2, Rom. xi. 33, Phil. ii. 6–8, and Wisdom iii.
4–8 (if *De Laude Mart.* can be quoted as Novatian's) will
probably lead to the conclusion that Novatian and Cyprian as
well as Speculum and Hilary do in reality quote from one
version. If however this be so we can already see going on in
Novatian that process by which the African version developed
into the European. In Matt. v. 8 and John i. 1 we already see
the version losing its distinctive 'Africanisms,' and in Ps. xliv. 8
and cix. 1 we have conspicuous agreements between Novatian,
Speculum and the A text of Cyprian against Cyprian himself.
We have already noticed that the later modification of Cyprian's
text in Gen. xlix. 10 appears already in Novatian, and in Gen.
xxxii. 30 though Cyprian's rendering cannot be quoted, *uisio* of
Novatian, Speculum and Ambrose seems to be a correction as
compared with *facies* of Lugd. or *aspectus* of Augustine. In

fact though it is not very obvious in Gen. xxxii. 24–31, Novatian often has very close relations with Speculum (as in John xiv. 7) and is perhaps on the whole no further removed from the Cyprianic text than Speculum is. The quotations of Novatian frequently introduce particles which are not by any means 'African,' but which become more common in the later European forms of the version, such as *nec quisquam* (καὶ οὐδείς), *ita, itaque, ideo, uero* and *-que*.

HILARY. Hilary's quotations are marked by considerable variety of character. At times he has clear connection with Augustine against the European texts, as in Gen. xxi. 17–18 against Novatian, and Deut. xxxii. 36 against Lugd.; but for the most part he has more agreements with the European texts than with Augustine. Connections with Ambrose, Lucifer, Speculum and Lugd. are frequently obvious (*e.g.* with Ambrose in Gen. xviii. 14), but in Deut. at least we frequently find that Hilary opposes them, as if in this book he used a less revised Latin text. Thus he differs several times from Speculum, Lugd. and Ambrose in Deut. xxxii. 2; and in Deut. vi. 4 and 5 (*uiribus* and the omission of *deus* and *dominus*), and in Deut. xxxii. 39 (*interimam* and *uiuificabo*) he agrees with Tertullian or Cyprian against the later authorities. Where the European texts differ he sometimes agrees with Ambrose and Jerome against Lugd. or Speculum (as in Deut. x. 12–13) but at other times with Lugd. against Ambrose (as in Deut. xxxiii. 16); in Gen. ix. 6 a clear connection with Speculum against Ambrose and Lucifer is seen in the addition of *anima*. In Num. xxv. 11–13 Hilary's seems to be the earliest of the texts quoted (which are all European). Ambrose, Lugd. and Jerome are evidently later, Lucifer occupying an intermediate position; the scribe of one MS of Hilary has inserted the rendering given by Lugd. and Ambrose. In Deut. x. 13 Hilary's vocabulary is again somewhat earlier than that of the other European authorities.

On two occasions Hilary shows a knowledge of alternative texts. His quotation of Deut. xxxii. 43 in *De Trin.* iv. 33, though in other respects differing from Lugd., agrees with it both in the order of *filii* and *angeli* and in having the singular *eum*, but when quoting the verse again on Ps. lxvii he gives the other order and has *eos*, following apparently a different Greek reading. The second example is in his quotations of Gen. xxxv. 1; both quotations are found in *De Trin.*, one being very much like Speculum, the other more like Cyprian and Augustine.

In spite of the difficulty of connecting Hilary's text intimately with any of the remaining Latin texts, there can be no doubt that his version is also fundamentally theirs. Such quotations of his as that of 1 Cor. xv. 53–55, for example (*De Trin.* xi. 35), are evidently from the same version as Cyprian's. Moreover his changes in the Cyprianic text are of the same kind, and sometimes agree exactly with those made by Lucifer, Speculum and the A text of Cyprian. Revision of the Cyprianic text is seen in Hilary's removal of *nequam* from Matthew and *facinus* from Isaiah, in the rarity of *quasi* and *quomodo* and in the substitution of *apponere, esca, excelsus, intrare, mandare, mandatum* and *ualde* for the 'African' equivalents found in Cyprian. In some places however Hilary retains the Cyprianic *fortitudo, natio* and *quoadusque*, and he does not use the late *quemadmodum*. The transition of his text from the Cyprianic to the European type is shown in the use of *claritas, gloria* and *honor* and of *perficere* and *consummare* in turn. On the whole Hilary's text is close to that of Lucifer and Speculum, but he seems rather nearer to Cyprian in point of vocabulary than either of them.

IRENAEUS AND TYCONIUS. The Latin version of Irenaeus has some very clear agreements with Lugd., e.g. *cum ui potestatem exercebant et in odio* (Iren. *odium*) *eis adducebant uitam* (Ex. i. 13–14), and *concupiscens* and *malefeci* (ἐπιθύμημα and ἐκάκωσα) in Num. xvi. 15; in some places however it probably depends directly on its Greek original and not on an Old Latin version, while in a few others it agrees with Cyprian or Mon. and seems to contain survivals of the more primitive Old Latin. Tyconius differs much from Lugd. in Ex. i. 6–10, but in other places (*e.g.* Ex. iv. 23) shows less divergence from that MS.

CHAPTER III

THE GREEK TEXT UNDERLYING
THE OLD LATIN VERSION

(a) The influence of the " B " type and the " A " type
of Greek Text

THROUGHOUT the greater part of the Heptateuch A and B
stand at the head of two opposing groups of Greek uncials,
each representing types of text both ancient and widely
known. In Ex. B is very much alone among the uncials; in
Num. it is frequently but not consistently followed by N and G;
in Deut. it is again very much supported by these two, and also
to a much greater extent by Θ; in all three of these books AFM
are closely connected. In Josh. F is more closely and NΘ less
closely related to B, but the opposition of B and AM is as
clearly seen as in former books. In Lev. and Judges the relations between the Greek uncials are very different and over the
greater part of Gen. B is missing[1].

Each of these Greek texts, represented respectively by B
and A, had its influence on the Old Latin version, over one
hundred[2] perfectly clear agreements with each group being
found in the four books Ex., Num., Deut., and Josh., which
will be first considered. Agreements of the Old Latin with B
are frequently omissions from, only occasionally insertions into,
the text of A; the agreements with A are often insertions, and
rarely omissions.

The influence of the two types of text however varies very
considerably from book to book. In Ex. the Latin version has
twice as many agreements with AFM as with B, and an equally
close agreement with AMNΘ is seen in Josh. In Num., on
the other hand, the agreements of the Old Latin (at least in the
case of the Old Latin MSS) with B (often of course with N and G)
are more striking and numerous than with the other uncials;

---

[1] See an article 'On the classification of the Greek MSS of the Hexateuch'
in the *Journal of Theological Studies* for April 1925.
[2] This number could be doubled by including smaller agreements which
probably, but not undoubtedly, imply a relation between the texts.

and in Deut. the agreement of the Latin version with BΘ becomes even more marked. In this book the connection of the Old Latin with B (normally including Θbwgnua₂) is much closer than anywhere else in the Heptateuch.

A selection of the agreements of the Old Latin with each group of uncials follows, those examples for the most part being chosen for which more than one Old Latin text can be quoted.

Agreements between the Old Latin and B

Gen. l. 1 Lugd., Ottob. with BDL*bnwd*₂ omit ἐπί.

Gen. l. 16 Lugd., Spec. with B*ackmowxb*₂*c*₂ παρεγένοντο λέγοντες for παραγενόμενοι εἶπαν.

Ex. xii. 48 Mon. with B*fioqrs* ποιῆσαι for καὶ ποιῇ.

Ex. xiii. 12 Mon., Amb. with BM(mg)*nv* Philo ἀφελεῖς for ἀφοριεῖς.

Ex. xvii. 6 Mon., Ottob. with BM(mg)*fioqr* insert μοῦ.

Ex. xxxiv. 12 Lugd., Wir. with B*ao* σοι for ποτέ.

Ex. xxxvii. 6 Lugd. with B*ahnxy* κεφαλίδας, which the other Greek mss conflate with ψαλίδας of *dpt*.

Ex. xxxviii. 2 and 3 Lugd., Mon. with B*abdhnx* and B*abhptx* have omissions.

Num. ii. 3 Lugd. with B*a*₂ κατὰ νότον for πρῶτοι. G conflates the two, but the obelus shows that the former is the true LXX.

Num. vi. 19 Lugd. with B*a*₂ and margins of *svz* εὐχήν (no doubt correctly) for κεφαλήν.

Num. x. 9 Lugd., Amb. with BFM etc. σημανεῖτε for σαλπιεῖτε.

Num. xi. 11 Lugd. with BN*dghknpta*₂ ὁρμήν for ὀργήν.

Num. xvi. 31 Lugd. with BG*dgnptmrxa*₂ omits τῶν ποδῶν.

Deut. ix. 15 Lugd., Mon. with BΘ*bwgnua*₂, G*cxdpt* having one (Hexaplaric) insertion, and AFMN etc. another.

Deut. xi. 31 Lugd. with B*dm* κατοικήσετε. F*b*₂ have κληρονομήσετε, other Greek mss conflating the two.

Deut. xii. 14 Lugd. with BΘ*gn* φυλῶν for πόλεων.

Deut. xvii. 5 Lugd., Luc. with B*kua*₂ omit a long clause which appears in other mss in two forms—one (Hexaplaric) in G*coptx*, another in AFMNΘ etc.

Deut. xviii. 19 Lugd., Cyp. with BΘ*abguwa*₂ ὅσα. G*cox* prefix πάντα, AFMN etc. τῶν λόγων αὐτοῦ.

Deut. xxxi. 5 Lugd., Mon. with BΘ*bgmnuwa*₂; expanded in different ways by GN*cdkoptx* and AFM etc.

Deut. xxxi. 12 Lugd., Wir., Luc. with BΘ*bglnuwa*₂ ἐκκλησιάσας and ὑμῶν for ἐκκλησιάσατε and σοῦ.

Deut. xxxi. 21 Lugd., Wir., Mon. with BΘMN*aghklnqrua*₂ omit a long clause which may be a Hexaplaric insertion in AF etc.

Deut. xxxii. 14 Lugd., Luc., Mon., Hil. with BF*gilnx ἔπιεν for ἔπιον.

Deut. xxxiii. 6 Lugd., Amb. with BFΘ and most cursives omit συμεών.

Josh. viii. 10 Lugd. with Bru omit both τοῦ λαοῦ and Ἰσραήλ.

Josh. xix. 29 Lugd. with Bhqr λέβ for τοῦ σχοινίσματος.

Josh. xxiv. 22 Lugd. with Bn κυρίῳ for τὸν κν (a clear connection because the dative is not natural).

Agreements between the Old Latin and A

Ex. ii. 18 Lugd. with Abdotw and margin of jvz, Ἰοθόρ for ῥαγουήλ.

Ex. xvii. 9 Mon., Cyp., Ottob. with AMejsvzgklwya₂ omit δυνατούς.

Ex. xxii. 18 Wir., Prisc. with AFM etc. περιβιώσετε for περιποιήσετε.

Ex. xxii. 25 Wir., Spec., Amb. with A*F*Mdpthlwa₂b₂ λαῷ for ἀδελφῷ.

Ex. xxxiii. 8 Lugd., Luc. with AF etc. omit three words.

Ex. xxxiii. 18 Lugd., Wir., Aug., Tert. with AFM etc. δόξαν for σεαυτόν of Bahr.

Ex. xxxiii. 19 Lugd., Wir., Aug., Amb. with AFM etc. καλέσω for λαλήσω of Bahu.

Ex. xxxiv. 26 Lugd., Wir. with AFM etc. εἰσοίσεις and ἐψήσεις for θήσεις and προσοίσεις of Ba.

Ex. xxxv. 23 Lugd., Wir., Aug. with AFM etc. insert πᾶς.

Num. ii. 17 Lugd. with AM etc. τάγμα for ἡγεμονίαν.

Num. ix. 21 and 22 Lugd., Aug. with AFM etc. have insertions not found in BNbirwa₂ and BNdgnptira₂ respectively.

Num. xvi. 5 Lugd., Amb. with AFHM etc. insert negatives opposing BGNxa₂.

Num. xviii. 1 Lugd., Aug., Or.-Lat. with AFGHN etc. ἁμαρτίας for ἀπαρχάς of BNorua₂.

Num. xxxi. 28 Lugd., Mon. with AF*HM etc. ὄνων for αἰγῶν of BNorua₂.

Num. xxxiv. 29 Lugd., Mon. with AFfilmyb₂ καταμετρῆσαι for καταμερίσαι.

Deut. x. 20 Lugd. with AΘdptesvzfiᵃr adds μόνῳ; the combination AΘ is rare in Deut. and probably the insertion is from vi. 13.

Deut. xix. 14 Lugd. with AMNmorxa₂ πρότεροι for πατέρες.

Deut. xxiv. 15 Lugd., Spec., Aug. with AFMNΘ insert a negative which is omitted by Bbwx.

Deut. xxxiii. 10 Lugd. with AFbw ἑορτῇ for ὀργῇ.

Josh. viii. 5 Lugd., Aug. with AFMNΘ etc. πᾶς ὁ λαός for πάντες.

Josh. viii. 27 Lugd., Aug. with AMNΘ*abloxyb*₂ omit πάντα ἅ.

Josh. x. 8 Lugd., Aug. with AFᵇNΘ etc. ὑποστήσεται for ὑπολειφθήσεται.

Josh. xv. 18 Lugd., Aug. with ANΘ*klmuyb*₂ εἰσπορεύεσθαι for ἐκπορεύεσθαι.

Josh. xxiv. 27 Lugd., Cyp., Aug. with AMNΘ etc. have οὗτος for αὐτός, omit αὐτῷ, have ὅσα for ὅ τι and ὑμᾶς for ἡμᾶς.

The connections of the Old Latin with B in Josh. are fewer and less convincing than elsewhere, but the above lists amply justify the claim that in each of these four books of the Heptateuch both types of Greek text have deeply influenced the Latin version.

In all the passages so far adduced there is no variation in the existing Latin authorities, but such variation is found at times, most conspicuously when Augustine's text is compared with the Old Latin MSS. The following list gives a selection of the more noticeable differences between Augustine and the MSS which seem to be due to the use of different Greek texts.

Ex. iii. 8 Lugd. has καὶ εἰσαγαγεῖν αὐτούς with B[1]: Aug. omit with AFM[1].

Ex. x. 1 Mon. has ἐσκλήρυνα with B: Aug. ἐβάρυνα with AM.

Ex. xviii. 21 and 25 Mon. omits γραμματοεισαγωγεῖς with BFᵇ *Mabhmqux*: Aug. has it with AF*.

Ex. xxvi. 7 Lugd., Wir., Ottob. have σκέπην with BM: Aug. σκέπειν with AF*abjtxb*₂.

Ex. xxvii. 9 Lugd. omits three words with B*h*: Aug. has them with AFM.

Ex. xxxi. 2 Lugd. (*Uri qui dicitur Or*) and xxxv. 30 Lugd., Wir. (*Uri qui est Or*) follow B*ahnox*, which have τὸν "Ωρ for υἱοῦ "Ωρ: Aug. follows AFM.

Ex. xxxiii. 19 Lugd., Wir. with B*aru* have ὀνόματί μου κύριος: Aug. omits μου and has κυρίου with AF*M: Amb. has κύριον with *bwdnptkxd*₂.

Ex. xxxvii. 14 Lugd. with B has σκηνῆς: Aug. with AFM αὐλῆς.

Num. v. 7 Lugd., Mon. with B have ἐποίησεν: Aug. ἥμαρτεν with *Aaehjsvz* and M (mg).

---

[1] Unless specially stated uncials thus quoted are supported by several cursives.

Num. viii. 19 Lugd. with BN omits three words: Aug. inserts with AFM.

Num. viii. 24 Lugd. with Bga_2 Philo has ἐνεργεῖν: Aug. with AFM has λειτουργεῖν λειτουργίαν ἐν ἔργοις, conflating ἐνεργεῖν with λειτουργεῖν of N$dnpt$.

Num. xxviii. 13 Lugd. with B*FHK: Aug. repeats δέκατον with B^{ab}AMN$cxya_2$.

Deut. vii. 1 Lugd. with B$bcuwxa_2$ has ἐὰν δέ: Aug. (et erit cum) follows the majority.

Deut. vii. 1 Lugd. with B*N$ejsvzdptb_2$ has μεγάλα: Aug. with AFM combines this with πολλά, the reading of B$^{a\Theta}cgnxa_2$.

Deut. xv. 7 Lugd. with BΘgna_2 has ἀποστέρξεις: Aug., Tert. ἀποστρέψεις with AFGMN.

Deut. xx. 16 Lugd. with B$\Theta dglmn$: Aug. has a long insertion with AFMN.

Deut. xxiv. 13 Lugd., Spec., Amb. with BΘ have ἐνέχυρον: Aug., Jer., Tert. ἱμάτιον with AFM (N conflates the two).

Deut. xxx. 13 Lugd., Tert. with BΘ ἀκουστὴν ἡμῖν ποιήσῃ αὐτὴν καί: Aug. with AFGM has ἀκούσαντες αὐτήν.

Josh. vi. 26 Lugd. with B$gkmnru$ omits ἀναστήσει καί and inserts ἐναντίον κυρίου with B: Aug. in each case follows AFMNΘ.

Josh. xvii. 16 Lugd. with Bhq omits οἱ υἱοὶ ἰωσήφ: Aug. with AGNΘ.

Josh. xxii. 8 Lugd. with Bhr σίδηρον: most cursives add χαλκόν: Aug. with AN$\Theta luyb_2$ omits both.

Josh. xxii. 30 Lugd. with B inserts Ἰσραήλ: Aug. omits with AN$\Theta aluya_2b_2$.

Several important conclusions are suggested by the above lists. We notice first that the third list supplements the first in providing several more agreements between the Latin MSS and B in Ex. and Josh., showing that even if in these books the connections of the MSS with the A text are more numerous than with the B text, yet there is a real connection with the latter, though not so close a one as in Num. and Deut. Again while the four Latin MSS, Speculum, Lucifer and Cyprian practically always agree in the Greek text followed, Augustine has many clear differences from their text, the examples from Deut. xv. 7 and xxiv. 13 suggesting that we may look rather to Jerome and Tertullian for Old Latin support for Augustine's type of text. A comparison of the first and second lists will show that while Augustine (where extant) almost always agrees with the Latin

MSS when they follow A, he has few significant agreements with them when they follow B; and the third list shows that in all books there are many passages in which the MSS follow B but Augustine follows AFM; while on the other hand it would be difficult to find anywhere in the Heptateuch a clear instance of Augustine following B and the other Latin authorities A. In the chapters of Ex. where no Latin MS exists we find Augustine again has numerous agreements with AFM whereas agreements with B (such as the omission of ὕδωρ in Ex. xv. 23 with Bqr) are rare.

It is not altogether easy to decide what is the cause of these differences between Augustine and the other Latin authorities. The fact that Augustine has no Latin support in these divergences from the MSS except occasionally in Jerome and Tertullian (who would both have been familiar with a Greek text) suggests that Augustine may have made the alterations himself from a Greek text differing from that which underlay the current Latin version; there are clear indications that the Old Latin version known to Augustine was nearer to the text of B than that which he himself would adopt, and that the Greek MSS with which he was acquainted were rather of the AFM type. In Ex. iii for example he notices that the Latin version inserts *ego* in *v.* 11 and *deus ad Moysen* in *v.* 12, but that the Greek omits both and has *quia* in *v.* 11 where the Latin has *ut*. The Latin version was therefore in harmony with B in all three respects, and Augustine's Greek was the Greek of AFM— in *v.* 12 of AFM$la_2b_2c_2$ only. Again in Ex. x. 23 he notices that the Latin text inserts the words *tribus diebus* which are absent (he says) from the Greek. They are in fact absent from most Greek MSS, but B$fioqrs$ have them and so has Mon.

Most of the passages quoted from Augustine in the above lists are contained in his treatises *Quaestiones* and *Locutiones* where it is almost certain that he would be using a Greek MS constantly, and it would therefore be reasonable to suppose that some of these alterations in the Latin text were introduced by him from the Greek MS before him, a MS which was evidently of the AFM type. A similar use of a Greek MS to amend the Latin text seems indicated in the case of Augustine's treatise *De Gen. ad Litt.* For example in quoting Gen. i. 14 in that treatise he inserts the words *in inchoationem diei et noctis* which are absent not only from *De Pasc. Comp.* and Amb. (*Hex.* iv. 3) but also from Augustine's quotations in *De Gen. con. Man.* and *De Gen. Imperf. Liber.* The words are also absent from most Greek MSS and it seems certain that Augustine derived them from a Greek MS before him which contained the insertion found in AD*lnr* only. Again in Gen. iii we find in *De Gen. ad Litt.* the words *ab omni ligno paradisi* in *v.* 1 and *a fructu ligni* in *v.* 2, but *quod est in paradiso* is used for the first and *ex omni ligno* for the second by Luc., Amb. (*De Para.* 12) and by Augustine himself in *De Gen. con. Man.*; it seems likely that the latter is in each case the true Old Latin and that the former was derived by Augustine from a MS before him giving the readings now found in A*a*D*Eghjoqsuxy* and D*Eghnqrxy* respectively. These examples afford sufficient justification for arguing that in *Qu.* and *Loc.* and in *De Gen. ad Litt.* Augustine's departures from the normal Old Latin may be due to his use of a Greek MS from which he introduced corrections into the current Latin text; but on the other hand our examination of *Qu.* and *Loc.* showed that Augustine almost certainly preserved the vocabulary of the Old Latin version, and it may seem unlikely that he would keep to the Latin in this respect and yet so often assimilate its text to his Greek MSS. Hence it may seem more likely that a definite revision of the Old Latin had taken place in which a Greek MS of the AFM type was used to correct the text of the Old Latin; a revision which might have taken place during, rather than before, the time of Augustine since not only *De Pasc. Comp.*, Ambrose and Lucifer but also Augustine himself in his earlier works used the unrevised Old Latin. That there was such a revision of the Old Latin is supported by the evident fact that Augustine several times shows a knowledge of alternative current Latin renderings depending on different Greek texts. In Ex. viii. 26 for example he notices that some Latins inserted a negative and though this might have been done independently, yet it probably indicates dependence on a Greek MS like *bwfms*—cursives with some of which, as we shall see later, the Old Latin frequently has undoubted connections; it is clear however that he also knew of a Latin text which followed most Greek MSS in omitting the negative. Augustine's knowledge of different Latin renderings is clearly seen in other places also, as *e.g.* in Lev. vi. 22 and xxv. 23, so that it seems likely on the whole that in *Qu.* and *Loc.* he was not so much translating for himself as using an Old Latin text which had been revised not only in its Latinity but also to conform the text to what was then considered a superior Greek text.

Ex. xxxiii. 2 is especially noteworthy in this connection. Augustine quotes it twice in *Qu.*, once in Ex. and once in Josh., and not only do his two quotations differ from one another but both differ from Lugd. in the Greek text presupposed. The first part of the verse reads as follows in various Greek and Latin authorities:

'I will send my angel before thy face'—B*cnr*,
'I will send before thee my angel'—*x* Lugd., Mon.,
'I will send my angel before thee'—AF*M etc. Aug. (*Qu., Ex.*),
'I will send before thy face my angel'—*ahkmoqu* Aug. (*Qu. Josh.*);

and in the same verse in a list of the nations to be dispossessed we have:

'Canaanites' omitted—B*bquwy,
'Canaanites' added at the end and 'Gergashites' transposed from
    fourth to sixth—*xegjnsvz* Lugd., Mon.,
'Canaanites' added at beginning—AFM etc. Aug. (*Qu. Ex.*),
'Canaanites' added at end—*afhior* Aug. (*Qu. Josh.*).

We notice that in neither respect is B followed by any Latin authority, but that the Latin MSS in both follow *x*, a cursive with which the Old Latin has a peculiar connection. In his discussion of the verse in its proper place in Ex. Augustine follows in each respect his usual Greek MSS AFM; but when quoting it in *Qu. Josh.* he follows a fourth form which also has Greek support. It does not seem likely that the variations in *Qu. Josh.* are due to the quotation being made from memory; the support of the same Greek cursives (*aho*) in each part of the verse seems to show that he is following a genuine Latin text; and had the quotation been from memory we should have expected the order of the words in the first part of the verse to correspond with that in B*cnr* since this is the order adopted in what would be the best known occurrence of this phrase (in Matt. xi. 10). It seems therefore that we have here evidence for three Latin renderings each founded on a distinct Greek original.

(b) The influence of the leading types of Greek Text in Leviticus and Judges

The text of Leviticus requires separate notice owing to the unusual grouping of the Greek uncials. In this book, and in this book alone in the Heptateuch, B is generally supported by A, frequently also by NG and the cursives hya_2. The Latin MSS have several clear coincidences with this group, but the places in which they oppose it are considerably more numerous. A few examples are here given:

Lev. xiv. 36 Lugd., Mon. have οἰκίαν with BAF instead of ἀφήν of GMN.

Lev. xx. 21 Wir., Spec., Tert. omit καὶ ἀνήρ with BAN$bcwxa_2$.

Lev. xxvi. 18 Lugd., Aug. omit πληγαῖς with BA$bwgn$.

Lev. xxvii. 2 Lug. omits ἄνθρωπος with BANhya_2b_2.

and on the other side

Lev. iv. 24 Lugd., Wir., Mon. with F^{b}GM have ἁμαρτίας for ἁμαρτία.

Lev. v. 6 Lugd., Wir., Aug. with FM omit three words.

Lev. xi. 35 Lugd., Wir., Mon. omit ταῦτα twice, opposing BAya_2 each time.

Lev. xiv. 39 Lugd., Mon., Tert. omit οὐ opposing BA$axya_2$.

Lev. xiv. 45 Lugd., Mon., Spec. insert τῆς οἰκίας opposing BAN$hmsxya_2$.

Lev. xxvi. 39 Lugd., Aug. (*Impf. Jul.*) have a long insertion with FM and most cursives; G$cghnx$ have it later.

Lev. xxvii. 33 Lugd., Spec. insert οὐδὲ πονηρὸν καλῷ opposing BAN$bhya_2$.

Lev. xiv. 42 is especially noticeable; Lugd. and Mon. have *lapides alios*; Tert. has *lapides politos et solidos*, not only representing ἀπεξυσμένους which is in all Greek MSS (G sub —) but also reading στερεούς for ἑτέρους with BAy only. Tertullian of course might be using a Greek MS and not the Old Latin version but it seems likely in any case that Mon. and Lugd. represent a late post-Origen Greek text which has been brought into harmony with the Hebrew.

But if Tertullian, in this place at least, inclines towards BA as compared with the MSS, it is quite clear that Augustine inclines very much towards FM; at least a dozen clear examples of this could be quoted, but nearly all are insertions made by FM and Augustine into the text of BAG. For example:

Lev. ix. 4 Aug. inserts *a bubus* with FM: Lugd. follows BAG.
Lev. xi. 34 Aug. inserts *uobis* with FM: Lugd., Mon., Wir.
follow BAG.
Lev. xi. 47 Aug. inserts *instruere filios Israel* with FM: Lugd.,
Mon. follow BAG*abcwya*$_2$.

Only in one place (x. 18) does Augustine follow BA where
the other Latin texts (Lugd. and Ambrose) do not, and this
exception is apparent rather than real because here F agrees
with BA, so that the agreement of Augustine with BA loses
its significance. Augustine's divergence from BA is also clear
in chs. xxi to xxv where no Old Latin MS exists for comparison;
here he has many clear coincidences with FM against BA (see
e.g. xxiii. 15, xxiv. 15, xxiv. 17, xxv. 2), while the only clear
connection with BA is found in xxi. 10 (*uestimenta* for *sancta*)
and the force of this example is again lessened by the fact that
this is another place in which F agrees with BA. In view of
this general agreement of Augustine with FM it is noticeable
that where these uncials are Hexaplaric (as in Lev. v. 2) he
agrees with the Latin MSS in following BA.

This agreement of A with B against FM, which is the normal
thing in Lev., is found occasionally in Ex. also. Where this is
the case Lugd. often agrees with A and B (*e.g.* in Ex. iv. 27 and
vi. 22), but has also a large number of agreements with FM,
most of which are merely additions to the text of BA, though
one or two are of greater interest. For example in Ex. iv. 23
Lugd. has *tu uero noluisti dimittere*, and since Tyconius agrees
(except in having *autem* for *uero*), this evidently represents the
original Old Latin which here followed FM, for BA have εἰ
μὲν οὖν μὴ βούλει ἐξαποστεῖλαι. In Ex. iv. 17 Lugd. agrees
with Augustine in omitting a clause with F*M*lwxya*$_2$*b*$_2$*c*$_2$; but
just as Augustine shows more agreement with AFM than
Lugd., so he has also more agreements with FM against BA;
for example Augustine's *eloquens* in Ex. iv. 10 apparently represents εὔλογος of F*M, but Lugd., Ambrose and Jerome
have *dignus* which more probably represents ἱκανός of BA; and
in Ex. vii. 9 Augustine's omission of *in terram* brings his text
into agreement with FM where Lugd. follows BA. One other
example may be added from Exodus because it introduces other
Old Latin authorities and suggests that these agreements of the

Old Latin with FM in some instances come down from the primitive Old Latin version—the agreement of Mon. and Cyprian in reading ὑπό in xvii. 10 where BA*lsya*₂ read ἐπί.

The combination of BAF against the other uncials, of which two examples have been quoted from Lev., occurs also a few times in Num., and here again (*e.g.* in xx. 12, xxvii. 18 and xxxi. 54) we sometimes find Augustine following BAF while Lugd. follows MN or GMN. In each case Lugd. probably represents an inferior Greek text, but in view of Augustine's comparatively slight connection with B it is probable that the presence of these readings in his text is to be connected with their presence in AF rather than in B.

The Old Latin text of Judges also requires separate consideration because although the Greek uncials AMN seem to be closely related when compared with B, yet A diverges so widely from MN that the relations of the Latin texts to each of the three groups B, A, MN need to be distinguished.

Lugd. certainly has a number of readings in agreement with B, and supported by a group of cursives of which the most constant members are *fimoqrsu*. Most of the examples given here will illustrate at the same time how Augustine keeps to the reading of AMN.

Jud. i. 3 Lugd. *aduersus Channaneos* with B: Aug. *in Chananaeo* with AMN.

Jud. i. 18 Lugd. *nec* and *fines* (each thrice) with B: Aug. *et* and *finem* with AMN.

Jud. vi. 21 Lugd. *ascendit* with B: Aug. *accensus est* with AMN.

Jud. vi. 26 Lugd., Spec. omit ὄρους with B.

Jud. viii. 33 Lugd. has *Bahalim*, which is like B: Aug. *Baalberith* with MN (A is similar).

Jud. i. 27 is not so clear; Lugd. has *abstulit*, apparently following B, while Augustine has *hereditauit* with AMN, but in *v.* 21, where the same variation is found again in the Latin authorities, A and a few cursives agree with Lugd., and BMN with Augustine. Though therefore we can count this as an agreement of Augustine with MN, Lugd. cannot definitely be considered as following either A or B—the cursives *dek* being the only Greek MSS which agree with Lugd. in both verses. Such connections of Lugd. with B are in any case not frequent—most of the principal ones are mentioned above—but Augustine has even less agreement with B than Lugd. has; where Lugd. and Augustine exist together they can be quoted as clearly agreeing with AMN time after time, but for agreements with B we have to go to such uncertain points as the omission of γῆν in xi. 29 and of πᾶς in vii. 6. In xvi. 26 both Lugd. and Augustine evidently read ἄφες for ἐπανάπαυσον and omitted ποίησον, but the force of this example is quite discounted by the fact that not only a larger number of cursives than usual but also M agrees with B; so in xv. 10 where Augustine (here differing from Lugd.) definitely reads *et dixerunt uir Iuda* he again follows a reading found in M as well as B.

A few readings of Lugd. and Speculum (where Augustine is unfortunately missing) are of special interest on account of their apparent superiority to the readings of most or (in one case) of any of the Greek uncials. In xv. 4 Lugd. and Speculum omit καὶ ἔδησεν with AG. The insertion of these words in B was probably due to the alteration of the preceding καὶ συνέδησεν to καὶ ἐπέστρεψεν to agree with the M.T., while their presence in M creates a redundant phrase. Here A and G with Lugd. and Speculum seem correct, but in the next verse Lugd. and Speculum seem to preserve the true LXX and all the uncials appear to be wrong. The following are the various readings:

B ἐκάησαν ἀπὸ ἅλωνος καὶ ἕως σταχύων ὀρθῶν.

M ἐνεπύρισεν τοὺς στάχυας ἀπὸ στοιβῆς καὶ ἕως ἑστῶτος.

AG ἐνεπύρισεν τοὺς στάχυας καὶ τὰ προτεθερισμένα ἀπὸ στοιβῆς καὶ ἕως ἑστῶτος.

Lugd., Spec. *succendit spicas eorum et quae metita erant.*

A and G evidently are conflate, and as τοὺς στάχυας καὶ τὰ προτεθερισμένα is under an obelus in G it is almost certain that these words, which appear to be the source of Lugd. and Speculum, give the original LXX, which therefore survives entirely in AG and partly in M but conflated with another reading, which may be Theodotion's. Another agreement of Lugd. and Speculum with A where it alone of the uncials preserves the true LXX is probably to be found in vi. 26. There the three words τῷ ὀφθέντι σοι, contained in A, a dozen cursives and some versions are marked with an obelus in the Syro-Hexaplar, and not finding a place in the M.T., seem unques-

tionably part of the true LXX, so that their absence from
BMN is to be reckoned as a Hexaplaric omission. But if
Lugd. in these places thus agrees with A against BMN when
A has the superior reading, we shall immediately show that it
also frequently follows M and N where these two uncials preserve the true LXX and both B and A are wrong; and the theory
suggested by these conclusions, that in the book of Judges Lugd.
represents a text of the LXX which on the whole is superior to
that of any of the surviving uncials, has other support also.

We now consider some of the places in which A differs from
MN and both Lugd. and Augustine can be quoted. If Lugd.
and Augustine agree they occasionally follow A—e.g. in *pugnare*
in viii. 1 and in reading *sex* instead of *sexaginta* in xii. 7; but they
more frequently agree with MN especially when MN preserve a
superior text. Thus they omit καθὼς καιρός in xiii. 23, and
δεύτερον in vi. 25, in both of which places B and A seem to
have been influenced by Hexaplaric insertions; in iii. 31 they
represent with MN what is apparently the true LXX reading
(ἐκτὸς μόσχων), for B seems to follow Theodotion and A conflates the two. Occasionally (as in xiii. 6) Lugd. agrees with
MN, and Augustine follows BA; but on the whole Augustine
everywhere has a remarkable connection with MN (and the
cursive *y*) which is not shared by Lugd. *Habitantes* in v. 7 is
a clear agreement between Augustine and MN*akmyb₂* (Lugd.
potentes) and others are to be found in omissions in i. 10 and 12,
iv. 8 and 20, and viii. 26, and insertions in i. 19 and iii. 21.
In several of these places MN*y* are the only Greek authorities
for Augustine's reading; in v. 7 Lugd. follows B or cursives,
in iii. 21 and viii. 26 it agrees with A, and in some of these
places both A and B agree with it. An interesting example is
provided by xi. 8 and 9; Augustine definitely reads *caput* in
the former verse and *princeps* in the latter, following MN*dk
ptvya₂b₂*. B has ἄρχοντα both times, while A*abcghlnowx* agree
with Lugd. in reading κεφαλήν in each verse. Occasionally B joins MN and Augustine, and Lugd. follows A in an
inferior text, as in xi. 34 where with AK and some cursives
and versions it adds a gloss ἀγαπητή.

A further point of agreement between Augustine and MN
is provided by the numerous conflations which they have in

common, which suggest that though MN frequently preserve the superior text, yet in some respects Augustine in following them represents a later type of text than Lugd. Several of these conflations are of interest. In i. 20 Lugd. (*et abstulit inde tres filios Enoc*) follows Abckx; instead of this Bfioq have τῶν υἱῶν 'Ενάκ; Augustine with MN and the rest of the cursives gives the reading of B followed by that of A (*tres ciuitates filiorum Enac et abstulit inde tres filios Enac*). If the obelus of the Syro-Hexaplar is to be trusted A and Lugd. here represent the true reading of the LXX. In ii. 3 B has οὐ μὴ ἐξαρῶ in place of a longer clause in abdgknptvw which Lugd. renders *non adiciam transmigrare populum quam dixi excludere*— Acl have the same clause with ἐξολεθρεῦσαι in place of ἐξῶσαι. To the end of this—which he has exactly as Lugd. except for *eicere* in place of *excludere*—Augustine adds the reading of B (*non auferam*) exactly as MNhioryb₂. The obelus of Syro-Hex. again indicates that A and Lugd. give us the true LXX, and probably Lugd. is superior to A in representing ἐξῶσαι instead of ἐξολεθρεῦσαι. In vii. 6 Lugd. (*lingua sua*) agrees with Aabdglnptvw; B and a dozen cursives (practically the same group as follows B in ii. 3 above) have an entirely different reading (ἐν χειρὶ αὐτῶν πρὸς τὸ στόμα αὐτῶν) which agrees with the M.T. Augustine combines part of the reading of B with that of A, having *manu sua lingua sua*; this, he says, is the reading of the Greek and it is as a matter of fact the reading of MNmyb₂. Augustine however notices that several Latin MSS have *lingua* only and this (the reading of Lugd.) would again seem to represent the true LXX. In v. 8 Augustine again exactly agrees with MN in the position of *ut panem hordaceum*, in having *tunc* (τότε) and in combining the two renderings of the second line of the verse found in B and A. The rendering of A, due to a wrong pointing of the Hebrew, is evidently the earlier and is followed by Lugd. In the third line of the verse Augustine is missing, and the present text of A is (if we accept the conjecture of Ewald) due to a combination of the two readings σκέπην ἐὰν ἴδω καὶ σιρομάστην, and σκέπη ἐὰν ὀφθῇ καὶ σιρομάστης. If this be so the Ethiopic which represents ἀνήφθη depends ultimately on the second, but MN which have νεανίδων on the first. The Latin version, as represented both by Lugd. and the Commentary of Verecundus, was evidently based on the reading of A. Verecundus has *tegumen iuuencularum iaculantium accensus est et iaculauit*; Lugd. (*tegumen iuuenum merronum incensum est et errauerunt*) has corrected the unsuitable feminine *iuuencularum* but otherwise represents the earlier form if *merronum* (probably for *errorum*) and *errauerunt* are, as seems likely, due to רֹמֵחַ being read as the Pual of רָמָה. It is interesting to notice that *abcx*, though independent of B, have preserved ἐὰν ὀφθῇ as well as νεανίδων. The cursive *l* has ἐὰν ἴδω νεανίδων and also ἀνήφθη, Theodoret has ἐὰν ἴδω only. The presence of ἐὰν ἴδω or a corruption of it in all MSS (except those which follow the late B), while ἐὰν ὀφθῇ and ἀνήφθη are absent from many, including MN, suggests that ἐὰν ἴδω may be the original LXX, though found only in Theodoret and (with the addition of a corruption and a doublet) in *l*. The obelus of Syro-Hex. may also be taken as evidence that ἐὰν ἴδω rather than ἐὰν ὀφθῇ is the older reading.

(c) Variations in the Latin MSS supported by leading uncials

The readings quoted thus far show that where there are two well supported Greek readings Augustine (and perhaps Tertullian) quite frequently follow one, and the other Latin authorities the other. It is also clear that where Augustine thus differs from the Latin MSS he consistently tends to agree with A rather than with B, and in Lev. and Jud. (and at times in other books too) with FM or MN rather than AB. Except in the case of Augustine, such a divergence between the Latin authorities is comparatively rare, though a sufficient number of such variations occurs to make a considerable list when they are collected together. The following list contains the chief of these passages in which different Greek readings, each with good uncial support, are followed by different Latin authorities, the reading agreeing with B being put first in each case.

Ex. xii. 46 Cyp. with BF: Mon. inserts eight words with AM.
Ex. xvii. 6 Mon. with Bq Philo: Ottob. inserts ἐλθεῖν with AF (M inserts ἐκεῖ).
Ex. xvii. 10 Mon. with B: Ottob. omits ἐξελθών with AF*M.

Ex. xxxii. 20 Mon. ὑπό with B*fit: Lugd., Wir., Aug. ἐπί with AFM.

Ex. xxxii. 24 Mon. with Bckmqua₂: Lugd., Wir., Aug. omit εἴ with AFM.

Ex. xxxiii. 13 Lugd. with BM: Wir., Aug. (Qu., De Trin.) omit τὸ μέγα with A*F*.

Ex. xxxiv. 7 Wir. ἀνομίας with B: Lugd. ἁμαρτίας with AFM (perhaps from xx. 5).

Ex. xxxix. 10 Mon., Wir. with B: Lugd. inserts κύκλῳ with AFM.

Lev. v. 4 Wir. with BA: Lugd., Aug., Or.-Lat. omit πρὸ ὀφθαλμῶν with FGM and the M.T.

Lev. v. 16 Wir. with BAbhwya₂: Lugd., Or.-Lat. omit αὐτό with FGM (as redundant).

Lev. vii. 4 Lugd. with BAbwya₂: Wir., Or.-Lat. insert ἀπ' αὐτοῦ with FGM.

Lev. xiii. 2 Mon. ἀχθήσεται with BAGabchkwya₂: Lugd. ἐλεύσεται with FM.

Lev. xviii. 5 Lugd. ἃ ποιήσας with BANhr*y: Wir., Luc. with F (influenced probably by New Test.).

Lev. xix. 16 Mon., Spec. (Cod. Sess.) ἐπιστήσῃ with BANhnᵃya₂: Luc., Spec. (other MSS) ἐπισυστήσῃ with FGM.

Deut. xxii. 8 Lugd., in two small points, with BΘ: Mon., Aug. with AFMN each time.

Deut. xxii. 21 Mon. αὐτὴν ἐν λίθοις with BΘ: Lugd., Aug. with AFMN.

Deut. xxviii. 14 Lugd. οὐδέ with BFNqua₂: Mon., Luc., Aug. ἤ with AGMΘ.

Deut. xxviii. 56 Wir. with BGΘcgnx: Lugd. inserts σφόδρα with AFM.

Deut. xxxi. 20 Lugd., Wir. with BΘ: Mon. inserts three words with AFMN.

Deut. xxxi. 21 Lugd., Wir. with BΘbcfx: Mon. inserts four words with AFMN.

Deut. xxxi. 23 Lugd., Wir. with Bbcowx: Mon. inserts Μωυσῆς with AFMNΘ.

Deut. xxxi. 23 Lugd., Wir. with BNk: Mon. inserts υἱῷ Ναυή with AFMΘ.

Deut. xxxii. 20 Lugd. inserts ἡμερῶν with BΘgl: Mon. omits with AFMN.

The preceding table reveals some interesting facts; after what has been already said we are not surprised to find that Augustine appears seven times with AFM but not once with B. If, as appears probable, the readings of B are on the whole superior to those of A, it agrees with our previous estimate of Mon. to find that in Ex. and Lev. this MS is found seven times with B and only once with A and then only in a part of Ex. in which Mon. has a later text, and in which it is Cyprian (presumably representing the earliest Old Latin) who is in agreement with B. In Deut. on the other hand Mon. decidedly inclines to A (seven times out of eight). It might be argued that here B is inferior to A and that of the four omissions in B in Deut. xxxi. 20–23, three are of the nature of Hexaplaric omissions made to bring it into agreement with the M.T. Unfortunately the evidence of G is not here available, but it is more likely perhaps that as there are signs in these later chapters of Deut. that Mon. has been revised in Latinity, so it has also been revised in its text, and that in the readings just quoted from Deut. xxxi and xxxii Lugd. and Wir. really are nearer the primitive Old Latin than Mon. If however Mon. has been revised in these chapters from a MS of the AFM type the revision has been only very partially carried out, for on the whole even in these last chapters of Deut. the connection of Mon. with BΘ is very noticeable.

(d) The influence of other uncials on the Latin text

So far we have only noticed the two or (in the book of Judges) three leading types of Greek text which are widely spread and evidently both ancient. There can however be no doubt that in several places the Old Latin text depended on a Greek original which is now found in a much less weighty group of MSS. In some places where we have only one Latin text which may be late, or where the Latin authorities vary, it may be uncertain whether such readings are part of the original Old Latin version, but in other cases the reading doubtless found a place in the earliest form of the Latin version. Considering the wide difference between Augustine and the other Latin authorities, the agreement of Augustine with the MSS very much increases the probability of such a reading being the true Old Latin. Later in this chapter we shall indicate the amount of connection between the Latin version and certain groups of Greek cursives but here a selection of readings may be given in which the Latin authorities agree with groups consisting of one (occasionally two) uncials—presumably inferior uncials—and a few miscellaneous cursives which do not form one of the distinctive cursive groups. The occasional importance of this class of agreement will be seen from a reading in Lev. xii. 4 and 5 on which we can quote Augustine's comment. Mon. and Lugd. have *mundus* following G*ejsvzacob*$_2$, and Augustine notices that in spite of its difficulty this is the reading of the Old Latin, though some Greek MSS have *immundus*. The latter is in fact the reading not only of some but of nearly all Greek MSS including BAFM, but nevertheless it seems to be a correction. The most correct rendering of the original is καθαρισμοῦ which is found in *bwgn* in *v.* 4, and *dpt* in *v.* 5, and seems due to a revision from the Hebrew. The history of this rendering can therefore probably be reconstructed as follows: through the noun being mistaken for an adjective, *mundus* was the original LXX rendering, though it is preserved only in the Old Latin and a group of ten Greek MSS which in themselves would seem worthy of little consideration; *immundus* though appearing in practically all Greek MSS is a correction made without reference to the Hebrew by one who saw that *mundus* was unsuitable; later the 'Lucianic' or 'Hesychian' revision made with the help of the Hebrew substituted the correct rendering now found in the seven cursives (*bwdgnpt*) which are generally supposed to represent these later versions.

Among readings of this kind few have such interest as the one just noticed; of the following selected examples some are evidently late and inferior readings, but in others we have a remarkable consensus of Latin testimony which suggests that the reading in question probably found a place in the original Latin version, though poorly supported in the Greek.

Ex. xxv. 33 Lugd., Wir., Ottob. omit four words with F*ejsvz lwxa*$_2$*b*$_2$.

Ex. xxviii. 39 Cyp., Lugd., Aug., Amb., Jer. have καί for ἤ with M*l*, margins of *sz*, Eth.

Lev. xx. 27 Wir., Aug. have αὐτῷ for αὐτῶν with F*acklmuvx*.

Lev. xxvi. 24 Lugd., Or.-Lat. omit θυμῷ with G*efx* (so Lugd. with *fi*n* in *v.* 28).

Num. i. 4 Lugd., Aug. read κεφαλήν for φυλήν with F*f, Boh.—apparently an ancient reading, originally a doublet of ἀρχόντων (רֹאשֵׁי).

Num. iv. 44 Lugd., Mon. insert a word with A*abhkklw*.

Num. viii. 15 Lugd. inserts a word with F(mg.)N (obviously a late insertion).

Num. xi. 25 Lugd., Mon. insert *in castris* with Ncgnd₂.

Num. xxxiv. 12 Lugd., Mon. read κατά for καὶ τά with G only.

Deut. xii. 30 Lugd., Aug. read μή ('lest') for οὐ μή (imperative) with Θbwejsvzgnua₂ (Gcdoptx have μήποτε: B is missing here).

Deut. xxviii. 27 Lugd., Mon. Αἰγυπτίων for Αἰγυπτίῳ with FᵇNbcfilmrw.

Deut. xxxii. 10 Lugd., Mon., Verecundus γῇ for τῇ with F only.

Josh. v. 4 Lugd., Aug. read τοῦτον δέ for ὃν δέ with N only (dgptw τοῦτον τόν).

Josh. vii. 15 Lugd., Luc. add διὰ κ̄ῡ with Fejsvzfira₂.

Josh. x. 12 Lugd. adds a clause with Fᵇdgnptejhikrwa₂ (evidently an inferior addition).

It is not to be inferred from this list that dependence on such inferior Greek MSS is common in the Old Latin; the many additions for example found in NΘ and GΘ in Deut. have scarcely affected the Latin at all.

In other places where the MSS have readings of this kind Augustine differs from them, following the reading supported by the majority of the Greek MSS. In the first of the following examples Wir. and Ambrose may quite well preserve the original Old Latin, in the second also Augustine seems late, in the third and fourth Lugd. is evidently inferior, but in the others it is very doubtful which of the Latin readings is the original.

Gen. xl. 13 Wir., Amb. omit *eius* and transpose *Pharao* with Dy: Aug. with AEM.

Ex. vi. 20 Lugd. ἕξ with Abwhpt: Aug. ἑπτά with FM and the M.T.: Bfir have δύo.

Ex. vi. 18 Lugd. corrects 130 to 133 with FᵇMdptejsvfirackmx: Aug. with BAF*.

Deut. v. 14 Lugd. has *qui intra ianuam* with MN (probably Hexaplaric): Aug. with BAFΘ.

Num. xxxi. 29 Lugd., Mon. κ̄ω̄ for κυρίου with Gdflma₂: Aug. with BAFHMN.

Deut. ii. 30 Lugd. omits σηών with AΘgn: Aug. with BFMN.

Deut. xxviii. 56 Lugd., Wir. put ἀπαλότητα before τρυφερότητα with GΘbwgnejsuvza₂: B (only) omits the former, Aug. with AFM puts it second.

In the following examples Mon. seems inferior to the Patristic quotation, but each is from that part of Mon. which has many other marks of lateness.

Ex. ix. 15 Mon. θανάτῳ with M: Jer. (Is. xviii) θανατώσω with
BA.

Ex. xii. 46 Mon. *efferentur* with F*: Cyp. *eicietis* with BAM.

On the other hand we sometimes find that Augustine follows
a reading supported by one, apparently inferior, uncial and a
few cursives, where the MSS represent the more widely supported Greek text. In each of the following instances Lugd.
(and in the first Wir. also) is extant and follows the common
Greek text.

Ex. xxv. 23 Aug. omits *byssus* and transposes clauses with
F*la_2b_2.

Lev. xiii. 11 Aug. has οὐκ for καί with F*ejsvzfilox.

Lev. xiii. 45 Aug. repeats *immundus* with F*M*loqu*: the other
reading (of Lugd.) is also known to Aug. '*in alio graeco.*'

Lev. xiii. 55 Aug. has *tactus aspectum suum* with F.

Num. xvi. 30 Aug. knows a Latin based on χάσματι of Gcxy,
but in Greek seems to know only φάσματι on which Lugd.
is based.

Deut. xx. 4 Aug. has futures for infinitives with M*fhqr*.

Other examples could be given, but these are sufficient to show
that besides having an occasional knowledge of texts like those
of G and M, Augustine in many places used a text which is
more nearly represented by F than by any other surviving Greek
uncial. Another good example can be quoted from Ex. xxi. 8,
where no Old Latin MS is extant, but Augustine's text—*non
adnominauit eam*—agrees with F* alone among Greek uncials.
That his text also had a close connection with M can be seen
from two of his readings in Ex. viii, where again no Old Latin
MS is extant. In *v.* 25 he remarks that the Latin has *euntes*, but
the Greek reading is equivalent to *uenientes*; evidently his Old
Latin was based on ἀπελθόντες, which is preserved in M and
ten cursives—BA and the other cursives having ἐλθόντες. In
v. 29 he quotes *a Pharaone et a seruis eius*, which though found
in M and several cursives is very different from the reading of
BA; in the latter case we may infer from his comment that his
Latin and Greek MSS agreed.

It remains to notice a few places where there is divergence
between the Latin MSS so that readings similar to those we have
just been considering are found in one but not in all. A case
of special interest occurs in Lev. xviii. 7. The second half of

this verse appears in Wir. as *mater enim tua est, non deteges turpitudinem eius*, which practically agrees with almost all the Greek MSS. The last word of the first half of the verse is ἀποκαλύψεις and Lugd., Augustine and the uncial F have (by homoeoteleuton) omitted the words which follow, the second half of the verse appearing as *confusione enim* in Lugd., and as *turpitudo enim eorum* in Augustine. The three omissions might have been considered independent of one another except for two things; one, that Lugd. and Augustine both insert *enim*, which, though it has a place among the omitted words, is not represented in this position in any other authority, and the other, that F with one cursive (*h*) has αὐτῶν for the last word and not αὐτῆς, and as Augustine definitely explains why *eorum* and not *eius* is here used it appears that a connection between Augustine and a MS like F is probable. A few other instances of similar divergence between the MSS are added:

In Ex. xvi. 29 Ottob. with F*abckoq* conflates two readings of which one is found in Mon. and most Greek MSS (including BAM) and the other in an inferior group of cursives and the margin of M[1].

In Lev. iv. 23–24 Lugd. has a passage consisting of a dozen words written twice, and on the first occasion it inserts into the passage the words *pro peccato* corresponding to an addition in F*bMdptfi lmoqrub*$_2$. That the words are a subsequent insertion into the text of Lugd. is clear not only from the fact that Mon. and Wir. omit them, but also because, in Lev., Lugd. generally uses the earlier *delictum* (*e.g.* twice in these two verses) instead of *peccatum*.

In Lev. xi. 27 Lugd. has πᾶν ὅ for πᾶς ὅς of Mon. Whether the change in Lugd. is independent of the Greek or is derived from the reading of F[b] and a dozen cursives it is clear that Mon. is the earlier.

In Lev. xi. 42 Lugd. and Wir. read αὐτά but Mon. αὐτό. The reading of Lugd. and Wir. may be due to the Greek reading found in F*ejsvzgnkl* or due to independent revision but again Mon. is evidently earlier.

In Ex. xxii. 20 Wir. adds ἑτέροις with A*bwfirx* and some Greek Fathers and Egyptian versions. Here no other Latin MS is extant, but Cyp., Spec. and Aug. omit the word, so that Wir. evidently represents a late alteration.

The chief point of interest in these five examples just given is that Lugd. if it exists gives the later Latin text in each case,

[1] The Cambridge Septuagint seems to be wrong in giving Mon. as a supporter of this latter group.

and Mon. the earlier. Wir. once has the earlier in comparison with Lugd., but twice has the later as compared with Mon. and Cyprian. We have here another indication that Mon. represents the earliest text of the MSS and Lugd. the latest, Wir. occupying an intermediate position.

A number of readings can be quoted in which the Latin version, or some representative of it, has curious agreements with B (frequently B*) which are found in practically no other text. The following are examples:

Ex. xxiii. 2: Spec. has *excludere* which may be connected with ἐκκλεῖσαι found in B only. Luc. and Aug. agree with all other Greek MSS in using *declinare*.

Ex. xxiii. 19: Ottob. and Amb. (*Ep.* 35) omit τῆς γῆς with B*e only. Spec. represents the words.

Lev. xi. 13: Lugd. inserts a relative *quae* with Arm., Eth. and B only. The word would not easily be inserted afterwards, so that here Lugd. seems to represent the original Old Latin. It is curious that Mon. and Wir. (which omit *quae*) insert *quia* with no Greek authority a few words further on. It would appear that Mon. and Wir. have transposed and altered the word to a form and place in which it was more suitable.

Num. xii. 6: practically all the Greek MSS here have κυρίῳ, but Mon. and Lugd. have *domini*; the genitive might easily have been introduced in translation or transcription but a genitive seems to have been the original reading of B, and is also found in the Latin Origen. Most of the MSS of Spec. omit the word; the only one which has it (*Cod. Sess.*) has a genitive which is placed before *in uobis*, evidently to connect it more closely with *propheta*. Aug. (*De Gen. ad Litt.* xii. 27) has a nominative, as G only among Greek MSS, and this he transposes, apparently to connect it closely with the subject of *cognoscar*. Since no Latin authority represents the dative and four have a genitive it appears that a genitive, whether based on the reading of B* or not, was the original Old Latin.

Deut. xxiv. 18: Spec. with B*, Arm. only omits καὶ μνησθήσῃ. Since Julian (*apud* Aug. *Op. Impf. con. Iul.* iii. 13) also omits the words it seems a genuine Old Latin omission. Lugd. also indirectly supports the omission, for in that MS *et scito* (which agrees with no Greek MS at all) has been inserted to fill the gap.

There are several other connections of this kind between the Latin version and B in Deut., frequently having the support of an Egyptian version, but often no other Greek support at all; n many instances however the Latin texts differ among themselves. Thus in Deut. xxviii Mon. inserts *omnes* in *v.* 9, omits *et facere* in *v.* 13, and has a nominative *dispersio* in *v.* 25, in each case with B only, but Lugd.(with Lucifer in the second and Jerome in the third) follows the usual Greek text. That these agreements of Mon. with B may represent the original Old Latin is suggested by the fact that three similar examples can be cited from Cyprian. In Deut. xiii. 18 Cyprian omits πάσας (B*u*), in xxiv. 16 with Lugd., Speculum and Augustine inserts ἐν (B only) and in xxxiii. 9 omits αὐτοῦ twice with Speculum and Augustine (B*d* and B*mq*); Lugd. has the commoner text in xiii. 18 and also in xxxiii. 9, where with Ambrose and Irenaeus it makes the sentence smoother by inserting *suo* and *suae*. In Deut. iv. 8 Lugd. and Speculum seem to show a knowledge of the reading of B**km* (ὑμῖν) for they conflate it with the usual Greek text ἐνώπιον ὑμῶν. Lugd. has several agreements with Ba_2 only (*e.g.* Num. i. 2, xiii. 33, Deut. vii. 12) and a few with B*k* only (*e.g.* Deut. xxvi. 10).

(e) The text of Genesis

In the preceding pages very few readings have been quoted from Genesis, for of the uncials which have been compared with the Latin in the other books of the Heptateuch BFG and N are missing over the whole or nearly the whole of this book, so that our usual division of the Greek texts becomes quite inapplicable. It seems moreover that the character of A may be different here from what it is in the later books. Here indeed as elsewhere *y* is a very close follower of A, but agreements of A with small groups of cursives are very common in Gen., though elsewhere in the Heptateuch A is generally supported by other uncials and a majority of the cursives. Certainly the Latin version has much less connection with A in Gen. and this in spite of the fact that here Augustine (whose connection with A is so obvious elsewhere) is frequently the sole authority for the Old Latin version. It follows therefore that M is the only uncial which we can quote in Gen. with any probability that it stands for the same type of text as it does in the other books.

A few examples of correspondences between the Latin version and various uncials or groups of uncials are given here.

With A:

Gen. i. 11 Aug., Tert., Or.-Lat. omit κατὰ γένος with A*aej loqd₂.

Gen. xxx. 21 Lugd. inserts a clause with A only.

With E:

Gen. i. 14 *De Pasc. Comp.* Aug., Ambrstr., Niceta, Or.-Lat. represent ὥστε φαίνειν with E*n*. Ambrose's *ad illuminationem* may come directly from εἰς φαῦσιν and not through the Old Latin.

Gen. vii. 23 Aug. (*Loc.*) has ἐξηλείφθη for ἐξήλειψεν with E*dmpqud₂*.

With M:

Gen. xiii. 5 Amb. (*Abr.*), Vindob. σκηναί for κτήνη with M*ace hjmoqu* (E*n* conflate the two).

Gen. xv. 17 Aug. (*De Ciu. Dei*), Amb. (*Abr.*) insert ἤδη with M*bgw*.

With combinations of Uncials:

Gen. xi. 4 Aug. (*De Ciu. Dei*) ἑαυτῶν for ἑαυτοῖς with AE*ir*ᵃ and margins of *js*—against M.

Gen. xxxi. 32 Lugd. transposes two sentences with DEL*bwdptf ikrs* (against AFM).

Gen. xxxv. 2 Aug. (*Qu.*) inserts *qui uobiscum sunt* with DL*egj dnptfhir* (against AEG).

Gen. xli. 4–5 Wir. has insertions as EM*dnpegjfiko* (especially *dnpefk*) against AD.

Gen. xliii. 16 Lugd. inserts *isti* with DLM*befgjs* (against AF).

Gen. xliii. 27 Lugd. has ζῆν for ζῇ with FM*degjlmnpquxa₂c₂d₂* (against AD).

There are many other places in which the Old Latin clearly opposes A; *e.g.* Augustine (*Loc.*) inserts *lauare* with DM in xxiv. 32, Augustine (*De Ciu. Dei*) and Philo-Lat. have the perfect for future tense with DEM in xxvi. 24, and Ambrose (*Patr.*) has ηὔξησεν for ὕψωσεν with EM in xli. 52. It opposes both A and L in xix. 30 where Augustine (*Qu.*) and Jerome have *ascendit* with DEM, and in xli. 27 where Ambrose (*Jos.*) adds a clause with DEM.

In some places different Old Latin renderings agree with different Greek uncials:

Gen. ii. 15 Aug. (*Doct. Chr.*), Tert. have *finxit* with AE: Aug. (*Litt., Man.*), Amb. *fecit* with M*hmnq*.

Gen. xii. 1 Amb. omits *uade* with ADa*hrt*: Cyp., Spec., Aug., Jer., Or.-Lat. insert it with EM (evidently the true O.L.).

Gen. xvi. 2 Amb. (*Abr.*) 'second' person with AM*dptfir*: Jer. (*Heb. Qu.*) 'first' with D.

Gen. xvii. 12 Lugd., Amb. insert three words with A: Aug. (*Ciu.*) omits with M*acehjlmoqux*.

Gen. xvii. 20 Hil. *et* with A*df*: Aug. (*Ciu.*) *ecce* with M (*acmoqux* have both).

Gen. xviii. 5 Aug. (*Max.*) inserts three words with AM: Spec., Amb. (*Abr.*) omit them with D*ahmo*.

Gen. xxii. 2 Aug. (*Trin.*) inserts *ibi* with A: Cyp., Amb. (*Abr.*) omit it with DM*bwdpefjlsd*$_2$.

Gen. xxvii. 28 Lugd., Aug. (*Ser.*), Amb. insert ἄνωθεν with A*efgijr*: Cyp., Philo-Lat., Tert., Iren., Aug. (*Ciu.*) omit it with DEM.

Gen. xxxii. 27 Aug. (*Max.*), Nov. σοῦ with ADEL: Lugd., Spec. σοί with GM*bkouwxc*$_2$.

Gen. xxxii. 29 Aug. (*Max.*) omits a clause with ADEGM: Lugd., Spec. have it with L*cdfkmpx*.

Gen. xli. 30 Amb. (*Jos.*) omits a clause with ADM: Aug. (*Qu.*) has it with EL.

An examination of these readings will lead to the conclusion that Augustine shows more dependence on EM than on AD, while Ambrose, besides the connection which all the Latin authorities show with M, has points of contact with A and D rather than with E. The whole question of the Latin and LXX texts of Gen. however is likely to prove one of exceptional difficulty.

(*f*) *The influence of the cursive groups on the Latin text*

Among the MSS of the LXX there have been identified certain groups of cursives representing peculiar types of text, which are of special interest because attempts have been made to trace in some of them the 'Lucianic' or 'Hesychian' recensions of the LXX. In the following pages an attempt will be made to estimate the amount of connection between each of these groups of cursives and the Old Latin version.

(i) *bw*

The two cursives *bw* have been supposed to incorporate many readings of the Lucianic recension. They certainly have very many readings peculiar to themselves among Greek MSS, and the great majority of these have had no influence on the Latin version. The following readings however seem to indicate an occasional connection between some of the Latin authorities and these two cursives: Gen. xvi. 4 Lugd. represents ἐκάλεσα instead of ἐκάλεσεν; Gen. xvii. 6 Lugd. and Ambrose (*Abr.*) have *erunt* though Augustine, both in *De Ciu. Dei* and in *De Gen. con. Man.*, follows the common Greek reading ἐξελεύσονται; Gen. xix. 12 Lugd. and Augustine (*Con. Max.*) represent εἰσί instead of ἔστιν τις; Gen. xxvii. 28 Lugd., Philo-Lat., Cyprian, Hilary, Ambrose, Irenaeus all omit καί though Augustine (*De Ciu. Dei* and *Ser.*) retains it. In these four places *bw* are the only Greek MSS which support the Latin reading in question, but occasionally there is some slight additional support from other Greek MSS. Thus Lugd. presupposes αὐτοῦ for τούτους in Gen. xxix. 13 with *bwg*, inserts τοῦ τόπου with E*bw* in Gen. xxxi. 48, and in Gen. xlvi. 27 Lugd., Ambrose (*Hex.*) and Jerome (*Heb. Qu.*) omit two words with *bwi**; in Gen. xxxi. 48 (the only one of the three for which he can be quoted) Augustine follows the usual Greek reading. Several coincidences with these cursives are also found in Num.; *e.g.* in vi. 21 Lugd. gives ὅσα for χωρὶς ὧν, and in xxii. 20 οὕτως for τοῦτο; Augustine is not extant for the first and agrees with the common Greek text in the second. Two other agreements of Lugd. with *bw* in Num. are seen in συναγωγήν for παρεμβολήν in xvi. 46 and δοκεῖ for ἀρέσκει in xxii. 34, but these are supported by marginal readings in M*z* and M*vz* respectively, and the former agrees with the M.T. In Num. vii both Lugd. and Mon., like *bw*, frequently insert *obtulit* at the beginning of verses, *e.g.* of *v.* 43. The Latin MSS however make the insertion more regularly than the Greek cursives and possibly independently of them. Lugd., Mon. and *bw* are also the most conspicuous supporters of the change from *consideratio* and *considerare* to *numerus* and *numerare* in chs. iii and iv. These changes are sometimes made in the Bohairic, in the margins of M*svz*, and occasionally in the uncials AHM, so that they might be explained as independent substitutions of a well-known explanatory gloss, not uniformly made in any MS and on the whole made in different places in the different MSS both Greek and Latin. However *bw* and the two Latin MSS are the most constant in making these alterations, these alone *e.g.*

changing the first verb in iv. 46 though leaving the second unchanged. On the whole it seems that in Gen. and Num. at least a common peculiar tradition has affected these cursives and some of the Latin texts. The same thing seems to have happened occasionally in Deut. In xxviii. 22 Lugd. evidently read φόβῳ with *bw* and the Armenian; B omits the word and two MSS read πόνῳ but otherwise all the MSS have φόνῳ. In vi. 9 Speculum and Ambrose have *in ianuis tuis* with *bw* only; Lugd. here omits the three words, but in xi. 20 depends on the same reading, which is there found in *ua₂* and the margins of *vz* as well as in *bw*; again Augustine follows the common Greek reading τῶν πυλῶν ὑμῶν. Two readings of Mon. in Deut. may show the influence of these cursives. In x. 7 Mon. inserts *ubi*, and though the text is rather confused, this seems connected with the insertion of οὗ in *bw*; Lugd. however omits the word. In xxii. 15 *eicient* of Mon. seems to depend rather on ἐξάξουσιν of *bw* than ἐξοίσουσιν of the other Greek MSS; Lugd. (*proferre*) again represents the usual Greek.

In Lev. and Ex. traces of the influence of the text of *bw* are rarer; we may however mention καί for ὅς in Lugd. and Augustine in Ex. ii. 1; the insertion of a negative, apparently intended as a correction, in Lugd. (not Mon. or Wir.) in Lev. xi. 24 with *bwx*; ἤ for εἰς in Lugd. in Lev. xiii. 25; and καί for οὐδέ in Augustine and Tertullian in Lev. xxi. 11.

The few agreements of these two cursives with Augustine can easily be set down to accidental coincidence, but their influence on the MSS seems too great to be attributed to chance; the way in which other Latin texts (except Augustine) agree with the MSS where they can be quoted, is against attributing the connection to a subsequent emendation of the Latin text from a late Greek tradition. Mon. seems very primitive in Deut. x. 7, and *eicere* (xxii. 15) is a genuine Cyprianic word, so that altogether it seems likely that these readings agreeing with *bw* belong to the original Old Latin version. Augustine's divergences from the other Latin texts in these places would doubtless be due to the same revision which, as we have seen, brought his text into harmony with the AFM group of uncials elsewhere. This support of the Latin version would indicate that a few at least of these *bw* readings are earlier than the Lucianic recension.

(ii) *dgnpt*

There are many readings peculiar to the five Greek cursives *dgnpt*; there are many also which are confined to *gn*, and yet others peculiar to *dpt*. These last seem to possess a character of their own[1], but the two groups *gn* and *dgnpt* seem to represent the same type of text and their readings may be considered together.

Lugd. has an undoubted connection with this group of cursives in Josh. and Jud. In Josh. xv. 18 Lugd. has *consilium dedit illi dicens pete a patri tuo agrum*, exactly following *dgnpt*; Augustine has *consilium habuit cum eo dicens petam patrem meum agrum*, with the other Greek MSS. So in xxii. 8 Lugd. has *ite in domos uestras* with *dgnpt* and Kw (which have a close connection with these five cursives in Joshua), but Augustine again follows the other Greek MSS with *abierunt in domos suas*. In these instances Lugd. and the five cursives seem to have been corrected, in the first to agree with Jud. i. 14, and in the second to agree with the M.T., so that the reading followed by Augustine would seem to be the true LXX and also therefore the original Old Latin. Josh. xxiv. 27 however points decidedly the other way; here Lugd. and Cyprian have *recesseritis* with *gnptw*, while Augustine and the rest of the Greek MSS have *mentiti fueritis*. The agreement of Cyprian seems to show that Lugd. and the five cursives here represent the older Latin text (which also differs more widely from the M.T.) and furnishes evidence that Augustine has been corrected from Greek MSS. In Josh. viii. 22 Lugd. has *inter Istrahel in medium* with *gnw* (Augustine *inter medium castrorum*), and in *v.* 27 reads κτηνῶν with *gn*, Augustine and most Greek MSS combining this with σκύλων—the reading of B and two cursives. The following are noticeable agreements between Lugd. and these cursives in parts of Josh. where Augustine is missing; Lugd. and Lucifer in vii. 14 have *tribus quae ostensa fuerit per dominum* (Luc. *deum*) with *gnptw*, the other Greek MSS having ἣν ἂν δείξῃ κύριος; Lugd. and Speculum in xxiv. 19 have ὑμᾶς for οὗτος with *gnptw*; Lugd. in xi. 14 has *quemquam spirantem* with K*gnptw*, and in xii. 7 has *in Macho et dimidium Galaad* with

---

[1] See the article already referred to in the *J.T.S.* for April 1925.

K*dgnpt*—the spelling *Macho* indicating a closer connection with K*gn* than with *dpt*. It will be noticed that though Lucifer and Speculum where extant agree with Lugd., Augustine on every occasion for which his evidence is clear differs from Lugd.

In Judges these five cursives are members of a larger group which includes also *lovw*. These nine cursives have very many distinctive readings which though supported by no uncial (except K) give us a fourth type of text in this book, almost as distinctive as those of B, A and MN, and sometimes apparently, as in Jud. vi. 2, superior to all of them. With this group of MSS Lugd. has remarkable agreements (*e.g.* in Jud. vi. 2 just mentioned), but again Augustine, as the following readings will show, does not share in these agreements. In ix. 34 Lugd. adds *in campo*, and in v. 31 has *fiant* for *pereant* with this group, Augustine following the usual reading in each place. In x. 1 Lugd. conflates *uir Issachar* with *filius Charreon*, the latter being evidently derived from ῦῦ κάριε which these nine have in place of the former; Augustine here follows MN etc. Lugd. has an alternative rendering of the Hebrew in v. 29 and 30, a rendering which is not found elsewhere except in the eight cursives *dglnptvw* (here without *o*) in which it is given after the common Greek rendering of these two verses. Augustine does not quote from vv. 29 and 30, but in v. 31 he has *sicut ortus solis* following the usual Greek text, Lugd. having *cum oritur sol*, and the eight cursives again combining both renderings. In this passage Lugd. and these eight cursives seem to represent an ancient alternative rendering, perhaps even the original LXX, since the renderings in the other Greek MSS seem like corrections to agree with the M.T. Lugd. agrees with a smaller group (*glnw*) in iv. 13; in vi. 34 with *glnw* and *irux* it reads *induit* (ἐνέδυσεν), Augustine again following the other Greek MSS in having *confortauit*.

In the five books of the Pentateuch the connection of the Latin version with these cursives is much less conspicuous. The agreements in Lev. may be taken first because here Augustine has a note on such a reading. In Lev. vi. 22 Lugd. had *ponetur*, evidently representing ἐπιτεθήσεται. Most Greek MSS have ἐπιτελεσθήσεται which might have been read as ἐπιτεθήσεται by a translator, but *dgnptkw* have the latter, and the rendering of Lugd. is more likely to have been made from such a MS. Augustine has *consummabitur*, but knows of *imponetur* as another Latin rendering, though he does not seem to know of the variant in the Greek. The only other place where Augustine shows knowledge of a reading of this kind is in Lev. xvi. 16, where Augustine and Lugd. have *pro sanctis*, showing that the Latin version was derived from περὶ τῶν ἁγίων which survives only in *gn* and the margins of M*vz*. Augustine notes that his Greek MS reads τὸ ἅγιον, but apparently this (the reading of nearly all Greek MSS) had not found its way into the Latin version. In Lev. xi. 33 Lugd., Mon. and Wir. have *confringetis* with *gnx* and the Armenian: here again it seems that we have a primitive Latin connection with these cursives, and in Augustine's *conteretur* a correction from the common Greek text. The other examples from Lev. however suggest that these *dgnpt* and *gn* readings were not always part of the original Latin version. In xi. 36 Lugd. and Wir. have an addition of three words which are also found in *dgnpthk*, but Mon. is free from the insertion; in xii. 4 a word added by Lugd. and *dgpt* is not found in Mon. or Augustine; and in xi. 21 Lugd. seems to follow *gn* and M(mg.) in having *a* (ἀπό), whereas Mon. (*super*) agrees with the common reading ἐπί. Mon. is so clearly primitive in these chapters of Lev. that it seems likely that the original Old Latin is represented by that MS in these three places, and that the *dgnpt* readings are subsequent alterations in the Latin.

Apart from Lev. xi. 33 the clearest example of such a reading in Mon. is found in Num. xxxv. 4, where τείχους is added with *gnpto*; Lugd. doubtless had the same reading, for *extremorum* is evidently a corruption of *extra murum*; in Num. however Mon. cannot claim to represent the original version. Lugd. has several other examples in Num.; in xvi. 37 it has *sanctificatae sunt* with *gnb₂*, in xx. 13 *maledictionis* with *gno* and the margins of M*sv*, in xxx. 4 *et* with *dgnpt*, Augustine having *sanctificauerunt*, *contradictionis* and *aut* with the great majority of Greek MSS. There are fewer examples of the influence of these cursives in Gen. and Ex., though in Ex. xxv. 28 Lugd. and Ottob. insert three words with M*dnpt*, and in Ex. xxx. 31

Lugd. inserts a word with F^b*dnpt*; in the former place Augustine is missing, in the other he follows the other Greek MSS. Lucifer has additions in Deut. xxiii. 6 (*usque*), xxv. 15 (*et bene tibi sit*) and xxviii. 12 (*tibi*), all corresponding to additions in Θ*dgnpt*, and transposes *omne* in xxviii. 12 with Θ*gn*. All of the additions however could be easily made independently, and Lugd. is in each case free from them, while in xxviii. 12 Mon., Ambrose and Lugd. all agree against Lucifer. Lugd. however agrees with Lucifer in omitting κατά with Θ*gn* in xix. 20, and in reading πρόσταγμα with Θ*g* (B πρᾶγμα, AFGMN ῥῆμα) in xvii. 10.

Summing up, then, the influence of these cursives is strongest in Josh. and Jud., less evident in Lev., Num. and Deut. and quite inconspicuous in Gen. and Ex. In Lev. (where alone they are noticed by Augustine), in Josh. and in Jud. it would seem that some readings of this kind were found in the Latin version from the earliest times; the evidence for this however is less clear in Num.; in Deut. most of the readings in agreement with these cursives seem late and inferior, while the two quoted from Ex. are obviously so.

The readings contained in *dpt* but not in *gn* are of a different kind; they have been supposed to represent the Hesychian revision, and if this be so it is clear that the Hesychian text had practically no influence on the Old Latin. The only agreement of a Latin text with this group which seems worth mentioning is the change from the first person to the third made by Lugd. in Josh. xxiii. 3 and 4, but even here since *n* is partially affected by the change, the example might come rather under the heading of agreements with the whole group *dgnpt*. Here also it is noticeable that Augustine differs from Lugd. Other agreements are so trivial compared with the numerous peculiar readings of these cursives, that we can safely say that whatever text these cursives represent it had less influence on the Old Latin than almost any other. In Num. a few readings contained in *dpt* are supported by Ba₂ only among Greek MSS. Such a one occurs in Num. vi. 18, where B*dpta*₂, Cyril and Egyptian versions read ὑπό for ἐπί. The agreement of B as well as Lugd. makes us doubtful whether such a reading is Hesychian, though its other supporters are Egyptian. Even this however is rather an exceptional case; more typical of this kind of reading would be 'three hundred' for 'two hundred' (B*dgnpt*, Arm.) in i. 33 and ἀπ᾽ ἐμοῦ for ἀπὸ σοῦ (B*dgnpta*$_2$, Cyril, Arm.) in xvii. 5. In both these instances Lugd. supports the reading quoted but the agreement of *gn* and the Armenian as well as B makes it even more doubtful whether they can be classed as Hesychian.

(iii) *ejsvz*

The cursives *ejsvz*, with which are often associated *gn* in Ex. and *u* in Deut., form a clearly recognisable group, with which each of the principal groups of Latin authorities has connections, fairly clear if not numerous. For example Jerome's quotation of Deut. ix. 4 and 5 (*Adu. Pel.* 2) has *eos* for *gentes illos* and *eorum* for *harum*, Mon., Lugd., Augustine and Ambrose agreeing against him. In Num. ix. 13 Augustine repeats *homo*, in Num. xxi. 13 omits ἀπάραντες, and in Deut. xi. 4 has *in tempore suo*, Lugd. differing in all three places. The MSS also have some fairly obvious connections with this group; in Deut. xxxi. 16 Lugd., Mon. and Wir. all omit ἐκεῖ and insert *in eam* with them; in Deut. ix. 1 Lugd. and Mon. seem to follow them in reading σοῦ for μᾶλλον ἢ ὑμεῖς and in Josh. viii. 24 Lugd. represents τῇ ἐρήμῳ of *efhjsvz* and M(mg.) for τῷ ὄρει. In none of these three places is any Latin authority besides the MSS extant, but in Ex. xxxiii. 19 where Lugd. and Wir. agree with M(mg.)*jsvzx* (προπορεύσομαι for παρελεύσομαι) they are followed by Ambrose and Tertullian though not by Augustine. It is noticeable however that *x* supports this reading, for a connection with this cursive is obvious in the Old Latin in other places also. Mon. agrees with *egsz* in Ex. xxxvii. 20 in inserting *filius Or*; Mon. however puts *Or* before *Uriae*, whereas the cursives put it after, as it is in the M.T. The addition in Mon. seems clearly to be a later insertion into the Latin version so that Lugd. is here superior.

In Gen. *e* and *j* (frequently joined by *g*) form a group, for the most part distinct from *svz*, and a few coincidences with these can be quoted. Lugd. inserts τούτοις with *egj* in xxxii. 20; in xxviii. 11 Lugd. and Augustine (*De Unit. Eccl.*, but not *De Ciu. Dei*) add λίθον; in i. 26 Augustine *De Gen. con. Man.* (but not Ambrose or Augustine *De Gen. ad Litt.*) inserts *et ferarum* with *ejv*. Here may be noticed two readings in the margins of *jv*, both obviously late, which have found their way into Latin texts. In Gen. i. 11 Ambrose (*Hex.* 3) adds *secundum genus*, and in Gen. xxxvii. 28 Ottob. changes *Madianei* to *Ismahelitae*; Lugd. however is free from the latter and Augustine and Tertullian from the former (which may be Hexaplaric).

The margins of *svz* (sometimes with the margin of M and sometimes without *s*) have already been quoted as occasionally in agreement with *bw* or *gn*. There are also a few agreements between certain Latin texts and these cursives in places where neither *bw* nor *gn* agree. In Num. iii. 16 Lugd. represents κατὰ τὸ ῥῆμα of *g* and mg. of M*svz* for διὰ φωνῆς; in Deut. ii. 30 Lugd. with *x* and mg. of M*sz* inserts *fines*, which Augustine omits; in Lev. iv. 33 Lugd. inserts *in loco sancto* with *b₂* and mg. of *svz*, Wir. being free from the insertion; in Lev. xx. 21 Wir. has *erunt* for *morientur* with mg. of *svz*, but here also the Latin texts vary, Tertullian and Speculum following the usual Greek reading; in Josh. ix. 7 Lugd. and Or.-Lat. with mg. of *vz* have βιβλίῳ τοῦ νόμου for νόμῳ Μωυσῆ. In Josh. xvii. 16 there is more variety of reading; Augustine following ΑΝΘ reads *qui habitat in Baethsan*, but something has evidently dropped out here: Β*hqr* before ἐν βαιθαισάν insert ἐν αὐτῷ: the Hexaplaric MSS insert ἐν τῇ γῇ ἐν ἐμοί, where ἐν τῇ γῇ is evidently a correction from the Hebrew, but ἐν ἐμοί seems to have remained from an earlier LXX text, for it is found in a majority of the cursives as well as in Lugd., Or.-Lat. and the Armenian. After *in me* Lugd. has *qui sunt* (*qui habitat in me qui sunt in Abaethsam*), which would seem to be connected with εἰσίν found in *a₂* and mg. of *vz*. It will be noticed that Augustine gives no support whatever to readings of this class.

(iv) *qu*

The Latin version seldom shows any connections with the peculiar readings of *qu*. In Lev. v. 16 Lugd. evidently follows a primitive Latin error in reading καιρῷ; Wir. has corrected it but though καιρῷ is only found in *qu*, κριῷ could easily be confused with it. In Ex. xxxv. 34 Wir. inserts a relative *quae* in the same place as *qu*; the Latin here however is very confused and Lugd. has no sign of the pronoun. In Ex. iv. 5 Lugd.

inserts *et dixit illi* with these two cursives, and Augustine notices that the words were inserted in the Latin, though not in the Greek; the insertion however is an easy and natural one.

Occasionally the Latin agrees with readings found both in *qu* or (in Deut.) *ua₂* and the margins of *svz*. Thus Lugd. has ἔσονται for φεύξονται with *qu* and mg. of *svz* in Lev. xxvi. 36, Lugd. and Lucifer seem to read ἰδεῖν for εἰδέναι with *u* and *z*(mg.) in Deut. xiii. 3 (though Augustine and Cyprian have *scire* not *uidere*), and Lugd. in Deut. xxix. 5 has ἐπαλαιώθη with *ua₂* and mg. of *vz*; in the last case however the word might easily be repeated from the preceding clause and Augustine represents κατετρίβη with the other Greek MSS.

(v) *fir*

That there is a connection between the Latin version and the text preserved by the cursive *r* seems certain.

In Gen. iv. 5 Augustine, Ambrose and Lucifer all depend on the reading ἐλυπήθη instead of ἐλύπησεν τόν. This reading is found in *r* only among Greek MSS, but it is ancient as it occurs not only in the Armenian and Egyptian versions but also in Clement of Rome. In Gen. xxviii. 14 Lugd. and Augustine (*De Unit. Eccl.*) follow πληθύνειν, the reading of *r* and Philo, and therefore also an ancient variant. Augustine however quoting the verse in his other works has the usual πλατύνειν. In Gen. xxx. 11 Augustine states that the Latin rendering is *beata* or *felix facta sum* but that the Greek has εὐτύχη, a reading preserved in *r* only. Neither Lugd. nor Jerome however agrees with him here, for Lugd. has a verb with most Greek cursives and Jerome has *in fortuna* apparently with ADEM*lqu*. In Deut. ii. 33 Lugd. follows the text εἰς τὰς χεῖρας ἡμῶν which is the reading of *r*, Arm., Eth. BAFN have πρὸ προσώπου ἡμῶν and ΘM conflate the two.

In view of these four remarkable coincidences it seems that Mon., Wir. and Augustine probably preserve the true Old Latin in Ex. xxxii. 28 ('twenty-three thousand' not 'three thousand') though supported by *r*, Cyril and the Bohairic only. If so Lugd., Lucifer and Ambrose depend on a corrected reading and Tertullian must have got his reading from a Greek MS.

The cursive *r* is however one of a group *fir* (often with *k* in Lev. and Num.) which has many distinctive readings, and with which Latin quotations at times agree. In Num. xxxi. 21 Lugd. and Mon. have ἄρχοντας for ἄνδρας with *fik*, and in *v.* 35 ἄρσενος for ἀνδρός with the same group. In the latter place Augustine has *uiri*; but in Gen. xviii. 11 in *Loc.*, *Qu.* and *Con. Jul.* he follows *fir* in reading ἐν ταῖς ἡμέραις αὐτῶν for ἡμερῶν. In Gen. xxix. 3 Lugd. reads ποιμένες for ποίμνια with *ir* and Egyptian versions; in Gen. xxxvii. 30 Lugd. and Ottob. have *introibo* with *i* only, and the alteration from πορεύεσθαι to εἰσπορεύεσθαι is not natural here; in Deut. xxiii. 3 Ambrose (*Lk.* and *Ps. xlviii*) and Or.-Lat. have *usque ad tertiam et quartam generationem* which, though the reading of no other MS whatever, is found in *i* and the Ethiopic combined with *decimam* of Lugd., Mon., Augustine and Jerome and the Greek MSS. In Lev. xi. 22 Lugd. and Mon. insert a negative with *i*ᵃ*k* and Egyptian versions only. Additions of the nature of glosses are frequent in this group of cursives; such additions may sometimes be made independently by different authorities, but several are common to this group and Latin MSS. Wir. and Ambrose thus add κακόν in Gen. xl. 15, Lugd. has additions in Ex. ii. 23, xxv. 25 (with Ottob.) and xxx. 38; similar additions in Lugd. in Gen. xlvi. 31 and l. 10 are absent from Augustine.

(g) The influence of other cursives on the Latin Version

There are other single cursives with which the Latin Version has at times some curious connections, the most noticeable of such connections being with h, m, n, o, w, x, a_2 and b_2.

Lugd. inserts clauses in Lev. vii. 1, xiii. 39 and xiv. 10 corresponding to insertions in the cursive h; the agreements, especially the first, are too long and too close to be due to accident. In none of these places is there any other Latin text extant, but Wir. as well as Lugd. has such an insertion, though a rather shorter one in vii. 15; in this instance *dgnpt* have the insertion later in the verse but Augustine omits the words. Lugd. also repeats the second half of Lev. xviii. 17 between *vv.* 15 and 16; *bwgn* however as well as h make this insertion, but Wir. omits it. In no other book than Lev. is there any sign of a special connection between the Latin version and h, and in these places it is probably due to a late assimilation to an inferior Greek text.

Among agreements with *m* we may probably reckon two peculiar readings of Wir. in Ex., for although in each case one other cursive agrees with *m*, they are cursives which seem to have no other special connection with the Latin. In Ex. xxii. 28 Wir. and Filastrius insert ἀλλοτρίους with *km*, and in Ex. xxxii. 24 Wir. adds *et demserunt* with *cm*, Sah., Eth. These additions however seem to be no part of the original Old Latin, for though Augustine's reading in the first place might be a correction, the reading of Mon. and Lugd. in the second may be taken as the true Old Latin and they omit the words. The other probable connections with *m* are all in Deut. In Deut. xxiii. 15 Speculum omits four words with *m* and in Deut. xxvii has a repeated *fiat* half a dozen times, though all the MSS except *m* have the word only once in each place. Again these seem to be later alterations in the Latin, for Augustine in the first place and Lugd. in both follow the majority of Greek MSS. Two other passages may be quoted. In Deut. xi. 28 Lugd. and Tert. (*Scorp.* 2) insert a negative with *lm*, and in Deut. xiii. 13 Cyprian and Lugd. have *nostis* representing οἴδατε of *hm* rather than ᾔδειτε of the other MSS. Perhaps in both cases the Latin is independent of the corresponding cursives, but they provide good examples of the unity of the late Latin text of Lugd. with the primitive Old Latin of Cyprian and Tertullian.

The most noteworthy correspondences of the Latin with *n* occur in Ex. In Ex. xxiii. 21 Cyprian, Tertullian, Ottob. and the ancient treatise *Adu. Iud.* all represent αὐτῷ for σεαυτῷ with *n* only, and it is clear that this was the primitive Old Latin text. Hence we have here a clear example of a correction from the Greek in Augustine for he has *tibi*. In Ex. xxxii. 1 Mon. and Cyprian have *uir* for *homo*; the two words are so regularly used to translate different Greek words that it seems likely that here again there is a relation between the primitive Latin and *n*; if it be so Wir. and Lugd. show a correction to the usual Greek reading for they have *homo*. Lugd. and Wir. have a correspondence with *n* in Ex. xxv. 40 in the omission of ὅρα which however finds a place in Ottob. In Ex. xxxiv. 7 Wir. inserts *purificationem* which however is found not only in *k* and M(mg.) as well as in *n*, but also in *dpt* in a slightly different place. The word is missing in Lugd. as well as in Augustine and so may be another late insertion.

With *o* there is one noticeable agreement in Num. xxxiii. 1, where Mon. and Lugd. both represent οἱ ἐξελθόντες for ὡς ἐξῆλθον. In Josh. v. 3 Lugd. adds a clause *et posuit grumos praeputiorum* which is found in *w* only. The other probable coincidences with *w* are all in Ex. In Ex. v. 1 Lugd. and Or.-Lat. represent λατρεύειν for ἑορτάζειν, in Ex. xxii. 21 Wir. and Speculum add *et uos*, and in Ex. xl. 27 Lugd. inserts *cum autem*; in each case *w* is the only Greek MS representing the reading in question but in the last example at least (where Mon. and Wir. differ) the text is probably not that of the original Old Latin.

We have already given one example of the influence of *x* on the Latin in a coincidence of Mon., Lugd. and Irenaeus with it in Ex. xxxiii. 2; another is probably to be seen in the omission of a word in Mon. and Lugd. in Ex. xxxii. 34. Most of the Latin coincidences with *x* however are found in Lugd. only, as in Ex. xxxii. 3 and 4 where Mon. differs, in Ex. xxxv. 20 where Wir. differs, and in Ex. xxix. 10 where Augustine differs. In Lev. xi. 8 Lugd. conflates *abominamini* of *x*, M(mg.) and *z*(mg.) with *non tangetis*, the reading of Wir. and all other Greek MSS. Evidently Lugd. here represents a late modification, but as in some of the examples from Ex. the connection with the Greek text represented by *x* is clear. We have also an omission in Lugd. and *x* in Jud. i. 10, but the omission is also made by b_2, a cursive with which Lugd. has a remarkable connection in the preceding verse.

The reading of Lugd. in Lev. viii. 17 is evidently due to κρέα being read as κέρατα, and the reading of Speculum (*Cod. Sess.*) in Ex. xxxiv. 14 seems due to ζηλωτόν being read as ζηλῶ τό. In the case of the latter this would imply that Wir. and Lugd. and the other MSS of Speculum as well as Augustine used a text which had corrected the primitive error. Both mistakes might have arisen from a misreading of the ordinary Greek text, but in each case a_2, and a_2 alone, preserves the blunder among Greek MSS.

One connection between Lugd. and b_2 is particularly interesting. In Jud. i. 9 Lugd. has *habitantem in monte et austrum quae pertundebant ad eum usque ad afilioten*. The readings of all Greek uncials and most cursives (τὴν ὀρεινὴν καὶ τὸν νότον καὶ τὴν πεδινήν) exactly represents the M.T. and is followed by Augustine. A few cursives however comprising *defsz* as well as b_2 add καὶ πρὸς ἀπηλιώτην, words which are evidently presupposed by Lugd. The source of *pertundebant* however is found only in b_2 which has τὸ ὄρος καὶ τὰ παρατείνοντα καὶ τὰ πρὸς ἀπηλιώτην, a reading referred to in a Hexaplaric note in *z* as being that of 'οὐδεὶς τῶν τεσσάρων.'

It will be noticed that apart from this curious connection with b_2 and the additions in Lugd. from the text of *h* in Lev., the chief agreements with single cursives are in Ex. and are with *m*, *n* and *x*, which may occasionally be joined by *k*. As a matter of fact it is clear without any reference to the Latin version that there is a peculiar relation between these four cursives in Ex., none the less real because on the whole *n* shares the text of other groups of cursives, *dpt*, *ejsvz* and especially *g*. In spite of their different relations these four cursives seem to preserve an early common element which has also left its influence on the Latin version (see *e.g.* also Ex. xxx. 20 κάρπωμα *knx*, Lugd.).

This group has a specially strong claim to be regarded as the origin of the Old Latin in a few places where it is joined by *bw*. Thus in Ex. xxxii. 26 Mon. and Wir. insert εἰ with *bwkmx*, and though Lugd., Lucifer, Augustine and Ambrose all omit it, the insertion is probably part of the original Latin text. So in Ex. xxxv. 21 Lugd. and Wir. read οἷς for ὧν with *bwnx* though Augustine follows the usual Greek reading.

The various groups of cursives enumerated earlier sometimes combine in their peculiar readings.

In Num. for example *dgnpt* or *gn* often combine with *ck*, Arm. This has the appearance of a Hexaplaric combination, especially as some of their common readings are insertions into the common text, but the evidence of the M.T. and of G where extant (*e.g.* in xix. 10) seems to show that these are not always Hexaplaric insertions. In xix. 10 (twice), xxiii. 28 and xxviii. 25 Lugd. has clear insertions with this group; in the last two Augustine is not extant but in the first he follows the Greek uncials.

In Lev. *gn* (or *dgnpt*) and *bw* frequently combine. Lugd. (often with Wir. if extant) has several agreements with this combination, a conspicuous one occurring in Lev. xviii. 14 where Wir. and Lugd. have *accedes* but Augustine *introibis* with the uncials. The same combination of *gn* with *b* (*w* is missing) seems to be the origin of the Old Latin in Josh. i. 8 where Lugd. and Lucifer have *dirigam uias tuas*, the other Greek MSS being expanded here. There are many other places in which a combination of cursives including *bw* may preserve the text on which the Old Latin was based. A few examples are worth giving here:

Ex. viii. 26: Aug. notices that some Latin MSS inserted a negative, and some made the sentence interrogative; apparently he knew some also which literally rendered the Greek text. The negative is found in *bwfms* among Greek MSS.

Ex. xii. 5: Cyp., *De Pasc. Comp.*, Amb., Niceta and Priscillian all represent ἄμωμος, though this word is found in no uncial, and only a dozen cursives (including *bwdnpt*). This may however be a very early Latin conflation due to τέλειος (rendered *perfectus*) being here used instead of the usual ἄμωμος, and made independently of the Greek conflation. Aug. alone omits the Latin equivalent of ἄμωμος, evidently after reference (made by himself or some predecessor) to the Greek text. Amb. (*Abr.* i. 5) has an even fuller text, adding *mundus* to *consummatus* (the later equivalent of *perfectus*) and *sine macula*.

Ex. xii. 10: Cyp. and *De Pasc. Comp.* have αὐτῶν for αὐτοῦ with *bwfi*ᵃ*lr* Sah.—a small point but perhaps significant considering the early date of the Latin text they represent and the frequency with which such readings appear in the later Latin MSS.

Lev. vi. 10: here again Aug. testifies to a reading of the kind under review, for he takes ὁλοκάρπωσιν (*bwfhix*) as the normal reading, and refers to κατακάρπωσιν, which all the uncials give, as being found *in quodam graeco*. Lugd. agrees with him if we may assume that κατακάρπωσιν would have been transliterated as it is in *v*. 11.

Lev. xviii. 30: Lugd. and Mon. follow *bwcg* and mg. of *svz*, for *obseruationes* implies φυλάγματα, not προστάγματα.

In Lev. xxv. 23 Augustine again shows knowledge of a reading of this kind (*profanationem* = βεβήλωσιν) which is found in N*bwdhptub*₂ and the margins of M*sv*. He expresses a preference for this reading, though of course not on textual grounds; but that it is inferior is probable not only from comparison with the M.T. but also from the agreement of Lugd. with the alternative *confirmationem* (βεβαίωσιν) which Augustine also knows. In Deut. Lugd. has some agreements with combinations of cursive groups which include bw (*e.g.* in ii. 5, ii. 22 and xxix. 15).

In Gen. these combinations of cursive groups without uncial support are particularly common, bw being frequently of the number but *fikr* and *dgnpt* being even more conspicuous in such groups. There can be no doubt that Wir. in Gen. xl has connections with such a group, *e.g.* in *in domo lacus* in *v.* 15 with *dnptbwfikv*, and in *generibus* in *v.* 17 with *dgnpt bwfikrc$_2$ej*. Agreements of Lugd. with such groups may be seen in Gen. xxxi. 17 (*dptfikr*), in Gen. xxxi. 26 (*dhptfi^{a}kr*) and, with Ottob., in Gen. l. 24 (*fikrbwn*). Two cases may be quoted in which such readings in Lugd. are not supported by Mon. In Lev. xiv. 28 Lugd. makes a considerable transposition and alteration to agree with *svzfiorqub$_2$*; and in Num. iv. 47 reads *sanctorum* with *dgknptqub$_2$s*(mg.)*z*(mg.), Mon. having *operum* with all the uncials. The generally primitive character of Mon. in Lev. suggests that in the first place it gives the primitive reading of the Latin version, and the same is probably true in Num. though the same reason cannot be alleged.

In a few places the Latin version has remarkable connections with the readings of various miscellaneous cursives which do not seem to form a recognisable group. A few such readings in which Augustine is extant or makes notes on the text are here mentioned; it will be noticed that in all except the last example x is among the group supporting the Latin reading, so that it is possible that we have here further examples of the influence of the text preserved by this cursive on the Old Latin. In Gen. xv. 13 Augustine (*Qu.* and *De Ciu. Dei*) and Tyconius omit the third verb ταπεινοῦν with *hoqux*. It seems that a conflation has here made its way into nearly all Greek MSS, but without affecting the primitive Latin. Ambrose (*Abr.*) and Jerome (*Ep.*) insert the third verb doubtless to bring the Latin into harmony with the current Greek. In Ex. xxiv. 19 Augustine (*De Trin.* ii. 15) follows the reading λίθον with *eklmx* Philo-Lat., but Ottob. represents πλίνθου; *De Trin.* is however one of the works in which Augustine would be most likely to follow the Old Latin, so that we may have here another example of the influence of a *kmx* reading on the Latin. In Ex. xxviii. 21 Augustine follows a few cursives ($fioxa_2b_2$) in reading γενέσεις for ὀνόματα; Lugd. agrees with the majority of the MSS, A$ybwqu$ being conflate. In Ex. xxxii. 24 Mon., Wir. and Lugd. have *aurum* following $flnxb_2$, and this, Augustine says, is the Latin rendering though the Greek has *aurea*. A somewhat larger collection of cursives (thirteen) omit υἱός in Gen. xvii. 17, and this was doubtless the reading followed by the Old Latin, for the word is omitted in Lugd., Ambrose (*Abr.*) and Augustine. Evidently in many of these places the Old Latin preserves a very old LXX variant, and in some of them Augustine, though he uses a revised text as a rule, bears witness to the fact that such readings preserved in the Latin MSS are genuine primitive Old Latin readings. In Jud. i. 16, where Augustine is not extant, the reading of Lugd. (*Amalec*) goes back to a primitive misreading of the Hebrew, which in *defsz* Sah. is conflated with τοῦ λαοῦ, but is preserved in its original form only in Lugd.

Another place in which Lugd. (with the Ethiopic version) is the only authority preserving the original LXX may be noticed here; it will also well illustrate the superiority of the Latin MSS over the text of Augustine. In Ex. xxx. 10 the uncials AFM followed by most Greek cursives and by Augustine have ἀπὸ τοῦ αἵματος τοῦ καθαρισμοῦ τῶν ἁμαρτιῶν τοῦ ἐξιλασμοῦ, the cursives *cmnsvz* agreeing except that they have τοῦ καθαρισμοῦ after τῶν ἁμαρτιῶν; *l* has τοῦ ἱλασμοῦ before, and τοῦ καθαρισμοῦ after. All of these are conflate, and the Hexaplaric *k* which omits καθαρισμοῦ and the Syro-Hex. which marks it with an obelus indicate that this word was the one originally in the LXX; hence Lugd. (*de sanguine peccatorum purificationis*) and the Ethiopic, which reverses the order of *peccatorum* and *purificationis*, alone represent the true reading of the LXX. It is possible that B would have preserved the correct reading had it not omitted some words here, for it contained the word καθαρισμοῦ.

(h) *Hexaplaric influence on the Latin Version*

We come at last to consider the relation between the Old Latin and the Hexaplaric group of MSS. Commencing with Mon. we are not surprised to find that Hexaplaric influence is seen most clearly and frequently in this MS in Ex. ix to xx, and in Num., where we have already found grounds for believing that Mon. represents a comparatively late form of the Old Latin. Of the dozen Hexaplaric readings in Ex. ix–xx may be mentioned insertions in ix. 25 and xii. 32 (the latter misplaced), an alteration in x. 13, and an omission in xviii. 8—the last with an unusual group of Greek MSS, $Fhla_2b_2$, but marked with an obelus in v. In Num., where Lugd. and Mon. agree very closely, Hexaplaric influence is seen in both MSS in an omission in xxxi. 21, and in insertions in xxxiii. 38, xxxiv. 2 and 14, and xxxvi. 9. We notice however that most of these insertions find a place also in the *dgnpt* group though these five cursives are not on the whole Hexaplaric in Num. In v. 3 Mon. adds *et mittite*, evidently Hexaplaric, where Lugd. has the true LXX; but in iv. 44 Lugd. has an Hexaplaric omission from which Mon. is free. The absence of any other Hexaplaric reading in either Latin MS in the early part of Num. suggests that the omission in iv. 4 which they both share with $Bbwdgnptfikra_2$ was made in some MSS of the LXX before the time of the real Hexaplaric omissions. The few examples cited do not of course make the Latin MSS Hexaplaric in Num., for against these half dozen Hexaplaric readings can be set dozens of passages in which Hexaplaric changes have left no trace on either Mon. or Lugd.

In those parts of Mon. in which a more primitive type of text is preserved, there are thirteen more readings which appear to be Hexaplaric (two in Ex., seven in Lev.—of which three are in ch. iv—and four in Deut.); three are insertions and ten omissions, but two of the insertions are rather uncertain. In Ex. xxxii. 8 and Lev. xiv. 41 Mon. and Lugd. are supported in their additions by the great majority of the Greek MSS and it may be that the Greek MSS which make the omissions ($Bdptafls$ and $BAhya_2$) accidentally lost both the clause (by homoeoteleuton) in the former passage, and the easily spared word in the second. Of the ten omissions we might easily attribute to accident the omission of *delictum* in Lev. iv. 20, of the second *ante deum* in Lev. iv. 4, and of the second *sacerdos* in Lev. xiv. 38. None of these three omissions is made in Lugd., and though each is marked with an obelus in G, the fact that each is omitted by some cursives which are not given to Hexaplaric omission shows how easily the omissions could be made; accidental also could be the omission of ὑμῖν by all three MSS (or rather by a common ancestor of the three) in Lev. xi. 42, an omission found also in the non-Hexaplaric b_2; and the clause omitted by Mon. (not Lugd.) in Deut. xxviii. 24 may be another example of omission by homoeoteleuton. This leaves in Mon. one case of insertion and five of omission which are not easily explained away, but it is noticeable that three of these six readings are found in Deut. xxviii and xxx where an admixture of later elements in Mon. has been suspected on other grounds. These six readings are as follows:

Ex. xxxiii. 3: Mon. and Lugd. omit three words with x (marked with obelus in Syro-Hex.). The omission is not a natural one and could hardly be accidental, so that this seems a clear case, perhaps the clearest, of Hexaplaric influence in Mon.

Lev. iv. 23: Mon. omits *masculum* with kx, Arm., Eth. Lugd. has the word and it could easily be omitted by accident, but G being missing the authorities form a typical Hexaplaric combination.

Lev. xiv. 42: Mon. and Lugd. omit a word marked with obelus in G. Were there no clearer examples than this we might attribute this one also to accidental omission.

Deut. xxviii. 12: Mon. and Lugd. omit a long sentence with B*kx (marked with obelus in G). That the omission was made in the original Old Latin is indicated by the fact that Luc. and Amb. (*De Tobia*, 18), both of whom restore the clause, give it in entirely different words. Perhaps the words were absent from the original LXX and were therefore omitted from the Old Latin, but were inserted into the LXX from Deut. xv. 6 before Origen, and again omitted by him.

Deut. xxx. 16: Mon. inserts *praecepta* with AG$cjox$. Most Greek MSS insert it a little later; Lugd. omits it altogether with B$bwdkm$.

Deut. xxx. 18: Mon. and Lugd. have an omission with BΘgkm nrx Arm. Eth. This is a strong group of authorities but G and Syro-Hex. both mark the words with an obelus.

Considering the general lateness of Lugd. and the evidence that its text has been revised from the Greek we are not surprised to find numerous Hexaplaric readings in various parts of that MS. Many more examples occur in Josh. than in any other book but at least twenty clear cases can be counted in Num., and as many in Deut. Among the last we may notice Deut. xxiii. 2, where the words *et usque ecclesia domini*, which

seem to be derived from the Hexaplaric addition in *ox* and
Syro-Hex., do not appear in Mon. If the omission of *caelum et
terram* with B*GΘ*c* and the M.T. in viii. 19 is a Hexaplaric
omission it is noticeable that both Mon. and Speculum retain
the words with the LXX. In Lev. a few possible Hexaplaric
readings common to Lugd. and Mon. have been noticed, and
one or two more common to Lugd. and Wir. will be noticed
immediately, but there will then remain only one or two other
possible examples in Lugd. In Lev. vii. 8 Lugd. has an addition
hostiarum pacificarum eius which is found in *Gackdghnpt*; the
words do not appear in Wir. and are evidently a subsequent
insertion into the text represented by Lugd. in Lev., since
pacificus is used by Lugd. only two or three times in all, and
then probably only under the influence of the Vulgate. One
other reading marked as Hexaplaric may be quoted; in Lev.
xvi. 10 Lugd. with MN*dgnptejsvzqulmoxb*$_2$ Arm. adds a long
clause which is marked with an asterisk in M and *v*. This
clause has evidently been added from *v*. 22; it is not in
the M.T., nor in the regular Hexaplaric MSS *Gack* and this
suggests that the insertions indicated by asterisks in M and *v*
are not always of the same kind as those which are generally
called Hexaplaric. The rarity of Hexaplaric readings in the
Lugd. text of Lev. is interesting in view of the primitive character of the vocabulary of Lev.; on the other hand the insertions with *h* as well as some of those just noticed are evidently
of a late character and show that the text of Lugd. has not
always been left, even in this book, in its primitive state. In
Gen. and Ex. some clear examples of Hexaplaric readings occur
in Lugd. but they are not so numerous as in Num. and Deut.

Wir. (like Mon.) is remarkably free from Hexaplaric influence. Perhaps the only two clear examples are the omissions
of συνιέναι with *knx* Syro-Hex. (obelus) and Lugd. in Ex.
xxxv. 35, and of κύριος in Deut. xxxi. 11 with Lucifer: the latter
is marked with obelus in G and Syro-Hex., but is retained in
Lugd. In two other places Wir. agrees with readings which
have been marked as Hexaplaric in two cursives. In Lev. iv. 30
Wir. and Lugd. add a word which is contained in a dozen Greek
MSS and is under asterisk in *v* and *z*; the word however is not
found in the M.T. nor in *Gack*. So in Lev. xxii. 21 Wir.

adds a sentence with practically the same MSS, of which M as well as *vz* marks it with an asterisk. Here G is missing but *ak* do not contain the insertion. From these two passages and Lev. xvi. 10 (noticed earlier) it is clear that the Hexaplaric signs in M*vz* and in G*ack* stand for different things—at least in Lev.

In Ottob. may be quoted as showing Hexaplaric influence an addition in Gen. xli. 5, an omission in Ex. xxiii. 18 (which may be due to homoeoteleuton) and an omission with Lugd. in Gen. xlviii. 21. In Gen. xlix. 28 however where Lugd. follows *acm* Arm. in substituting φυλαί for υἱοί, and several Greek MSS conflate the two, Ottob. follows the true LXX.

The Hexaplaric element in Lugd. becomes more noticeable when we compare it with that in Augustine, for though Augustine's text where it differs from Lugd. depends so often on what seems to be a later type of MS, yet it is very much less influenced by the Hexaplaric MSS than Lugd. Nor is the larger number of Hexaplaric readings in Lugd. due to the fact that so much more of the Heptateuch is found in Lugd. than in Augustine, for in those verses in which both are extant, while Lugd. has twenty to thirty Hexaplaric readings from which Augustine is free, Augustine on the other hand has only six which are not found in Lugd. and five of these six are exceptional in that not only the regular Hexaplaric group, but also many (and in some cases most) of the Greek MSS have the 'Hexaplaric' reading. These five readings are as follows: the insertion of three words with all MSS except BFN*gilmnra*$_2$ in Num. xv. 28, the repetition of *ad parietem* with A and a dozen cursives in Num. xxii. 25, the omission of *omnem* in Josh. vi. 25 with AF^{b}MNΘ, and the omissions with BM of two words in Jud. xv. 10, and of ἑπτά in Jud. xvi. 11. The sixth example is in Deut. xxviii. 4 where Augustine adds three words with *cox* which are omitted by Mon. and Lugd. This is a typical Hexaplaric group of cursives, but this example, the only one of the six of any real significance, is not from *Qu.* or *Loc.*, but in a rather free quotation in *Cont. Adim.* 18.

Four other passages can be quoted in which Augustine has something like a Hexaplaric reading, but the Greek MSS supporting it are in three of these places different from or more

numerous than the usual Hexaplaric cursives. In Ex. iv. 6
Augustine states that the Latin version inserts *leprosa*; this
agrees with *cfipstxa*$_2$, the margin of F and the Syro-Hex.
(under asterisk), but his Greek MS agrees with Lugd. in omitting
it; in Ex. x. 1 Augustine and Mon. omit λέγων with *km* (Syro-
Hex. has obelus); in Lev. xxvi. 39 Augustine (*Impf. con. Iul.* 3)
and Lugd. have with FM an addition which the Hexaplaric
Gcghnx have later in the verse; and in Num. xviii. 1 Augustine, Lugd. and Or.-Lat. have an insertion with all Greek
MSS except BHN*kora*$_2$. Of these ten readings then, though
most resemble Hexaplaric readings, only two seem, from the
Greek MSS supporting them, to be really Hexaplaric—the omission of λέγων in Ex. x. 1, and the addition in Deut. xxviii. 4
in *Cont. Adim.* On the other hand Augustine avoids several
Hexaplaric readings which are supported either by Lugd. or
Mon. (as in Ex. xxxiii. 3) or by several Greek MSS; so that
though in some respects founded on a Greek text which seems
inferior to that underlying the Latin MSS there can be no doubt
that Augustine is exceptionally free from Hexaplaric influence.

Lucifer's text shows as much Hexaplaric influence as Lugd.
He has several Hexaplaric readings in common with Lugd., as
in Ex. xxxiii. 7 (*cmndpt*), Josh. vi. 20 (omission and inser-
tion), Josh. vii. 16 and 22, and probably Jud. vi. 16, besides
some in places where the MSS are free from them. Thus in
Ex. xxxiii. 8 Lucifer has a Hexaplaric reading with *kmx* Syro-
Hex. which is not found in Lugd., and in Ex. xxxiii. 5 and
Deut. xxxi. 9 others which are absent from Lugd. and Mon.
So in Deut. xxviii. 15 Mon. and Lugd. have *depraehendent* at
the end and *tui* (not *uestri*) at the beginning of the verse with
BAFMN and this would seem to be the true LXX: Lucifer
has *inuenient* and *uestri* with *GcoxΘdgnptbw*. The latter
seems Hexaplaric, and *v* is probably wrong in marking it as the
LXX, as it is evidently wrong in marking θάνατον sub ⳑ in
v. 21. The appearance of *thlipsin* in Lucifer in *v.* 20 is also
remarkable. It seems as if it can only be derived from ἐκθλῖψιν
noted in M as a variant for ἐκλιμίαν (possibly from Theodotion).
On the other hand in Josh. vii. 24 Lugd. has insertions which
seem to be Hexaplaric but are not found in Lucifer, and in
Deut. xvii Lugd. seems to have three Hexaplaric omissions with

B*x*, B and BAN*ry* only (*vv*. 8 and 10) where Lucifer has the fuller LXX text.

Quotations from the Heptateuch in Ambrose are comparatively few and short, but there are two or three places in which Hexaplaric influence seems to have affected his text. The insertion of *pater* in Gen. iv. 21 (*Hex*. i. 7) is made with a group of authorities (*cx*, Arm., Eth., Syro-Hex.) which seem Hexaplaric; the word however is found in Philo, and so appears to be an ancient insertion. Num. iii. 12 is twice quoted by Ambrose; in *De Off*. 50 he has the words *redemptiones eorum erunt isti* with Lugd., but in *Cain* ii. 2 he omits them, and as they are omitted in the M.T. and marked with an obelus in G, the omission seems Hexaplaric. In quoting Num. xxxvi. 8 (*Luc*. iii. 4) Ambrose has *uni ex populo et ex tribu patris sui*, and the words *ex tribu* are apparently connected with the insertion of τῆς φυλῆς in G*cx*, though there is no trace of them in Lugd. or Mon. In Deut. ix. 4 Ambrose (*Cain* i. 7) omits *bonam* with Lugd. and Mon., the cursives *kx* (G *sub* ÷) and the M.T., though Augustine (*Loc*.) retains the word with the LXX. That Ambrose is influenced by the Hexaplaric text more than Augustine is indicated by the fact that Augustine differs from Ambrose in the only two of the above places (Gen. iv. 21, *De Ciu. Dei*; and Deut. ix. 4, *Loc*.) where his reading exists.

Noticeable also are three passages in which Cyprian (or *De Pasc. Comp*.) agrees with Hexaplaric MSS. In Ex. xii. 3 both Cyprian and *De Pasc. Comp*. add *sibi*, and in *v*. 6 *De Pasc. Comp*. adds *diem*; in each case Augustine and Niceta omit the word and the insertion is supported by *ackmx* Arm. Syro-Hex.—a typical Hexaplaric combination. The third example is in Josh. i. 8 where Cyprian adds *in eo* which not only the Hexaplaric group but also F and some other cursives add. Any of these additions could be easily made independently, and even taken together they are hardly enough to cast doubt on Cyprian's independence of the 'Hexaplaric' text.

In some twenty places in the Heptateuch the Latin version seems to have been influenced by Aquila, Symmachus or Theodotion independently of Origen's work. In the Latin MSS this influence is less than that of the Hexaplaric MSS, but it is much more conspicuous in Cyprian. The evidence of Cyprian in fact shows that several of the readings attributed to these translators were not only known in the second century but were incorporated in the primitive Old Latin version. One of the clearest examples is in Josh. i. 8 where B has εἰδῇς, AFMNΘ have συνῇς, while *dgnpte* have φυλάσσῃς which is conflated with συνῃς in *fjsvz*. Both Syro-Hex. and the cursive *v* indicate that φυλάσσῃς was the rendering of the other translators and not of the LXX, but it was evidently the word before the Latin translators; Cyprian uses *obseruare*, Lucifer and Lugd. *custodire*, the regular 'African' and later equivalents respectively of φυλάσσειν. Almost as clear is Josh. v. 2 where BMNΘ, followed by Lugd., conflate the two renderings πετρίνας and ἐκ πέτρας. Augustine, following Aboxyb₂, has the latter only, which by the testimony of *v* and Syro-Hex. is the LXX rendering; Cyprian on the other hand with the cursives *dm* has the former only, the rendering of Aquila and Theodotion. A third example in Josh., the addition of *illuc* by Cyprian in xxiv. 26 with Aquila, Symmachus and Theodotion, is not so certain. The word is given in a dozen cursives and could be easily added independently; it is not found in Augustine or Lugd. Three readings of Cyprian in other books may be derived from these sources. In Gen. xxii. 2 *unicus* agrees with Aquila and Symmachus, but Augustine and Ambrose (*dilectus* and *amantissimus*) agree with the LXX. In Ex. iv. 11 *mogilalum* transliterates the rendering of Aquila, Symmachus and Theodotion, for a Greek word would scarcely be introduced to represent the LXX δύσκωφον. In Deut. xxx. 6 Cyprian (with Lactantius and Evagrius) has *circumcidit* which might have been derived from a book of testimonies, but is also found in Aquila; Augustine and Lugd. represent περικαθαριεῖ of the LXX.

To these six 'Hexaplaric' readings from Cyprian can be added two others from Tertullian which must be equally ancient. In Josh. x. 13 Lugd. follows the LXX but Tertullian has *ultus est populus de inimicis suis*; the insertion of *populus* with the omission of θεός appears in no Greek MS (*dgnpt* have both words) but is given in Syro-Hex. as the reading of Aquila and Symmachus. In Gen. vi. 2 the true LXX reading is evidently ἄγγελοι; this has less MS support than υἱοί but is used by Philo and Josephus and apparently Clement of Alexandria, while *vioí* seems to have been the rendering of the three other versions. If this be so the LXX reading is preserved in one MS of Speculum (*Cod. Sess.*) and used by Augustine (*De Ciu. Dei*) while *filii* was used in the other MSS of Speculum and by Tertullian and was known to Augustine. It would appear that the primitive Old Latin followed the LXX, while Tertullian used a different text which he probably derived from a Greek source, but which became current in Latin authorities at a later period.

A reading from Aquila would seem to have displaced the LXX reading in Lugd. and Augustine in Josh. xi. 19. Here there are four widely differing texts. One, with ἔλαβεν, preserved by B*ejsvzfirhoqu* seems to be the LXX reading; Theodotion's (παρέδωκεν) is found in AFGΘ; Aquila had παρεδόθη, a reading preserved in N*dgmnptwa*₂ and in Augustine and Lugd. (the only representatives of the Old Latin); the reading of Symmachus, which corresponds closely with the M.T., is added to Aquila's by *dgnptw* and in a different form by G*bchx*. The passage is noticeable for the departure of Augustine from the uncials AF which he generally follows so closely, and for the wide divergence of all the Greek versions, except Symmachus, from the M.T. Augustine has no other clear agreement with the other Greek versions against the LXX (Num. x. 17 and xix. 16 are very uncertain) but there are a few others in Lugd. In Josh. ii. 6 Lugd. conflates τοῖς ξύλοις, which comes from Theodotion, with the rendering of the other versions—FN and a dozen cursives having the same conflation. In Josh. xxiii. 13 Lugd. has πλευραῖς for πτέρναις; the latter is the LXX reading and as it remains in the Syro-Hex. it seems that we have not here a normal Hexaplaric alteration; πλευραῖς is given by a few cursives (*fgmnsvwz*) and both words find a place in *dpt*. In Gen. xlix. 26 Lugd., Ottob. and Ambrose (*Patr.* and elsewhere) depend on ἐπιθυμίας though this word (besides being noticed in M) is supported only by *finvz*, Theodoret and Chrysostom; all other MSS of the LXX have εὐλογίαις and this is followed by Rufinus (probably an indication that he used the Greek as well as the Old Latin); it is however very doubtful whether εὐλογίαις can be the original LXX reading, for it seems to have crept in from the preceding line. The addition of *fortis* in Lugd. in Num. xvi. 22

is supported by the Hexaplaric cursives *ck*; it is however found neither in G nor the M.T., and therefore may have come into Lugd. from one of the other Greek versions independently of Origen's Hexapla.

Mon. and Wir. seem to offer one example of such a reading. In Lev. xix. 37 they have *iustificationes* and *iustitias*, the early and late equivalents respectively of δικαιώματα. The reading of all Greek MSS is προστάγματα, but *s* and *v* give δικαιώματα as the reading of other versions. Wir. has added *mandata* evidently from a knowledge of the LXX reading.

(*i*) *Summary and Conclusions*

The first impression received from the study of the preceding pages will probably be that the version of Augustine must be founded on a different Greek text from that of the Latin MSS. The closeness of Augustine to FM in Lev., to MN in Jud. and to AFM elsewhere is indeed very remarkable; the MSS on the other hand are much less uniform in their tendencies; they have many more agreements with B in all books, and yet in many places have distinct connections with cursive groups, while they also have many distinct agreements with AFM, generally of course agreeing with Augustine in these last places. Among the cursive groups with which the Latin MSS have connections *dgnpt* or *gn* with *w* is conspicuous in Josh., and *dgnpt* with *lovw* in Jud. There are clear connections also with *bw*, with *nx* in Ex., *gnua₂* in Deut. and the margins of *svz* in Lev., Num. and Deut.; in these places as in those where the MSS incline to B Augustine generally retains a close connection with the AFM group of uncials. The group of cursives with which Augustine shows a greater tendency to agree (*ejsvz*) is one with which connections are comparatively few in Lugd. The group *fir* is the only one with which both Augustine and Lugd. show a decided connection.

On the other hand several striking agreements in text between Lugd. and Augustine have been quoted in the preceding pages. Among many significant common agreements with a minority of Greek MSS, those in Gen. xxviii. 14 (with *r* only), Num. i. 4 (with F*f only), Deut. xxiv. 18 (with B* only), Josh. v. 4 (with N only) and Josh. xi. 19 (with Aquila) stand out conspicuously, and Augustine's comments on the text frequently suggest that the real Old Latin text was more like that of the MSS than that which he selects (or makes) for his own use. We have for example quoted his comments on Ex. iii. 11 and 12 and Ex. x. 23 where he apparently knew of no Greek support for the Old Latin readings, and would probably have considered them as deserving alteration, but in each case B and the extant Latin MS support them. Again though he opposes Lugd. a dozen times at least when Lugd. follows the cursive group *dgnpt*, yet he knows that the readings of *dgnptkw* and Lugd. in Lev. vi. 22, and of M*vz*(mg.)*gn* and Lugd. in Lev. xvi. 16 are genuine Old Latin renderings. His short note on Ex. xxxii. 24 is especially instructive; here the three MSS in spite of their differences agree, first in *aurum* with *flnxb*$_2$ only, and then in having a third person verb which is now found in the Bohairic only. Augustine quotes as the Latin a text agreeing in both respects with them, while the Greek which he quotes agrees with the mass of Greek MSS. So in Ex. iv. 8, Lev. xii. 4 and 5 and Josh. v. 2 he supports readings given by cursive groups and the Latin MSS (and in the last case by Cyprian also) as being the Latin rendering, but mentions the alternatives as being found in some or all Greek MSS. The question whether the Old Latin version used by Augustine was in origin the same as that represented by the MSS must be settled only after a consideration of all sides of the question, vocabulary and style as well as text. The argument of the previous chapters has shown that the agreements between Augustine's version and that of the MSS almost demand a recognition of the unity of the version; and if this be so, while the differences in the presupposed Greek will be evidence of a revision which included a more or less systematic correction of the whole text, we shall probably accept the agreements in text as supporting a common origin. Augustine himself sometimes definitely refers to variants already in the Latin which seem to rest on different Greek texts (*e.g.* in Ex. viii. 26 and Lev. xxv. 23) so that we cannot attribute all Augustine's differences from the MSS to his own corrections of the Latin from Greek MSS before him. The paucity of support which Augustine receives from other Latin texts however seems to show that in his time the revised text which he used was not widely current.

Of the other Latin authorities the one which shows most difference from the MSS in the matter of the Greek text implied is Tertullian; and for the most part Tertullian's variations (like those of Augustine) are in the direction of the AFM group of uncials. Under these circumstances it is not surprising to find that Augustine and Tertullian sometimes agree against the other Latin authorities. In Deut. xv. 7 and xxiv. 13 for example they follow AFM but Lugd. (with Speculum and Ambrose in the second place) follows BΘ; in Deut. xiii. 4 and xxvii. 15 (where Augustine is missing) Tertullian (*Scorp.* 2) agrees with AFMN, but Lugd. and Speculum with B. Tertullian however shows a less consistent agreement with AFM than does Augustine; in Deut. xxx. 13 *e.g.* he agrees with Lugd. in following BΘ, and in Ex. xxxiii. 19 with Lugd., Wir. and Ambrose in following *jsvzx*, both being places in which Augustine follows his usual Greek text. Sometimes Tertullian even follows B where the MSS do not, as in Jud. ii. 15 where he is with B*aefjsz*, and in Lev. xiv. 42 where he follows BA*y*. Tertullian has several noticeable connections with later Latin authorities some of which suggest that he is using the same Latin version as appears afterwards in them; thus we have Deut. xi. 28 where Tertullian (*Scorp.* 2) and Lugd. with *lm* insert μή, Lev. xx. 21 where Tertullian (*Monog.* 7), Wir. and Speculum with BAN*bcwxa*$_2$ omit καὶ ἀνήρ, Gen. i. 11 where Tertullian (*Herm.* 22 and 29) and Augustine with A*aejloqd$_2$ and Or.-Lat. omit κατὰ γένος, Gen. ix. 5 where Tertullian (*Resurr.* 28), Ambrose (*Abr.* ii. 9), Irenaeus, Jerome and Augustine (*Cont. Litt. Pet.* ii. 92) omit two words with *fn*, and (most significant of all because Augustine differs) Ex. xxiii. 21 where Tertullian (*Marc.* iii. 16), Cyprian, *Adu. Iud.*, and Ottob. with *n* have αὐτῷ for σεαυτῷ.

Cyprian's text shows a much closer agreement with that of the MSS than Tertullian's—a fact supporting the common view that while Cyprian regularly quotes from the primitive Old Latin, Tertullian sometimes renders his Greek text into Latin for himself. Nearly everywhere Cyprian and Lugd. agree in text whether with B as in Deut. xviii. 18 and 19, or with A as in Josh. xxiv. 26 and 27. They even agree in coincidences with small cursive groups as with *gnptw* in Josh. xxiv. 27 and with *hm* in Deut. xiii. 13. Other cursives with which Cyprian seems to have coincidences are *fir* (Ex. xii. 10, *derelinquetis ex his*) and *n* (Ex. xxiii. 21 and xxxii. 1) and it has already been noticed that the MSS have some clear agreements with these. Cyprian agrees with Mon. against Lugd. in Deut. xxx. 19 (with BΘ*egn* Or.-Lat.) and in Ex. xxxii. 1 (with *n*); in each case the point is a small one but Lugd. corrects the readings to agree with the common Greek. Cyprian and Mon. have a clear coincidence in text in Ex. xvii. 9 (with AM and Ottob.), but in Ex. xii. 46 they have two divergences, Mon. first having a long insertion with AM and then an agreement with F*, being evidently inferior each time. In Deut. xviii. 18 and 19 where, as we have just noticed, Cyprian and Lugd. have clear connections with BΘ, it is remarkable that Lugd. more literally follows the Greek than Cyprian, so that if Cyprian's *ea quae* and *quisque* are the original Old Latin, Lugd.'s *secundum quae* and *homo quicumque* can only be attributed to revision from a knowledge of the Greek. Cyprian's renderings however are rather exceptional here and perhaps due to subsequent arbitrary alteration.

The most interesting point about Cyprian's text however is the frequency with which Augustine alters it; this is all the more remarkable when Lugd., Ottob. and Ambrose, which are distinctly European authorities, agree with Cyprian, and it provides a weighty argument for the view that the main revision of the Old Latin text affected Augustine only among our existing Latin authorities. The following are a few of the places in which Augustine thus alters a text which is evidently the true Old Latin. In Gen. xxii. 2 he inserts *ibi* against Cyprian and Ambrose, in Ex. xii. 5 he omits *immaculatus* (or *sine uitio*) against De Pasc. Comp., Cyprian and Ambrose, in Ex. xxiii. 21 he has *tibi* against Cyprian, Tertullian and Ottob., and in Josh. xxiv. 27 he has *mentiti fueritis* for *recesseritis* against Cyprian and Lugd. It is probably no mere coincidence that in Deut. xxx. 19 where Augustine keeps to the text of Mon. and Cyprian, and in Deut. xxxiii. 9 where he keeps to that of Cyprian and Speculum (though in each place Lugd. changes it), the quotation is not from *Qu.* or *Loc.* but from other works which more frequently seem to preserve earlier forms of the Old Latin.

If the text of Cyprian thus agrees so closely with that of the MSS, we expect to find that Lucifer, Ambrose and Speculum, which are so closely connected with Lugd., almost everywhere represent the same text as that MS.

The text of Speculum is almost everywhere in agreement with that of Lugd. whether with the B group of uncials, or with the A group, or with other uncials as in Gen. xxxii. 27 and 29, or with cursives only as in Josh. xxiv. 19, or where these two alone seem to preserve the original LXX as in Jud. xv. 5. The differences are in every case small and uncertain; *e.g.* if Lugd. (*appliciti eritis*) depends on *gn* in Josh. xxiii. 8, *adherebitis* of Speculum may be a correction from the Greek, but it might be an independent conformity to the usual expression. On the other hand if Speculum follows *m* in Deut. xxiii. 15 Lugd. would be corrected from the Greek; but again Speculum has in many places been arbitrarily altered and may be independent of this cursive here. Perhaps the transposition and omission which Speculum has in Jud. vi. 25 with *glnw* is more likely to be due to dependence on a different original, but in the absence of other clear instances we shall feel rather doubtful even about this. In Josh. x. 11 the agreements between Lugd. and Speculum are much more significant than their difference. Both have *et mortui sunt plures* with F^bgn, evidently the Hexaplaric variant (as the Syro-Hex. indicates) for the LXX καὶ ἐγένοντο (a dozen cursives conflate the two): the following participle, *morientes*, now becomes superfluous, and is dropped out by Speculum, F^b and *n*, though retained by *g* and Lugd.

Speculum has also noticeable agreements with Ambrose and Wir. (*e.g.* in Gen. xviii. 5 and Ex. xxii. 25) but Speculum and Augustine seem less close; they have several differences in Lev. xx. 10 and xxi. 7–8 which may be due to corrections of the text by Augustine or to arbitrary alterations in Speculum resulting in chance coincidences with various Greek MSS; if the former Speculum would seem in the second passage to have a connection with *k*.

The text of Speculum varies considerably in character; sometimes, as in the avoidance of a doublet with BF*achmr* in Ex. xxiii. 9, it seems good; but many alterations, which may sometimes have been made in it and the Greek MSS independently, bring it into agreement with inferior MSS (as in Ex. xix. 14, where Mon. is evidently preferable).

Though Lucifer and Lugd. agree on the whole even more closely than do Speculum and Lugd., they have more differences which correspond to differences in the Greek text. Obviously Lugd. and Lucifer are on the whole based on the same Greek text, but in the middle of passages where they agree almost word for word, we find an occasional difference corresponding exactly to a difference in the Greek MSS. Thus a slight examination of the parts of Jud. vi contained in Lugd. and Lucifer will show their practical identity; we have in both an agreement with *dglnptvw* in *v.* 2 in which these MSS alone retain a word which the obelus of the Syro-Hex. indicates to be part of the true LXX, followed by an agreement with B and a few cursives in which they do not seem to represent a true LXX text at all; and similar remarkable connections recur throughout the chapter. Yet in *v.* 4 Lugd. has *iumentum* with *dglnptvw* while Lucifer follows the other Greek MSS in having *asinum*, while in the next verse Lucifer inserts *et camelos suos ducebat* with the very same group (with Syro-Hex. under obelus) and Lugd. follows the common Greek reading. These however are the only obvious differences in text in the eighteen verses which Lucifer quotes from Jud., verses which contain a hundred considerable variations in the Greek text. So in the forty verses which Lucifer quotes from Josh., he shows exactly the same Greek text as Lugd. except in one or two places. Josh. vii. 17–18 will well illustrate both their general agreement and their occasional disagreement. Here with very slight variations both make three considerable insertions—*secundum uiros et ostensa est domus Zambri, et oblata est domus*, and *filius Charmi*; F*M*aiy*a*a₂ contain all three of these insertions, a few other cursives have one or two of them: and as G is missing they may be Hexaplaric in origin as each of them is under asterisk either in *vz*(mg.) or in Syro-Hex. The opening words of the first insertion are changed in Lucifer as in M*ahipty*a*a₂, to *per domus*, but when the insertions have once been made this change is a natural one; it might therefore have been made in Lucifer and M independently, but in any case Lucifer appears to be later than Lugd. In *v.* 24 on the other hand Lugd. seems later than Lucifer, both in giving the rendering *uallem Achor* (apparently from Symmachus or Theodotion) in place of *Mecachor*, and in inserting *et uestimentum et argentum et ligulam auream*; these words may have been repeated from *v.* 21, but that they are a later insertion (probably from a Hexaplaric source) appears from the use of *uestimentum*, for in *v.* 21 Lugd., like Lucifer, has *uestem*. In Deut. we have already noticed Hexaplaric influence in Lugd. in xvii. 8–10; the insertion of two words in Lugd. in *v.* 18 seems another indication that in this chapter Lucifer preserves the better Old Latin text. On the other hand, though both Lucifer and Lugd. are often assimilated to Θ*gn* or Θ*dgnpt* in Deut. (as in xiii. 1–3) yet the changes in this direction found in Lucifer only (*e.g.* in xxviii. 12–20 and xvii. 9–10) seem to be later modifications, whether depending on these MSS or independently made. Num. xxv. 12 and 13 afford an opportunity for comparison with Ambrose (*Ps. cxviii*) as well as Lugd., and bring out the close agreement between Ambrose and Lugd. Lucifer departs from the text of the other two in repeating *testamentum* (with AM), in having *cum ipso* for *post eum* (with AN*mnop*) and inserting *in* (with *dgnptcku*). In Lev. xviii. 4 and 5 Lucifer seems to agree with FM two or three times against Lugd. and Wir.; the agreement of Wir. and Lucifer against Lugd. in *v.* 5 is probably to be attributed to the influence of the New Testament form of the verse.

Ambrose, like Lucifer, shows a general close agreement with the text of the Old Latin MSS, with occasional clear departures from it. His close connection with Lugd. both in expression and in underlying Greek text is everywhere apparent, whether they follow B or A or other uncials (as in Lev. x. 18 and 19) or cursives. His agreements with Wir. in Gen. xl and Ex. xxii are also obvious, and he also closely follows the text of Mon. at least in the parts of Mon. which are European in character; a conspicuous example in Ex. xiii. 12 has already been given. Yet there are some places in which Ambrose and Lugd. follow different Greek MSS. In Jud. xv. 19 *aperuit* of Ambrose is evidently connected with ἤνοιξεν of AGM, but *scidit* of Lugd. with ἔρρηξεν of B. In Jud. xiv. 14 Ambrose twice refers to a reading *tristi*, in place of (*De Helia*, 11) or in addition to (*De*

Tobia, 15) *forti*; this seems to refer to σκληροῦ, which is found in *glow* in place of ἰσχυροῦ. Josh. xx. 4–6, omitted by Lugd. as by BNΘ, were evidently read by Ambrose (*Fuga Saec.* 2) as by A and most cursives. In Deut. xxxiii. 27 Ambrose's reading (*De Patr.* 9) *protegens deus initii* would probably be an equivalent of σκέπασις θεὸς ἀρχῆς which (except that they have θεοῦ in place of θεός) is the reading of B*FN*gmnrx*. It is possible that Ambrose comes nearest to the original LXX, though the Ethiopic alone supports the nominative *deus*. Later σκέπασις was made into a verb and σέ added as in AMΘ and the later hand of B, so that *coperiet te* of Lugd. seems to depend on a later Greek text. In Ex. xxxiii. 19 Ambrose has a text peculiar to himself among Latin authorities, Lugd. and Wir. agreeing with B, Augustine with AFM, and Ambrose with a few cursives (see page 84). The foregoing are clear divergences between the texts of Ambrose and the MSS, but on the other hand though in some respects Ambrose and Augustine have points of contact they do not seem to have a clear coincidence against the MSS in the matter of the Greek text used; more typical are the agreements against Augustine shown by Ambrose, with Lugd. in Gen. xvii. 12, with Speculum in Gen. xviii. 5 and with Cyprian in Gen. xxii. 2.

A few of the quotations of Ambrose show departure from a well-supported Old Latin text. In the following examples a reading obviously primitive survives in several later Old Latin authorities, but is not used by Ambrose. In Gen. i. 14 *De Pasc. Comp.*, Augustine, Or.-Lat. and Ambrosiaster all depend on the Greek reading preserved in E*n* only; Ambrose (*Hex.* 14) agrees with the other Greek MSS. In Gen. xii. 1 Cyprian, Speculum, Augustine, Jerome and Or.-Lat. all insert *uade* with EM; Ambrose (*Luc.* iii. 7) omits it with AD*ahrt*. In Deut. xxxiii. 9 Cyprian, Speculum, Augustine and Lugd. have *non cognouit* (or a synonym) either representing οὐκ ἐπέγνω (FM) or misunderstanding ἀπέγνω (BΘ). Ambrose (*De Off.*) substitutes *abdicauit* apparently from a knowledge of the latter Greek reading. In such passages the support of Cyprian and the concurrence of four or five Old Latin texts show that the reading in question was early and late and widespread and it seems more likely that Ambrose is correcting the Old Latin for himself from a Greek source than quoting another Old Latin version. This is not inconsistent with the conclusion already reached that Ambrose may sometimes follow the Old Latin when Augustine in such works as *Qu., Loc.* or *De Gen. ad Litt.* is making use of a Greek MS to amend his Latin text.

The three MSS evidently agree very closely in their text; even in Ex. and Lev., where Mon. differs so widely in its Latinity from the other MSS, the agreement between the texts of the three (or four if we include Ottob.) is extraordinary, especially when we consider the numerous differences Augustine has from them. Agreements between the three MSS have been enumerated above which follow not only important uncials and groups but also cursive groups like *gnx* or *ejsvz*. Lugd. and Mon. have been quoted as agreeing with single uncials like F, N or G, with *x*, with B*, with *gnpto* and *ejsvz*; Wir. and Lugd. as agreeing with *jsvzx*, *bwgn*, and *bwnx*, the third MS being missing in all these instances. Where they differ we find that in Ex. Mon. follows B and Lugd. and Wir. and Ottob. follow AFM nearly every time, and in Lev. Mon. follows AB and the others FM. In Deut. on the contrary though Mon. agrees several times with B, yet Lugd. (often with Wir.) agrees with B even more; evidently either B or Mon. represents an inferior text in Deut. There can be no doubt that the MSS which agree with B very frequently preserve the original Old Latin whether it be Lugd. (Lev. xviii. 5) or Wir. (Lev. v. 16) or Mon. (Lev. xi. 27 and 42); there appears to be an exception in Ex. xxxiii. 13, where Wir. and Augustine seem to have the older Latin reading with AF. Where Lugd. opposes Mon. and Wir. it seems uniformly inferior, except possibly in Lev. xi. 13; hence Mon. and Wir. may represent the primitive Old Latin in Ex. xxxii. 26 and 28, though the support for their readings seems weak, and four Latin texts oppose them in each place. In Wir. we have noticed several readings which are evidently inferior, notably in Ex. xxii. 20 and 28, xxxii. 24 and xxxiv. 7; many such agreements with late and inferior groups of cursives have been noticed in Lugd., and there are many others as *e.g.* in Ex. v. 11.

Doubtless the primitive Latin at times followed a text preserved in cursives only, but generally where the Latin MSS differ, the one following cursives only is inferior; thus Wir. and Lugd. seem inferior in Lev. xi. 36, Lugd. in Lev. xii. 4; Mon. seems inferior to Lugd. in Ex. xxxvii. 20, Mon. and Lugd. to Wir. in Lev. xi. 32. Lugd. perhaps preserves the true Old Latin and LXX reading (*acerbas*) in Deut. xxviii. 59 with Θ only; here unfortunately not only all other Latin evidence, but B* also is missing.

CHAPTER IV

THE STYLE OF THE MSS AND THEIR PLACE IN THE OLD LATIN VERSION

(a) Pronouns and adjectives

Iste. The use of *iste* for *hic* is a well-known 'Africanism.' It is found about fifty times in Cyprian, mostly in Ps., Is. and the Synoptic Gospels, and is replaced by *hic* six times in the A text, and often in other Latin texts. *Iste* is however occasionally found in later texts where earlier ones have *hic*. Thus Tyconius has *iste* in 1 Jn. ii. 3 though Cyprian has *hic*, and Lugd. has *iste* in Gen. xxxi. 13 where Novatian has *hic*.

Iste occurs seventeen times in Wir., three in Gen., once in Ex., eight times in Lev. and five in Deut.; and twenty times in Mon., sixteen in Lev., once in Num. and three times in Deut. It is noticeable that both in Mon. and Wir. the 'Africanisms' *iste* and *totus* are most common in Lev.; while from the latter part of Ex., which in Mon. is in most respects as primitive as Lev., both are almost entirely absent. We have here possibly evidence of an original diversity of usage in these books.

For *iste* of Mon. and Wir., Lugd. in Lev. generally substitutes *hic*; e.g. in ch. xi Mon. has *iste* five times, Wir. twice, Lugd. and Augustine not at all. *Iste* however is found in Lugd. frequently in other books. There are fifty occurrences in Deut., over forty in Josh., about twenty each in Gen. and Jud., but it is rare in Lev. and Num. and never used in Ex. Augustine uses it forty times in *Qu.* and *Loc.*, more than half of the occurrences being in Lev. and Num. The different distribution of the occurrences in Lugd. and Augustine is noticeable; the almost complete disappearance of this word from Lugd. Lev. and Num. (where Lugd. is most primitive) and its repeated use in Deut. (where Lugd. represents quite a late type of text) being most remarkable.

Iste is used by Jerome a dozen times in the Heptateuch, by Hilary, Ambrose and Tertullian three or four times each, by Speculum six times, three of which are in Deut. and agree with

Lugd. Novatian in this respect is more 'European,' for he uses *iste* only twice in all his Biblical quotations.

Istinc is used by Mon. and Lugd. in Deut. ix. 12; elsewhere both have the usual *hinc*.

Is, ille and **ipse**. *Ille* and *is* are almost synonymous in the Old Latin; *ipse* occurs with reflexive and intensive force, but is also used as a simple personal pronoun; in this section only the latter use is noticed.

In Cyprian *ille* is used about two hundred times, *ipse* about seventy-five. That these words are not distinctively late is also made clear by the fact that though Cyprian's *is* is in various parts of the Bible replaced by *ille* eight times in Speculum, seven times in Lucifer and seven in the A text of Cyprian, yet on the other hand *ille* of Cyprian is replaced by *is* three times in Speculum and twelve times in the A text of Cyprian, so that though a tendency to use *ille* can be seen in Lucifer, there are other late forms of the version in which the opposite tendency is seen.

In Wir. *ipse* is used nearly twenty times, *ille* about sixty. In Mon. there are about the same number of occurrences of *ipse* but about 100 of *ille*. Since Mon. is three times as long as Wir. this means that these words are relatively more frequent in Wir. than in Mon. (cf. Ex. xl. 13 and Lev. xix. 31 where Mon. has *eorum* and *eis* but Wir. *ipsorum*, the contrary never occurring). Lugd. in most parts has a marked tendency to use *ille*, but in certain books this pronoun is conspicuously rare. Except in the last three chapters *is* is almost always used in Lev., while in the last two chapters of Gen. and in the latter half of Deut. *ipse* is remarkably common—the last being all the more noticeable because in the early part of Deut. *ille* is as conspicuous as anywhere. Hence when we compare Mon. and Lugd. we get different results in different books. In Deut. ix and x Lugd. often has *ille* where Mon. has *is*, but in Lev. Lugd. often has *is* where Mon. (and Wir.) have *ille*, while in Deut. xxx–xxxii Lugd. several times has *ipse* where Mon. has *ille*.

A comparison of Lugd. and Augustine will show that Lugd. on the whole has a tendency to use *ille* and *ipse* where Augustine has *is*; in the quotations common to the two nearly one hundred examples of this could be found, the converse being rare except in Lev., where we have already remarked on the almost exclusive use of *is* by Lugd.

Ambrose shows a preference for *ille* in Gen. as compared with Lugd., using it about twelve times where Lugd. has *is*— the converse occurring only once; in the latter part of Deut. Lugd. has *ipse* seven times where Ambrose has *is*, but elsewhere there is little difference between the usage of Ambrose and Lugd. As compared with Lugd. Speculum has a preference for the shorter pronoun, having *is* twenty-one times where Lugd. has *ille* or *ipse*, the converse occurring nine times. The marked preference for *ipse* in the latter part of Deut. and for *is* in Lev. is evidently a peculiarity of Lugd., there being no support for it in any other MS or Father.

The use of these pronouns (generally *ille*) to represent the Greek article is considered 'African.' Cyprian thus uses them in Gen. iii. 17, xii. 1, xxii. 2 and xxxv. 1, and in these places they are removed by such later authorities as Augustine, Ambrose, Speculum and Hilary. This usage occurs three times in Novatian, one of which is in the Heptateuch (Gen. xxi. 17); it is found six times in Wir. and three in Ottob. but only four in Mon. (all in Lev. xiv); it occurs only rarely in Augustine —*e.g.* in Gen. xxxiv. 1, Ex. xxvi. 18 and (*De Gen. con. Man.*) Gen. iii. 24. There are probably fifty occurrences in Lugd., but several of these (especially in Deut.) are with proper names which are not declined where it serves to indicate the case— rather a different usage from the ordinary one.

The use of superlatives where they do not occur in the original is evidently primitive. Cyprian thus has *optimus* Ps. xxxiii. 13 (Speculum, Lucifer and A text *bonus*), *maximus* Matt. v. 19 (Speculum and A text *magnus*), *pessimus* 1 Cor. xv. 33 (Speculum and A text *malus*), and in the Heptateuch we have *dilectissimus* in Cyprian, Speculum, Ambrose in Gen. xxii. 12 and 16 (not Hilary, Augustine, Tyconius), *durissimus* in Cyprian, Speculum, Jerome, Augustine in Num. xvi. 26 (not Lugd.), *maximus* and *minimus* in *Ad. Nov.* in Deut. i. 17 (not Speculum, Lugd., Lucifer); doubtless also *optimus* in Aug. *De Gen. con. Man.* in Gen. ii. 12 is primitive (Ambrose and Aug. *De Gen. ad Litt. bonus*). Such superlatives are found in Mon. in Ex. xxxii. 21 (*maximus*, Lugd. and Wir. *magnus*), and in about a dozen places (several in Num. and Josh.) in various parts of Lugd., in one or two of which Augustine has the positive. Four such superlatives occur in Ottob.—Gen. xxxviii. 7 and 10, Gen. xli. 19 and Ex. xvi. 17; they are rare in later Fathers though we have examples in Ambrose Ex. xvi. 17, Augustine Deut. i. 35, Lucifer Deut. xxviii. 12 and Jerome Gen. xlvii. 9.

Si qui is used seven times by Mon., always in the primitive parts (Ex. xxxii, Lev. xix–xx and Deut. xxii). The form might of course only represent the preference of the scribe, but it is significant that Cyprian also frequently uses *si qui*, having it *e.g.* with Mon. in Ex. xxxii. 33, where Lugd. and Wir. (as elsewhere) have *si quis*. Perhaps *si quis* in Mon. in Deut. xxii. 28 rather represents the alteration of a scribe.

Quanta is used by Mon. for ὅσα seven times, and by Wir. three times. The single occurrence in Cyprian (Josh. xxiv. 27) is not sufficient in itself to mark it as 'African,' though here Lugd. and Augustine have replaced it, as they generally do, by *quicumque*. Augustine uses it half a dozen times (three in Num.), Lugd. a dozen; Speculum has it (with Lugd.) in Gen. xxxi. 12, and Lucifer (with Mon.) in Ex. xix. 4.

Mon., Lugd. and Ambrose frequently use *qui* for the compound relatives ὅς ἐάν and ὅστις ἐάν; Lucifer, Augustine and Wir. show a preference for *quicumque*. The latter however is not distinctly late, for Cyprian has it four times where Speculum has *qui*.

The expression *ad alis alium* is found in Wir. and Lugd. in Ex. xxvi. 5 and 6, *ex alis alium* in *v.* 3; Lugd. has *ab alis alio* Gen. xxxi. 49, *in alis alium* Ex. xxviii. 7, and *in alis alio* Ex. xxxvi. 11; Ottob. has *ex alis alio* in Ex. xxvi. 3. *Ad alis alium* and *cum alis alio* are found in Old Latin Gospel texts which seem to be European, and Augustine avoids these expressions in Ex. xxvi. 6, having *aulaeum ad aulaeum*. Mon. is missing in each of these places, but in Ex. xxxviii. 15 where Lugd. has *alii aliis* Mon. has *sibi*, which may be another slight indication that these peculiar expressions are European rather than 'African.'

Qualifying phrases commencing with the article and following a noun or pronoun are generally expanded into relative clauses: e.g. *omnia quae sunt in eo* is normally used by Mon., Wir. and

Lugd. for πάντα τὰ ἐν αὐτῇ. In Lev. xiv however Mon. three times has *sanguinis neclegentiae* (τοῦ αἵματος τοῦ τῆς πλημμελίας) where Lugd. has *sanguinis eius quod* (or *illius qui*) *est necligentiae*. So in Lev. iv and v Wir. frequently has *delicti* or *pro delicto* where Lugd. has *eius quod est delicti* or *quod est pro delicto*. Lugd. seldom has these abbreviated forms, and since the relative would hardly be omitted when once it had found a place in the Latin, Lugd. in these places appears to represent a deliberate correction by one who saw that the Latin did not make the meaning clear.

The Greek idiom by which a relative is attracted into the case of its antecedent is sometimes retained in the Latin version; four or five examples are found in Wir. and half a dozen in Lugd. A literal following of the Greek also accounts for such a phrase as *filii in quibus non est fides in ipsis*, in Mon. Deut. xxxii. 20. Augustine frequently notices such expressions in *Loc.*, but perhaps he is drawing attention to the repetition of the pronoun in the Greek and rendering the original literally for himself; thus *e.g.* he retains the full expression in Lev. vii. 25 and Num. xxiii. 13 where Lugd. shortens it. The second pronoun is omitted three times in Wir. and six in Mon., most of the latter being in Num. and the early part of Ex. By omitting the second pronoun in Lev. xi. 9 Wir. makes a great improvement on the literal rendering of Lugd. (*omnia in quibus sunt* for *omnia quaecumque sunt in eis*).

In Lev. xix. *vv.* 13 *sqq.* Mon. uses *tibi* five times for *tuus*. This is evidently a primitive mark, for in Cyprian we have *sibi* Ps. xxiii. 4 (Tyconius, Speculum and A text *suus*), *mihi* Is. lxvi. 1 (Novatian, Hilary and A text *meus*), *tibi* Matt. v. 43 (Luc. *tuus*); and further examples may be found in Cyprian in Bar. iii. 35 and Matt. xix. 19 and xxiii. 8. This use of *tibi* is found in the 'African' Gospels *k* and *e*, and in two MSS of Augustine (*Qu.*) in Lev. xviii. 20. A somewhat similar use of *tibi* for *tuus* is found in Augustine (*De Ciu. Dei* and *De Gen. con. Man.*) in Gen. xvii. 7; two other possible examples occur in the Heptateuch in Lugd. and Speculum Gen. xxxii. 27 and in Mon. Lev. xiv. 35, but in each of these places the Greek MSS are not unanimous.

(b) Nouns: use of the cases

The accusative of extension of time is very rare in the Old Latin as a whole, and as Cyprian does not seem to have a single example, it is probably a later correction where it is found. Wir. always has the ablative except in Lev. xxiii. 6 (*vii dies edetis azyma*). Mon. has the accusative twice (Num. xii. 14 and Deut. ix. 9), the ablative about twenty times. Lugd. has the accusative in these two places and occasionally elsewhere (*e.g.* in Deut. ix. 18 where Mon. has the ablative) but only about a dozen times altogether, nearly all of which are in Deut. and Josh.: in three of these Ambrose has the ablative, the accusative being as rare in Ambrose as anywhere. We find an accusative in Lucifer in Deut. xvii. 19, and one in Speculum in Ex. xxi. 21. Augustine has the accusative eight times in Gen. (*Qu., Loc.* and *De Ciu. Dei*), but only about half a dozen other examples are found in his Heptateuch.

In Ex. xxxiv. 23 Wir. and Lugd. have *per tria tempora anni*, though in the next verse Wir. has *tribus temporibus* and Lugd. and Augustine *tria tempora*. Such a use of *per* is found in Cyprian very rarely, and in Lugd. only about a dozen times. Except in the early part of Ex. Mon. avoids it altogether; in Lev. xii. 2 for example Mon. has *vii diebus* where Lugd. has *per* and Augustine *vii dies*; in Deut. xxii. 29 Mon. has *toto tempore* (Lugd. *omni tempore*) where Augustine and Ambrose have *per*. In the earlier chapters of Ex. Mon. has more variety of expression: we have *triduo* (Ex. x. 22), *per dies tres* (Ex. x. 23) and *per triduum* (Ex. xix. 15)—all for τρεῖς ἡμέρας; in the second place Augustine, and in the third Cyprian and Speculum have *tribus diebus*.

Grammatical blunders connected with the cases used after prepositions are frequent in the MSS. Prepositions which should take an ablative, such as *ab, cum, de* and *pro*, are sometimes followed by an accusative, and conversely *ante* is followed by an ablative. Such mistakes, often arising no doubt from the abbreviation for the accusative ending, are frequently found in inscriptions and are perhaps in many cases due to the scribes of the MSS. In many instances however they are evidently due to the retention of the case used in the Greek, and here we are doubtless correct in regarding them as survivals from the earliest form of the version. Thus Lugd. and Mon. have *ab unius mensis* in Num. iii, and *a xxv annorum usque ad l annorum* in Num. iv; Lugd. has *a xx annorum* in Ex. xxx. 14. These expressions are corrected by Augustine *e.g.* in Num. viii. 25 and xxvi. 2. Genitives after *audire* (or a compound) are found in Mon. Deut. xxviii. 13, and in Wir. Deut. xxviii. 45; these are corrected by Lugd., Lucifer and Ambrose, but Lugd. elsewhere has half a dozen examples of such genitives. Lucifer has one with Lugd. in Jud. vi. 10; and Augustine, though he nearly always uses the accusative, has two, one with Lugd. in Jud. ii. 20 (*Loc.*), and the other in Num. xii. 6 (*De Gen. ad Litt.*) where Lugd., Mon. and Spec. have the accusative. *Tangere* is followed by *ab* in Augustine Lev. v. 3 (Wir. and Lugd. acc.), and in Cyprian, Speculum and Augustine Num. xvi. 26 (Lugd. *ex*).

The Greek partitive genitive is generally replaced by an accusative; but prepositions (*ab, de* or *ex*) are used by Augustine Num. xx. 19 (Lugd. acc.), by Mon. (Lev. iv. 16 and 25 and xx. 3) and a few times by Lugd. Other cases which are retained from the Greek are genitives of measure in Wir., Lugd. and Augustine Ex. xxvi. 8, and double accusatives after *uestire* and *induere* in Mon., Wir. and Lugd. in several places, after *cibare* in Mon. and Lugd. in Deut. xxxii. 13, and after *multare* in Mon. and *condemnare* in Lugd. (ζημιοῦν) in Deut. xxii. 19, where Augustine has the ablative (*siclis*). A few alterations of cases seem to be attempts to make the meaning clearer; thus in Ex. xxvi. 1 (*et facies tabernaculum decem atriorum*, or *aulaeorum*) the genitive in Wir., Lugd., Ottob. and Augustine takes the place of a Greek accusative; in Lev. xxii. 27 Wir. uses nominatives *uitulus ouis haedus*, though Augustine retains the ungrammatical accusatives of the Greek.

The singular *lignum* is used in Wir. and Lugd. in Ex. xxxv. 33 (Augustine *ligna*) and by Mon. in Ex. ix. 25 for the Greek plural; with regard to *caro* the practice of Cyprian, Mon. and Wir. varies considerably, Cyprian *e.g.* having the plural in Ex. xii. 8 but the singular in Lev. vii. 19 and 20. Lugd. generally uses the singular, but Augustine, perhaps influenced by a knowledge of the original, nearly always retains the plural (*e.g.* in Ex. xxi. 28 and Num. xi. 21 and xix. 5).

Lugd. has several instances of inflected proper names which

are treated as indeclinable by Mon. and Augustine; only once or twice does Augustine inflect a name used indeclinably by Lugd. Perhaps the inflection is a sign of later emendation for in Num. xx. 25 Cyprian has *Eleazar*, but Lugd. *Eleazarum*.

(c) Verbs

Greek infinitives expressing purpose are sometimes represented by infinitives in Latin, but more often by *ut* and the subjunctive. In Cyprian *ut* takes the place of a Greek infinitive more than forty times, but in two places the A text, and in two others Lucifer restore the infinitive; on the other hand Cyprian twice has an infinitive where Lugd. has *ut*. There does not seem to be much difference between Wir. and Lugd. in this respect, but Mon. has the infinitive rather less than Lugd.; thus Mon. has *ut* in Lev. xi. 45 and Deut. ix. 1 where Lugd. has infinitives, but the converse does not occur anywhere. Augustine uses the infinitive more often than Lugd. especially in Deut. (*e.g.* in ix. 4 and 6 and x. 8); sometimes he may be literally representing the Greek; Lucifer also has three infinitives in Deut. where Lugd. has *ut*.

A more noticeable point about the rendering of the Greek infinitive is the frequency of the gerund and gerundive in Mon. About twenty examples are found altogether, all but two in the primitive parts, and eight in Ex. xxxviii–xl. Gerundives occur altogether nearly thirty times in Cyprian and three times in Novatian; *Ad. Nov.* introduces two into Gospel quotations, and they are often used by Tertullian (*e.g.* Gen. iv. 11, Ex. xvi. 3 and Deut. xiii. 5 and 9). They may therefore be primitive especially as they are sometimes removed from passages where Cyprian has them, by Augustine and Ottob. (Ex. xxiii. 20), Augustine and Lugd. (Deut. xxx. 6), Speculum (Rom. xii. 2) and the A text of Cyprian (Ps. lxvii. 8). Yet on the other hand we must notice that Speculum has a gerundive in Is. xxx. 1 and so has the A text of Cyprian in Ps. xviii. 6, though Cyprian has one in neither of these places.

Gerundives are rare in Augustine (though he has two in Jud.), and hence it is significant that the early *De Gen. con. Man.* has two in Gen. iii (*vv.* 6 and 24) which are replaced by infinitives in *De Gen. ad Litt.* Wir. has four examples; Lugd. has

about half a dozen in each book (though they are rather rarer
in Deut. and Josh.); Ambrose has one (with Lugd.) in Num.
x. 2, and Lucifer has two in Deut. (xiii. 9 and xvii. 7) where
Lugd. has infinitives. In Num. xxxi. 16 Mon. and Lugd. have
causa discedendi et contemnendi for τοῦ and the infinitive; this
use of *causa* and the gerundive seems early, a close parallel
being Cyprian's *potandae aquae causa* in Amos iv. 8. *In eo cum*
Mon. Lev. xviii. 28 (Lugd. *dum*) seems a primitive attempt to
represent ἐν τῷ before the infinitive.

Wir. has an 'accusative and infinitive' in Ex. xxii. 8; Lugd.
has the construction half a dozen times in Deut. and occasionally
elsewhere. It does not occur in Mon., but cannot be called late
for it is found several times in Cyprian, mostly in the New
Testament and sometimes (Lk. xx. 37 and 1 Jn. ii. 9) for a
Greek clause with ὅτι. Examples are found in both Augustine
and Ambrose in Gen. ii. 18 and xvi. 5 but they are rare in the
Heptateuch quotations of either. Tertullian has one in Deut.
xxiv. 1 (removed by Lugd.) and *Ad Nov.* one in Gen. vi. 5
(removed by Augustine).

The avoidance of participles has been called a mark of an
early text and the evidence of Cyprian and the MSS to some
extent supports this view. Cyprian does indeed on a few occasions introduce participles which are not in the Greek, and it
is possible to find quite a dozen in Cyprian which have been
replaced by clauses in Speculum, Lucifer, Tyconius, Lugd. or
the A text of Cyprian, but half of these instances are in
Speculum where the tendency to avoid participles is very pronounced indeed; and in about twenty places later authorities
substitute participles where Cyprian has clauses. Examples of
the restoration of participles not found in Cyprian are seen in
Ex. xix. 10 (Mon.), Josh. v. 2 and 13 (Lugd.), Gen. xii. 3
(Augustine and Ambrose) and Gen. xxxv. 1 (Hilary). In Ex.
xxxi–xl and Lev. Lugd. uses participles a dozen times where
Mon. avoids them, the converse occurring only three times; in
Num. and Deut. xxviii–xxxii where the text of Mon. is less
uniformly primitive we find six participles in Mon. which are
avoided by Lugd., the converse being found only twice. In
Mon. participles are also more frequent in the early part of
Ex., being found there not only for Greek participles, but

occasionally for principal verbs as in Ex. x. 7, x. 24 (where Augustine has *ite et seruite*) and xiv. 2. In view of these examples it is quite possible that *tollens*, Ex. xiii. 12, is really intended for a participle though Ambrose following the Greek has *tolles*; in Ex. xiii. 21 Mon. has a participle for the Greek infinitive. There is little difference between Lugd. and Augustine in the matter of the use of participles except that in Num. Augustine shows a preference for them as compared with Lugd. Ambrose, like Speculum, is inclined to avoid participles, but Lucifer seems to prefer them.

The future participle is very rare. In Lugd. it occurs several times in Deut. but not often elsewhere, and in no other MS or Father does it occur except rarely. Hilary has examples in Gen. xviii. 13 and 17, Augustine and Ambrose in Gen. xlix. 1, Speculum in Deut. viii. 20; Mon. has one in Ex. xix. 23 but avoids those used by Lugd. in Ex. xxxii. 13, and by Lugd., Lucifer and Augustine in Ex. xxxiii. 5. Novatian has two in St John, perhaps an indication of European revision.

The ablative absolute is not common, and its avoidance has been considered most noticeable in the early forms of the version. There are only about half a dozen examples in the whole of Cyprian, and about the same number in the Heptateuch quotations of Augustine. Wir. has four examples—Ex. xxxiii. 16, xl. 15 (with Mon.), Lev. v. 12 and xxii. 24; in the first three places Lugd. avoids the construction, in the fourth it is missing. Besides Ex. xl. 15 Mon. has examples in Ex. xxxii. 20, Lev. xix. 9 (with Speculum and Augustine), Num. xxxiv. 8, Deut. xxiii. 4 and xxxi. 27. In the first place Lugd. and Wir. have *sumens* (a later word than *accepto*), in the second Lugd. is missing, in the others Lugd. agrees with Mon. Mon. also introduces ablative absolutes twice where the Greek has a different construction (Ex. xvi. 13, Deut. ix. 17), but avoids them in Deut. ix. 9 with Lugd., in Ex. xii. 29 with Ambrose and Jerome, and in Ex. xvii. 12 where Cyprian has an ablative absolute. Speculum has four examples; Lugd. has over forty, the majority of which are in Gen., Num. and Deut. Lugd. has a dative absolute in Ex. iv. 21 and a genitive absolute in Deut. xxxiii. 5.

The insertion of the copula where it is not found in the Greek is apparently a mark of later texts. In Wir. it is found several times in Gen., and five times in Lev. where it does not appear in Lugd. In Lev. vii. 10 Cyprian as well as Wir. inserts it, and so does Mon. in Lev. xi. 46 and xii. 7; and since in all these places it does not appear in Lugd. it is clear that its omission is characteristic of Lugd. in this book. In other books however Lugd. often inserts it; Mon. does occasionally in Num. A clear distinction exists in Mon. in this respect between the earlier and later parts of Ex.; in the early chapters the copula is several times inserted, but in several places in the later chapters where Lugd. inserts it, it is not found in Mon.

In such verbs as *ire, delere, perire* Mon. generally uses the forms *deleam, periet, exiet, transiet* for the future, though we have *redibit* Lev. xiv. 39, and *peribitis* Deut. viii. 19 and 20. Lugd. has the forms with *b* more frequently, *e.g.* Ex. xxxii. 33, Deut. xxviii. 7, xxx. 18 and xxxi. 2, in each of which places Mon. has the shorter form; Augustine however has the longer forms even more regularly than Lugd. Speculum regularly uses the shortened form—an indication that *Cod. Sess.* probably preserves the true Speculum reading in Gen. xviii. 5. It is not clear whether either usage is to be considered more 'African' than the other; on the one side we can quote Lev. vii. 10 where Cyprian has *peribit*, but Wir. and Lugd. *periet*, but on the other side we have in Ex. xxxii. 33 *deleam* in Mon. and Cyprian but *delebo* in Wir. and Lugd.

A preference for the future perfect tense seems 'African,' for Cyprian has sixteen examples of future perfects changed by later authorities, eleven by Speculum, four by Lucifer, and two by Cyprian A text; the converse change is rare, though in Deut. xviii. 19 Lugd. has introduced a future perfect which is not found in Cyprian. Lugd. however shows a decided tendency to use them in Deut.; in this book it has five examples not found in Lucifer and seven not found in Mon., and everywhere shows more tendency to use them than Augustine. In Lev. however Mon. and Wir. have several which are removed by Lugd.

(d) Prepositions

In and **super**. In Wir. ἐπί is rendered *super* about forty times, *in* about thirty, and *ad* five (four of which represent ἐπί and the acc.). In Mon. *in* is used very nearly as much as *super* on the whole, and in some parts much more; *ad* is úsed a dozen times (generally for ἐπί and the acc.), *de* four times (Lev. xiv. 18 and three times in Lev. xi) and the dative without a preposition four times (all in Ex.). The simple dative, *ad*, and *de* scarcely occur at all in Lugd., *super* taking their place almost regularly. Cyprian has *ad* in Gen. xlviii. 17 and Josh. v. 14, Lugd. having *super* each time. Mon. and (to some extent) Wir. show a greater fondness for *in* than Augustine and Lugd.; thus eleven times in Lev. (five in ch. xi) and nine in Deut. xxii–xxxii Mon. has *in* where Lugd. has *super*, the converse being very rarely met with.

A preference for *super* has been regarded as 'African'— probably from the study of the Gospel texts, but in view of the character of Mon., there can really be no doubt that in the Pentateuch *in* is 'African.' We may notice especially such an instance as Deut. xxxii. 13 where Mon. has *in fortitudinem* and Lugd. *super uirtutem*—and *fortitudo* is certainly 'African.' As a matter of fact Cyprian also shows a decided preference for *in*; e.g. Hilary in Is. lxv. 16 and Bar. iii. 36, Cyprian A text in Ps. xlix. 5 and Tyconius in Ez. xxxvii. 14 all have *super* where Cyprian has *in*. Cyprian also has *in* in Ex. xvii. 9 where Mon. as well as Augustine and Ottob. have *super*, but this is just the part of Mon. in which we should expect to find the later usage. The following are other examples of variation in the Heptateuch: Gen. xxii. 2 Cyprian, Ambrose *in*, Augustine *super*; Ex. xxviii. 43 Cyprian, Augustine (*Parm.*) *in*, Lugd., Ambrose *super*; Gen. iv. 5 *Adu. Iud. in*, Lucifer, Ambrose *super*. On the other hand it should be noticed that later authorities sometimes replace Cyprian's *super* by *in*: thus we have Gen. xxii. 12 Cyprian, Speculum *super*, Hilary, Ambrose *in*; Ex. xii. 13 Cyprian *super*, Ambrose *in*; Deut. xiii. 9 Cyprian, Lugd. *super*, Tertullian, Lucifer *in*; and outside the Heptateuch, A text and Speculum in Lk. ix. 62 and Lucifer in Eph. v. 6 replace Cyprian's *super* by *in*. In this respect, as in some others, Wir. occupies a position between Mon. and Lugd., having *super* six times where Mon. has *in* (the converse occurring in Lev. xx. 3 only) but having *in* six times where Lugd. has *super*. A preference for *in* is seen in Ambrose in Gen. vi. 4 and vii. 22 (Augustine each time *super*) as well as in Gen. xxii. 2 and 12 and Ex. xii. 13 mentioned above.

With regard to *in* and *super* as prefixes of compound verbs the evidence is even more confusing. In Lev. iv–vi *e.g.* Wir. and Augustine use *superponere* frequently where Mon. and Lugd. have *imponere*. Augustine shows this preference for *superponere* everywhere, but Wir. uses *imponere* elsewhere (*e.g.* in Ex. xxv. 37). Ambrose uses *imponere* three times in Gen., Cyprian has three or four occurrences of each. In other words too Augustine shows the same preference for *super* as compared with Lugd.; in Lev. xxvi. 36 Augustine has *superducere*, but Lugd. *inducere*; in Gen. xxviii. 18 Augustine (*De Ciu. Dei*) has *superfudit in* but Lugd. *infudit super*.

A confusion between εἰς and ἐν is often found, sometimes doubtless due to a confusion between accusative and ablative which is found in most late Latin MSS and inscriptions. In some cases we have evidence that such mistakes persisted in the texts and were not due to individual scribes; thus in Ex. xxxv. 27 Wir. has *in umbonem et in manuali*; in Lugd. the second word is replaced by *logio*, but the ablative is retained. In Ex. v. 21 Augustine draws attention to the solecism *dare in manibus* which he says is less defensible since the Greek has εἰς. That the ablative here was not merely an eccentricity of Augustine's MS is shown by its appearance in Lugd.

Ad is used for εἰς three times in Wir. and six in Mon., but Mon. often has *in* where Lugd. has *ad* (five times in Lev. xii–xiv). Mon. has *per* for ἐν in Deut. xxviii. 7, 9, 25 and Deut. xxx. 16 (*per uias*), Lugd. having *in* each time. The use of *per columnam* by Cyprian Ex. xiii. 21, where Augustine, Ambrose and Mon. have *in*, suggests that this use of *per* may be 'African.'

The use of *de* four times in Mon. for ἐπί has already been noticed. *De* is also used sometimes for the Greek instrumental ἐν. This use of *de* is found in Mon. in Lev. iv. 6 (Lugd. ablative) and Ex. xxxviii. 10, four times in Wir. and a dozen in Lugd.; Augustine has it rarely but examples occur in Ex. xxi. 6 and (with Ottob.) Ex. xxvi. 34, though in all the places where Lugd. has it Augustine, if extant, either has *in* or omits the preposition.

Ante, coram, etc. As a rendering of a Greek preposition Wir. uses *in conspectu* twelve times, *ante* five times, *coram* twice and *palam* once; Ottob. has *in conspectu* four times, *ante* twice, *coram* twice, *palam* and *contra* once each. In Mon. *ante* is found twenty-six times (ten in Lev., ten in Num.), *coram* ten (chiefly in Num. and Deut.), *palam* seven (five in Ex. xii–xviii) and *in conspectu* or *in conspectum* seven (Lev. iv. 4, three times in Ex. x–xiv, and three in Deut. ix–x); *contra* is found in Num. xi. 20. Cyprian uses *coram*, *ante* and *in conspectu* about equally, *contra* three times in Josh. and Jud., but *palam* occurs in neither Cyprian nor Tyconius. A similar use of *ante*, *coram* and *in conspectu* with about equal frequency would probably be found in Speculum and Ambrose. It appears then that, with the possible exception of *palam*, none of these words is distinctively late or early and any variation in usage detected is more likely to be from one book of the Heptateuch to another than from one author to another. The large number of occurrences in Lugd. and Augustine will eliminate any possibility of accidental preponderance from the following tabulation of the usage of Lugd. and Augustine:

Lugd.

	Gen.	Ex.	Lev.	Num.	Deut.	Josh.	Jud.
Ante	31	1	65	35	3	12	7
In conspectu	7	35	1†	3	38	20	2
Coram	5	3	3†	31	12	9	10
Palam	—	8	—	—	13	—	—
Contra*	5	3	3†	27	1	6	—

Augustine (including the Genesis quotations in *De Ciu. Dei*)

	Gen.	Ex.	Lev.	Num.	Deut.	Josh.	Jud.
Ante	10	9	12	7	2	1	1
In conspectu	6	12	1	10	1	—	2
Coram	2	6	—	—	8	4	—
Palam	—	3	—	—	—	—	—
Contra	2	2‡	—	3	—	1	—

* There is a tendency to use *contra* for ἀπέναντι and κατέναντι but most of the occurrences in Num. are for the simple preposition.

† All in chs. xxv–xxvii.

‡ Once each for ἀπέναντι and κατέναντι.

Even if some occurrences have been overlooked in compiling this table it suggests some interesting conclusions.

Mon. and Lugd. agree in the frequent use of *ante* in Lev. and Num., and of *coram* in Num. and Deut., and in having *palam* and *in conspectu* almost restricted to Ex. and Deut. The only remarkable difference between the usage of these two MSS in fact is towards the end of Ex., where Mon. altogether avoids the *in conspectu* which is so common in Lugd. The distribution of the occurrences of *in conspectu* in Lugd. and Mon. would strongly suggest that this is a late or European word, were it not for its prominent place in Cyprian. A comparison of the usages of Augustine and Lugd. shows that in both *ante* is almost exclusively used in Lev.; the relative frequency of *in conspectu* in Ex., the restriction of *palam* to Ex., and the fact that half the occurrences of *contra* are in Num. are phenomena in Augustine which do not seem unconnected with the usage of Lugd. We have however striking differences between the two in the entire absence of *coram* from Augustine's Num., and the corresponding frequency of *in conspectu* there, and in the rareness of *in conspectu* and absence of *palam* in Augustine's Deut. It almost seems as if in Lugd. those features have been superimposed on Deut. also, which are characteristic of Ex. both in Augustine and Lugd. *Palam* is apparently not early, but it can hardly be called characteristically late for it does not seem to occur in Lucifer as a preposition, though he (with Lugd.) has *palam in palam* in Ex. xxxii. 11 (Augustine *facie ad faciem* or *os ad os*); it is in fact seldom found outside Lugd. Ex. and Deut. and Augustine and Mon. in Ex. i–xviii. In view of the frequency of *coram* in Lugd. Num. it may not be a coincidence that Ambrose regularly uses this word in that book; the preponderance of *ante* however in Lugd. Gen. is certainly not reflected in Ambrose.

Compound prepositions are found in most texts, but they are more common in the later ones. Thus *ab ante* is not found in Cyprian, but appears in Wir. (Lev. xix. 32), in the later parts of Mon. (Deut. ix. 3 and 4), occasionally in Augustine (*De Gen. con. Man.*, Gen. iii. 8) and half a dozen times in Lugd.—most of which are in Deut. and Ex., apparently the latest parts of that MS. Other compound prepositions are frequently met with in Lugd.; thus in Ex. xxxviii. 2 Lugd. has *de intus* and *de foris*, Mon. having *intus* and *foris*; we even have in Lugd. *de deorsum* (Deut. xxxiii. 13). One compound preposition, *desuper*, seems to be more characteristic of early texts than of late ones; thus we have *desuper* in Cyprian in Prov. viii. 28 replaced by *in summo* in Hilary and Speculum, and though Ambrose often shows a fondness for *desuper* (as in Gen. xxvii. 28 and Ex. xxv. 20 and 28), its place is generally taken in Lugd., Wir., Ottob. and Augustine by *a susum, desusum, a summo* or *in summo*. Mon. uses *desuper* three times in Ex. xxxviii–xl; it has *susum* in Ex. xx. 4, but this is a place where we should expect a later form in Mon.

Mon. on the whole shows a preference for simple verbs rather than for compound ones; in Lev. xi for example Mon. and Wir. have simple verbs three times where Lugd. has compounds. Ambrose and Lucifer also show a preference for simple verbs, each having half a dozen examples in passages where other Old Latin texts have compound verbs. Augustine also has several examples of simple verbs where Lugd. has compound ones, but this may be because it is in Lugd. that the tendency to use compound verbs is most conspicuous. Perhaps Cyprian and Wir. occupy rather an intermediate position in this respect, but Hilary often shows a preference for the compound forms.

(e) Conjunctions

Si autem and quodsi. *Si autem* is the usual rendering of ἐὰν δέ in all texts. It occurs regularly in Mon. (about twenty-four times) except in Ex. ix–xx, where *quodsi* is found (4/4). In Ex. xxii Wir. has *quodsi* eleven times and *si autem* twice; Wir. has *quodsi* also in Ex. xl. 31, and *si uero* in Ex. xxxiv. 20, but elsewhere *si autem* (ten times). Augustine (*Qu.* and *Loc.*) uses *quodsi* only four times, once in Ex. iv and three times in Ex. xxi. It therefore appears that in Mon., Wir. and Augustine alike *quodsi* is characteristic of the first half of Ex. In Lugd., chs. vii–xxv of Ex. are missing except for twenty-six verses of ch. xxi, but in these twenty-six verses *quodsi* is found twelve times, though it only occurs about another dozen times in the whole of the Heptateuch. Cyprian seems to use *quodsi* only in Deut. xiii. 6; in his only quotation from the early chapters of Ex. in which either of these words is used (Ex. xxii. 21) he has *si autem*. In Lucifer *quodsi* is used only a few times, one being in his quotation of Ex. xxi. 23; in Speculum it is found seven times in quotations from Ex. xxi to xxiii, but rarely elsewhere— only in Lev. xxvii. 31 in the Heptateuch. So too Ambrose uses it three times in quoting Ex. xxii but not often elsewhere. It is found occasionally in Hilary (*e.g.* in Gen. xviii. 21) and in some of the early European Gospel texts, and in Italian inscriptions of about 100 A.D., but its use in Augustine in the same places as the European authorities seems to show that it is not distinctly European. The persistence with which it recurs in Mon., Wir., Lugd., Speculum, Augustine, Ambrose and even Lucifer in certain chapters of Ex. seems rather to point to its being a characteristic of this part of the original Old Latin version which has been preserved by practically all authorities. We seem to have here a remarkable piece of evidence not only of the original unity of the version, but also of its lack of uniformity in different books of the Bible.

Sicut, tamquam, quomodo, etc.   *Sicut* is common in all stages of the Old Latin, but its various synonyms are very differently distributed.

In Cyprian we have *sicut* (fifty-four times), *quasi* (thirty-five), *tamquam* (twenty-one), *quomodo* (seventeen), *ut* (eleven), *uelut* (nine), *quemadmodum* (three—Matt., Jn., 1 Cor.), the A text replacing *quasi* (three times), *quomodo* (three times) and *uelut* (twice) by *sicut* or *tamquam*. In Tyconius *sicut* is used frequently, *quasi* and *uelut* half a dozen times each, *tamquam* and *quomodo* being rarer; *quomodo* and *quasi* are frequent in *k*.

The usage of the MSS is as follows: Wir. has *sicut* eleven times, *quemadmodum* six times, *secundum quae* (Ex. xxxix. 11), *tamquam* (Lev. xix. 34) and *quomodo* (Lev. v. 13) once each. Mon. has *sicut* thirty-one times, *secundum quae* thirteen (ten in Ex. xxxvi– xl), *tamquam* eight (five in Ex.), *quemadmodum* seven (five in Num.), *quomodo* three (all in Lev.), *secundum quae* twice (Ex. xxxii. 28 and Num. iv. 37) and *uelut* once (Lev. iv. 10). Lugd. has *sicut* nearly three hundred times (almost regularly in Gen. and Josh.), *quemadmodum* eighty-two (seventy of which are in Ex., Num. and Deut.), *quasi* thirty-one, *quomodo* seventeen, *secundum quod* sixteen (eight in Num.), *tamquam* twelve (five in Num. and four in Deut.), *secundum quae* four (all in Num.), *ut, prout* and *uelut* once or twice each. Ottob. has *sicut* seven times, *tamquam* six, *quemadmodum* three, *quasi* three (all in Gen. xli) and *secundum quod* (with Lugd.) in Gen. l. 6. The usage of Augustine is interesting for comparison. He has *sicut* forty-five times (almost regularly in Ex., Josh. and Jud.), *quemadmodum* eleven (seven in Gen. and Deut.), *tamquam* eight (most in Gen.), *quomodo* seven (five in Lev.), *secundum quae* three (all in Num.), *secundum quod* two (both in Deut.), *prout*, *ut* and *uelut* once or twice each. These figures apply to *Qu.* and *Loc.* only; in his other quotations, which are for the most part from Gen., he uses *tamquam* over a dozen times (six in *De Ciu. Dei*) and *quomodo* three or four: *quasi* does not occur in Augustine's quotations from the Heptateuch.

It seems an obvious conclusion that *quemadmodum* is late. This is made clear by its almost entire absence from the earlier authorities, and by its frequency in Lucifer and Lugd. (especially the late books). Its occurrences in Mon. are therefore noticeable, providing another indication that Mon. has a later text in Num. than in Ex. and Lev. *Quasi* is generally considered as a typical 'Africanism,' and this is doubtless correct; it occurs many times in Cyprian (Num. xxiii and xxiv provide several examples) in passages where Lucifer, Hilary, Speculum, Lugd., Tyconius and Cyprian A text use *ut, sicut* or *tamquam*; and in Gen. ix. 3 where used by Novatian (*Ad Iud.*) it is replaced by *sicut* in Ambrose and Lucifer. It would seem however that *quomodo* and *uelut* are equally characteristic of the early texts; both words, like *quasi*, are rare in Lucifer and Augustine (except for the five occurrences of *quomodo* in Augustine Lev.); they occur in Mon. only in Lev., and sometimes when used by Cyprian are replaced in Speculum, Lucifer and Cyprian A text by *sicut* or *quemadmodum*.

Tamquam cannot so certainly be considered 'African.' It is not common in Lugd., but it occurs frequently in Lucifer and Rufinus, and Augustine and Ambrose use it very much especially in Gen.; half the occurrences in Mon. are in the early part of Ex. where Mon. is certainly not primitive, and later authorities often substitute it for Cyprian's *quasi* (*e.g.* Lucifer, Speculum, Is. lviii. 2) or *uelut* (*e.g.* Ambrose, Gen. xlix. 9). The frequency of *secundum quae* (especially in Ex. xxxvi–xl) is one of the most noticeable usages of Mon. Wir. retains it once (xxxix. 11) but elsewhere, with Lugd., replaces it by *sicut* or *quemadmodum*. The exact expression occurs four times in Lugd. and three in Augustine (all in Num.), but *secundum quod* is more frequently met with in Lugd. and occasionally in Augustine, Lucifer, Hilary and Speculum. In spite of their non-appearance in *k*, Tyconius and Cyprian these may be early.

There does not seem to be much to suggest that particular renderings were characteristic of particular books in the version as a whole. The usage of Augustine and Mon. might suggest that *quomodo* was characteristic of Lev., but Lugd. does not support this as the majority of the occurrences in Lugd. are found in Jud. Lugd. and Augustine both show a tendency to use *quemadmodum* in Deut., but this can be explained by the fact that both have a later type of text in this book than in most others. We have however one or two striking coincidences in usage; thus *prout* occurs only once or twice both in Augustine and Lugd. and yet each has it in Deut. xvi. 10, and immediately afterwards each uses *secundum quod* which is equally rare in Augustine and not common in Lugd.

The usage of the other early Fathers may be noticed; Novatian altogether has *sicut* ten times, *quasi* five, *tamquam* five and *ut* three: the 'African' *quomodo* and *uelut* and the late *quemadmodum* do not occur. Hilary uses *sicut* in the great majority of instances, *quemadmodum* does not seem to be used at all, *tamquam*, *quomodo*, *quasi* and *ut* are found once or twice each. Tertullian uses *uelut* considerably, Irenaeus and Jerome frequently use *quasi*.

Quoniam and **quia**. A fondness for *quoniam* instead of *quia* had been noticed as a characteristic of Tyconius and is generally considered as 'African,' and the evidence of Mon. rather supports such a view. The two words occur in this MS altogether about an equal number of times, but *quia* is more common in Deut. and in Ex. ix–xx, *quoniam* in Ex. xxxi–xl and in Lev. In Wir. *quoniam* is found nine times and *quia* fourteen. In Lugd. *quoniam* is almost everywhere used in Lev. (25/27) and Jud. (81/92) and is fairly common in Num. (24/72) but is rare in Gen., Ex., Deut. and Josh. (about 45/300). In Augustine (*Qu.*

and *Loc.*) *quoniam* is relatively more frequent, being practically always used in Lev. and Jud., twice as common as *quia* in Num., and slightly more frequent than *quia* in Ex., Deut. and Josh. Only in Gen. is *quia* more common and there it much preponderates in *De Ciu. Dei* as well as in *Qu.* and *Loc.*, occurring in these three works fifty times, *quoniam* about half a dozen. Augustine and the MSS therefore preserve *quoniam* most frequently in just those portions in which other 'African' characteristics are frequently found.

It is therefore remarkable that in the Old Testament quotations of Lucifer *quoniam* is used much more than *quia*, the great majority of its occurrences being in Kings, Psalms, Ezekiel and Wisdom, where it is used almost to the exclusion of *quia*. When we examine Cyprian we find that each word occurs just over one hundred times, the occurrences being fairly evenly distributed except in Psalms, where *quoniam* is used thirteen times out of fourteen. Little of the books of Kings exists in Cyprian, and perhaps no stress can be laid on the fact that in Wisdom Cyprian uses *quoniam* four times and *quia* not at all, but in the case of Psalms at least the number of occurrences is great enough to allow us to conclude that there Cyprian's text showed an unusual preference for *quoniam*, which has survived in Lucifer's Psalms also. It certainly seems that the variation in the frequency of these words does not depend entirely on the date of the text, but that the rendering varied from one book to another, and that for this reason various texts show a preference for *quoniam* in the same book. Hilary's usage also seems to show that the relative distribution of *quoniam* and *quia* varied from book to book. On the whole Hilary uses the two about equally, but in John and Isaiah *quoniam* is more than twice as frequent as *quia*, while in Matthew and Paul the reverse is the case: and the number of occurrences is great enough to show that the difference is not accidental. That the difference is not only a matter of date is also shown by the fact that though thirteen instances occur in which Speculum or Lucifer changes Cyprian's *quoniam* to *quia*, there are eight in which Speculum, Lucifer or Tyconius changes his *quia* to *quoniam*. *Quoniam* is used by Novatian only four times out of twenty-four in *De Trin.*, but three times out of three in *De Laud. Mart.* Tertullian and

Irenaeus use *quoniam* more frequently than *quia*, but Speculum and Ottob. seldom use it. In Ambrose, though there are more occurrences of *quia* than of *quoniam*, the difference is not remarkable.

Quod is found only rarely in this connection, in Cyprian only twice altogether. It is found in Mon. three times (all in Deut.) and in Ambrose in Num. xvi. 3 and 9. Speculum has it in Gen. vi. 2 (with Tertullian), Gen. l. 15 and Deut. viii. 3, and Wir. has it once in Gen. It is perhaps not an accident that Augustine also has it four times in Gen. (and not elsewhere) and that the only occurrences in Lugd. besides two in Num. (one with Ambrose in xvi. 9) are about twenty in Gen.

Quare is used for διὰ τί in Mon. Ex. xviii. 14 and Num. xii. 8, as regularly in Cyprian, Augustine and Lugd. For ἵνα τί on the other hand Mon. uses *utquid* four times and *adquid* once. This agrees with the usage of Cyprian who has *utquid* and *adquid* but not *quare*, though the latter is introduced twice into the A text of Psalms. *Quare* also appears in Augustine and Ambrose, and a few times in Lugd. (but never in Num.). For τί in this sense Mon. has *quid* twice and *quare* once (all Ex. xvii–xviii); Cyprian uses *quid* (5/5) and so does Novatian (1/1) but Augustine and Lugd. often have *quare* (cf. Col. ii. 20—Cyprian *quid*, Speculum *quare*). Evidently the later authorities were inclined to use *quare* irrespective of the distinctions in the Greek.

Quando is used as a conjunction by Cyprian in Josh. xxiv. 27 (Lugd., Augustine *cum*), and in a few places outside the Heptateuch. This use of *quando* is found a dozen times in Lugd. and as many in Augustine (especially in Jud.), and occasionally in Speculum, Tertullian, Irenaeus and Jerome. *Ubi* is used as a temporal conjunction by Cyprian in Gen. xlviii. 17, Ex. xvii. 11 (Mon. *cum*), and a few other places; it is found occasionally in Lugd. and Augustine (chiefly in Josh.) and once in Ambrose (Gen. xvi. 5, Augustine *cum*). *Ut* also occurs at times in a temporal sense in most authorities, generally when the Greek has ὡς, though it is used a dozen times by Lugd. for a Greek participle in the latter half of Num. *Quomodo* is used in this sense by Cyprian in Josh. v. 13 (Lugd. *cum*), by Mon. in Lev. xiv. 34 (Lugd. *ut*), and a few times by Lugd. in Jud.; *quemadmodum* is thus used by Mon. and Lugd. in Deut. xxxii. 8.

Augustine has a marked tendency in most books to use *ita* where Lugd. has *sic*. *Ita* occurs half a dozen times in Cyprian and is a characteristic *k* word, and as we have *sic* in Lugd., Num. viii. 7, where Cyprian has *ita*, the latter has some claim to be regarded as 'African'; but the occurrence of *ita* in Speculum and Cyprian A text in 1 Cor. xv. 41 where Cyprian has *sic* points the other way. *Ita* occurs in Wir. only in Lev. xix. 34, and not at all in Mon., though *ita ut* (ὥστε) is found in Mon. in Deut. xxviii. 27 and twice in Wir.

Vel is used only twice in Cyprian, *siue* not at all, so that *aut* has a claim to be the typical early equivalent. *Vel* and *siue* are more frequent in Lugd. and Augustine, but are not found in Wir. In Mon. each occurs once in Num. and once in the early part of Ex., just the places where later forms might be expected; Speculum has *uel* as often as *aut*. *Vero* for *autem* also seems late, being found only once in Cyprian, but being substituted for *autem* several times in the A text. It is used in Mon. Ex. xviii. 22, xix. 24 and Deut. xxxi. 18. Novatian uses it in Gen. xxxii. 31, and it becomes more frequent in Lugd. and Augustine.

(f) *Primitive misreadings and misunderstandings*

There are numerous mistakes in the Latin version due to a misreading or misunderstanding of the original. In some instances these survive into texts of quite a late type, in others they are corrected by other, and obviously later, authorities. Mon. contains about a dozen such primitive errors:

Ex. xiii. 13. *Primitiuum filiorum non liberabis* is evidently due to the pronoun σοῦ being read as a negative οὐ.

Ex. xvi. 16. *In tabernacula sua* seems due to συσκηνίοις being read as, or taken as equivalent to, σκηναῖς. Ottob. agrees with Mon., but Aug. corrects the mistake.

Lev. xi. 35. *Expurgabuntur* is due to confusion between καθαιρεῖν and καθαρίζειν—the cursives *fn* have the same mistake. Lugd. replaces the 'African' word by its later equivalent *mundabuntur*, but Wir. corrects it to *deponentur*. Lugd. therefore shows revision of Latinity independent of the original, while Wir. shows revision from the Greek.

Lev. xviii. 19. Mon. and Wir. have *diuortio* misunderstanding the Greek; Lugd. and Aug. correct it, perhaps independently, as their renderings of the verse differ much.

Lev. xx. 2. Since *applicare* in Mon. renders προσάγειν, *qui applicati sunt* is probably due to προσγεγενημένων being read as προσηγμένων. Here again the emended reading of Wir. shows a knowledge of the original.

Num. v. 7. Mon. has *et quod imittitur et*, Lugd. *domino quod obicitur et* in place of τὸ κεφάλαιον καὶ τὸ ἐπίπεμπτον αὐτοῦ. *Imittitur* is doubtless due to τὸ ἐπίπεμπτον being connected with πέμπειν. The verb in Lugd. may be derived from Mon., for there are other examples of *mittere* being changed to *iacere*. In Lev. xxvii Lugd. again depends on a rendering which misunderstood this word, for it has *quod adautum fuerit* in v. 13 and *quod adiectum fuerit* four times (so Spec. v. 31); but in Lev. v. 16 Lugd. correctly has *quintam partem* (Wir. and Aug. *quintas*). In Num. v. 7 Aug. or his MS has corrected the reading from the Greek (*caput et quintas eius*). The asterisk under which G places κεφάλαιον is probably an error, but it is just possible that the Latin depended on a MS of the LXX which did not contain this word.

Num. xxxv. 3. *Super terminos* is due to the prefix ἀφ in ἀφορίσματα being read as ἐφ = ἐπί. Lugd. reproduces the same error.

Deut. x. 7. Mon. seems to have regarded εἰς as part of the proper name which follows and so has *isaegebaria*. Lugd. correctly has *in*.

Deut. xxxi. 20. Mon. has *descendent*, Lugd. *recedent*, Wir. *alienabuntur*. All three seem modifications of one mistranslation (perhaps *discedent*) due to κορήσουσιν or κορέσουσιν being connected with χωρεῖν. In the next sentence Lugd. has *discedent* for *dissipabunt* of Mon. and Wir. and this may be due to the repetition of this word from the preceding sentence.

It will be noticed that Wir. in the above list twice corrects the faulty rendering of Mon. and twice retains it, once where Lugd. and Augustine have corrected it, and once where though the Latin rendering has been changed it has not been corrected in either of the other MSS.

Wir. however has apparently four primitive blunders or mistranslations where the other authorities (including Mon. three times) have better renderings, so that considering the smaller extent of Wir. it has as large a proportion of primitive errors as Mon.

Ex. xxxii. 18. Wir. has *deprincipum* literally representing ἐξαρχόντων. Lugd., evidently taking *de* as a preposition, corrected the case of the noun and has *deprincipibus*, though when repeated just afterwards Lugd. retains the incorrect *deprincipum*. On the third occurrence Wir. and Lugd. both have *principatus*. Mon. suppresses the misleading prefix and has *principum* each time.

Ex. xl. 2. Wir., apparently reading νουμηνίᾳ στήσεις as νουμηνίας τῆς εἰς, renders *numeniae in.* Lugd. inserts the verb and omits *in*, but retains the genitive, and hence renders *nominiae statues*. Mon. is here the most correct of the three, rendering *in numenia constitues tabernaculum.*

Lev. v. 15. Wir. has *obliuio* taking λήθη as a nominative. Lugd. and Aug. correctly give *in obliuione.*

Lev. xi. 42. Wir. has *et omne* for διὰ παντός; Mon. and Lugd. have *semper*. Unless *et omne* is repeated from the previous clause, the reading of Wir. is due to failure to understand the Greek, and that of Lugd. and Mon. is a correction from the Greek.

It is noticeable that the primitive errors in Wir. are corrected by Lugd. more regularly than those in Mon.; and that Mon., in spite of its generally primitive character, has corrected them each time.

Lugd. however has several primitive errors which have been corrected in Mon. and (once) in Wir.; most of these are in Lev.:

Ex. xxxvi. 17. Lugd. inserts *secundum* before *lapidem* regarding κατά in κατάλιθον as a preposition; Mon. omits it.

Lev. v. 16. Lugd. has *tempore*, two cursives (*qu*) making the same confusion between καιρῷ and κριῷ. Aug. and Wir. have *ariete*, correcting the mistake from the Greek.

Lev. xiv. 36. Lugd. has *aperire*, apparently reading ἀποσκεπάσαι which is found in one cursive (*c*). Mon. has *emigrare de*, apparently from a knowledge of the true Greek reading ἀποσκευάσαι.

Lev. xiv. 48. Lugd. has *praeter genus*, reading παραγενόμενος as παρὰ γένους. Mon. (*aduenerit*) again shows knowledge of the true original.

Lev. xv. 2. Lugd. has *aut* taking ἡ as a conjunction instead of as the article. Mon. omits it.

Deut. xxxii. 27. Lugd. has *contra* for οἱ ὑπεναντίοι. Mon. more correctly has *aduersarii.*

Deut. xxxii. 29. Lugd. takes καταδεξάσθωσαν as derived from καταδιώκειν and has *subsequentur uos*. Mon. has *percipere.*

Considering the exceptionally early character of Mon. in Lev. it is remarkable that we should so frequently find in that MS corrections of primitive mistakes which survive in Lugd. It seems that a certain amount of correction from the Greek must have taken place at a very early stage in the history of the version; such early emendations may be already indicated by Cyprian's two quotations of Matt. viii. 12, in one of which he has *exibunt* and in the other *expellentur.*

Several other primitive errors of this kind can be quoted from Lugd. in places where the other Old Latin MSS are not extant. In all Lugd. probably contains forty examples as clear as those given above. They appear in all books, but especially in Lev. and Deut. The survival of so many primitive mistakes in so late a text as Lugd. Deut. is remarkable. The following list gives a selection from the most conspicuous examples:

Gen. xxvii. 39 *potu* for πιότητος (in *v.* 28 Lugd. has *pinguidine*); Ex. xxix. 27 and xxxvi. 3 *diuisio* for ἀφαίρεμα, evidently through confusion with ἀφόρισμα (Aug. has *demptio* correctly); Ex. xxxviii.23 *ascensum* for βάσιν (though this is so regularly rendered *bassem* that we wonder whether Lugd. read πρόβασιν with *x*); Lev. ii. 12 *ab initio* for ἀπαρχῆς; Lev. vi. 17 *mittetur* for πεφθήσεται (cf. ii. 4 *missum* for πεπεμμένην); Lev. xxv. 36 *zelabit* for ζήσεται (Amb. *De Tobia* has *uiuet*); Num. xviii. 8 *in senectute* for εἰς γέρας; Num. xix. 16 *pueri* for πεδίου (corrected by Aug.); Num. xxiv. 8 *cubitos* for τὰ πάχη (so Priscillian, but Cyp. *crassitudines*); Num. xxvi. 54 *plures in* for πλεονάσεις; Num. xxxv. 6 *ex* for ἕξ; Deut. ii. 4 and iii. 14 *montes* for ὁρίων; Deut. ii. 34 *ex quibus* for ἑξῆς (in iii. 6 Lugd. has *uno tempore*); Deut. vi. 7 *produces* for προβιβάσεις (Spec., Amb. *demonstrabis*); Deut. xii. 2 *super planam terram* for ἐπὶ τῶν θινῶν (Tert. *colles*); Deut. xiii. 5 *saluum te facere* for ἐξῶσαι; Deut. xiii. 16 *omne genus* for πανδημεί (Tert. *cum omni populo*); Deut. xvi. 1 *mensem iuniorum* for μῆνα τῶν νέων (Amb. *nouorum*); Deut. xix. 13 *auferens* for καθαριεῖς (by confusion with καθαιρεῖς, Luc. *mundabis* correctly); Deut. xxxii. 11 *confideat* for ἐπεπόθησεν (so Amb.—*confidit*—evidently connecting it with πέποιθα like the cursives *kv*); Deut. xxxiii. 21 *ab initio* for ἀπαρχήν (so Amb.); Deut. xxxiii. 26 *magnus et decens* for μεγαλοπρεπής (so Amb.); Deut. xxxiii. 28 *cum nebula roris* for συννεφὴς δρόσῳ (so Amb.); Josh. vi. 20 *coram aduersariis suis* for ἐξ ἐναντίας αὐτοῦ (so Luc.); Jud. i. 14 *suasit* for ἐπέσεισεν (three Greek MSS also have ἔπεισεν, but Aug. has *monuit*); Jud. vi. 4 *fines* for ἐκφόρια (so Luc., reading doubtless ὅρια).

It will be noticed by the above list that such errors are often corrected by the Fathers. Lucifer however retains the mistakes in Josh. vi. 20 and Jud. vi. 4, Priscillian retains one in Num. xxiv. 8, and Ambrose several in Deut. xxxii. and xxxiii. Deut. xxiii. 17 provides an interesting example of emendation without reference to the original. It would seem that the primitive rendering was *et non erit consummatus* (τελισκόμενος being confused with τελεῖν); this being evidently wrong Lugd. dropped out *non*, but the opponents of Augustine in *De Perf. Iust. Hom.*

(ch. ix) emended it by changing *consummatus* to *inconsummatus*, thus making the precept parallel to *tu autem perfectus eris*.

It is clear that in some points all three MSS represent a comparatively early form of the version. A writer like Augustine would doubtless often remove primitive blunders from his text, but on the other hand it seems likely that he would more often have noticed them in *Loc.* if they had been as common in his time as they are in the MSS. Even in Cyprian's text they seem less conspicuous, but perhaps it is natural that the tendency to remove these blunders would be less evident in the scribes of MSS than in the more literary Fathers of the times.

(*g*) *Over-literal renderings and transliterations*

Of similar import to the readings given in the last section are those in which the Greek is so literally rendered as to obscure the sense or spoil the style or grammar of the translation. Sometimes the improved Latinity of another MS more or less clearly indicates its later place in the development of the version. Some examples of a literal following of the Greek cases, which might have come under this heading, have been given earlier in this chapter. We begin this section with a few examples in which Mon. appears to preserve the original Old Latin rendering:

Ex. xl. 2. Mon. has *unus*, literally following the Greek. Wir. and Lugd. have *primus*—an improvement.

Ex. xl. 12. *Offerre* in Mon. seems a mechanical unintelligent rendering. It often correctly represents προσάγειν, but here is unsuitable and would not have replaced *adducere* if the latter had been originally in the version.

Lev. xi. 46. Mon. has *de pecoribus et uolucribus et totius animae*, relapsing in the last two words into the genitive of the Greek. Wir. and Lugd. replace the genitive by the ablative, and substitute *uolatile* and *omnis* for *uolucer* and *totus*. We have here weighty evidence that *uolucer* is 'African.'

There are however as many places in which Mon. has replaced a literal rendering, preserved in Lugd., by another word more in accordance with sense or Latin usage:

Ex. xxxii. 19. Lugd. and Wir. have *castrae*, the singular being probably due to Greek influence; Mon. has *castris*.

Ex. xxxix. 2. Lugd. has *a uisitatis uiris Synagogae*—a word for word rendering of the original. Mon. makes this more intelligible by substituting *a uiris uisitantibus Synagogam.*

Lev. xii. 2. Lugd. has *immundus*, not noticing that ἀκάθαρτος is here feminine; if Mon. has *immunda* it is evidently a correction.

Lev. xiv. 37. Lugd. has a genitive (*parietum*) after the comparative. Mon. corrects it to *parietibus.*

A few more such renderings in Lugd., in places where no other MS is extant, are added here:

Lev. vi. 40. Ἀναπεποιημένη is rendered *iterum factus*; two verses later *factus* alone is used by Lugd. and Wir.; in Num. *consparsus* is usual in Mon., Aug. and Lugd.

Deut. xvi. 18 etc. *Scribae inductores* is used for γραμματοεισαγω- γεῖς, though in Deut. i. 15 Lugd. attempts an explanation *aduocati qui causas inferrent.* Aug. on Ex. xviii. 21 mentions *doctores* as a Latin rendering.

Deut. xvii. 17. Μεταστήσεται is rendered *constabit*; Aug. corrects it to *discedat.*

Deut. xxviii. 55. Ὧν is literally rendered *quorum. De quibus* of Aug. is an improvement.

Augustine frequently gives literal renderings of the Greek in *Loc.* but sometimes he seems to be drawing attention to the different idioms of the Latin and Greek languages. In other places however he appears to be quoting a Latin version as when he gives *usque ad pecudem et repentium et uolatilium* in Gen. vii. 23, using a translation which relapsed into the genitive of the original since it did not notice that all three nouns were alike governed by ἕως. In Ex. xviii. 26 *causa* of Mon. is a decided improvement on the literal *uerbum* of Augustine which he seems to quote as the Latin rendering; these chapters of Mon. however are distinctly above the usual level of the Old Latin version in choice of words and general style.

It is natural to consider transliterations as marks of an early text, and so doubtless they generally are. There are however some instances in which though a Latin equivalent appears in the earliest texts, the Greek word reappears in the later ones; such technical terms as *euangelizare, baptizare* and *parabola* are often found in the late or European texts of the Gospels, though translated in the earlier ones. These examples are easily ex- plained by the growth of an ecclesiastical vocabulary into which Greek words were often incorporated, but such an explanation would not account for Cyprian's *horreum* being replaced by *apotheca* in Speculum in Matt. vi. 26. There are then exceptions to the rule that transliterations as compared with translations are early, but except in the case of the technical terms which are easily recognised, the rule will generally, and perhaps nearly always, hold.

Lugd. has an unusual number of Greek words in Lev. which are elsewhere translated; the following are some examples:

Afedrum (xii. 5) for which Mon. has *purgatio*.

Aporia (xxvi. 16) and *aportare* (xxv. 47—doubtless originally *aporiare*); for the verb Lugd. has *anxiari* in Gen. xxxii. 7, and for the noun, in Deut. xxviii. 22 Lugd. has *amentia*, Mon. *inopia*.

Clerus (xvi. 8), used also by Jer. in Gen. xlix. 14; otherwise *sors* is used from Cyp. onwards.

Cotula (xiv. 21) for which Mon. and Aug. use *hemina*.

Prosiali (xv. 8) for which Mon. has *saliuosus fuerit*.

In other books also Greek words are sometimes found in Lugd., though they are translated by Mon.:

Etphycarma (Ex. xxxii. 25); Wir. also has *epicharma*, but Mon. and Aug. use *in gaudium*.

Phyola (Ex. xxxviii. 23); Mon. here has *patera*, but *phiala* is used by Mon. (and Lugd.) in Num., and by Ottob.

Zona (Ex. xxxvi. 37), Mon. *cingula*; Cyp. uses both words, Lugd., Wir. and Aug. generally *zona*.

Anaphorus (Num. iv. 6), Mon. *balteus*, Lugd. also translating elsewhere.

Addiae (Deut. xxiii. 1) may also originally have been a transliteration; Mon. has *spado*.

In Num., Lugd. and Mon. several times agree in the use of Greek words which are elsewhere translated. Thus in addition to *phiala* just noticed we have

Bolides (xxxiii. 55); Mon. has *sagitta* in Ex. xix. 13.

Erythreum (ch. xxxiii); Lugd. prefers *rubrum* in Deut.; Mon. has *rubrum* in Ex. x but *eritreum* in Ex. xiii. 18.

Ortygomethra (xi. 31); Tert. also uses this word, but Amb. and Mon. in Ex. xvi. use *coturnices*; Aug. knows of both in Latin MSS.

The Greek words used by Mon. and translated by Lugd. are fewer: in Ex. xxxvi. 34 Mon. has *roiscus*, Lugd. *cirrus*; in Ex. xxxviii. 14 Mon. has *caulus*, Lugd. (and Wir. in ch. xxv) *scaphus*; in Deut. xxviii. 22 Mon. has *occhra*, Lugd. (apparently) *comestio*; in Deut. xxxi. 26 Mon. has *in plagio*, Lugd. *ab latere*.

Mon. has *epauleum* in Ex. xiv. 2, Mon. and Lugd. both translating in Num. by *uilla* or *stabulum*. Ottob. has *speroteres*,
charyssos and *thyisca* (Ex. xxv—translated by Wir. and Lugd.);
Wir. has *erysiue* in Deut. xxviii. 42.

In Lev. xi we have a long list of animals many of which would
be unfamiliar, and for several of these we have the Greek name
used in one (or two) MSS but translated in another (or others).
Lugd. alone preserves the Greek word in the case of *catirecten*,
arodium, *mygale*, *sphalax* and *calabotes*; for the last Wir., Mon.
and Novatian (*De Cibis Iudaicis*) all have *stelio*. *Upupam* and
saura are preserved in Mon. alone; for the former Lugd. here
has *paonem*, but uses *upupam* in Deut., for the latter Wir., Lugd.
and Novatian all have *lacerta*. Wir. also preserves four Greek
names which are translated by others, *opiomacem*, *strutionem*,
bruchum (so Mon.), and *attacum* (so Lugd.). It is noticeable
that Lugd. figures most in this list of transliterations and Mon.
least. That the translations are sometimes very early however
is shown by Novatian who translates all three of the above
which are used in *De Cib. Iud.* *Strutio* especially is noticeable,
for if this is the original Latin it was certainly being replaced
by *passer* at a very early date, the latter being used not only
by Novatian here but by both Novatian and Cyprian in the
First Gospel.

Augustine uses a few Greek words which are translated by
the MSS. In some cases he may be intentionally giving the
original word, but in some at least he is probably quoting a
Latin version; he thus has *spithamis* Ex. xxviii. 16 (Lugd.
palmum), *aspidisca* (for which Lugd. has *zonula* in Ex. xxviii
and *lamella* in Ex. xxxvi) and *peristomium* Ex. xxviii. 28 (Lugd.
orificium); he also has *chiliarchus* in Num. xxxi. 54 where Mon.
and Lugd. use *tribunus*, and *rhamnus* in Jud. ix. 15 where Lugd.
has *rubus*.

Greek words are occasionally found in other texts. In Gen.
xlix. 19 Rufinus as well as Lugd. has *piraterium*, Ambrose having
temptatio and Ottob. *temtaculum*; in Ex. i. 7 Tyconius has
cydaei fuerunt, Lugd. *diffundebantur*. The word *romphaea* seems
to have been a later reintroduction into the version; Jerome uses
it often and we find it in Ambrose and in Augustine *De Gen.
ad Litt.* in Gen. iii. 24, though the more primitive *De Gen. con.*

Man. has *framea*. *Machaera* is used by Ambrose in Gen. xxii. 6 and xlviii. 22, and by Augustine (*De Ciu. Dei* but not *De Trin.*) in Gen. xxii. 10; Cyprian uses *ensis, framea* and *gladius*.

(*h*) *Conflate readings*

If however Lugd. and Wir. preserve such early marks as primitive errors, over-literal renderings and Greek words as frequently as Mon., yet when tested by the frequency of con-flate readings, they appear to represent a considerably later text, for conflations though comparatively rare in Mon. are particularly numerous in the other MSS.

In Mon. we have the following:

Ex. x. 5: *fructiferum dans*—apparently a combination of two such readings as *fructiferum* and *fructum dans*.

Ex. xviii. 23: *in suum locum et in domus suas*.

Ex. xxxix. 9. Wir. has *et bases atrii* following M (αὐλῆς), AF having σκηνῆς. Mon. has *et bases atrii et tabernaculi testimonii*, which appears to be a conflation of the two. It is however more likely that the words *tabernaculi testimonii* have been transferred from *v*. 8 where Mon. omits them. On the other hand the omission of the clause in Lugd. is easier to account for if the text of Mon. is its original, for it then becomes a simple homoeoteleuton.

Ex. xl. 6. Mon. has *altare fructum pones primitiarum*, and *fructum* and *primitiarum* may appear to be separate renderings of καρπω-μάτων. Wir. has *frugum* here and *fructum* in *v*. 8, where Mon. repeats the same expression. There is however no evidence for *primitiarum* as a rendering of this word, and it seems rather that it was added to *fructum* as an explanation.

Deut. ix. 2. Mon. has *fili Aenac et unianimes sunt tu scis*, Lugd. *filios Senac quos tu scis*. Mon. seems to contain a conflation of the correct rendering of Lugd. with a primitive misrendering perhaps due to σὺ οἶσθας being understood as from συνειδέναι.

Deut. x. 6. Mon. has *et in Achi Misade*; *et in* may be due to Ἰακείμ being read as καὶ εἰς. Lugd. omits *et in* having *Lacu Man-sadae*.

Deut. xxxi. 20. This verse has been noticed already because all three MSS seem to reproduce a primitive error in taking κορήσουσιν as if derived from χωρεῖν. Mon. adds *ludentes* possibly due to another mistaken connection of the verb with χορεύειν.

Of these seven examples—the only ones to be found in Mon. —the first two are from chapters of Ex. which are evidently late, and the next two are more easily explained otherwise, so that, since the text of Deut. ix and x is also far from primitive, only one example is left from the older parts of the MS.

Conflate readings are more frequent in Wir. in spite of the much smaller extent of that MS. Of the seven examples which follow one or two might be classed rather as glosses or late additions but most are clearly conflate.

Ex. xxxiv. 9. Lugd. and Wir. have *iniquitates*, to which the latter adds *et iniustitias*.

Ex. xxxv. 21. *Quibus quod* (so also Lugd.—Aug. *quod* only) may be due to a combination of οἷς and ὄν, each of which is found in a few cursives in place of the usual ὧν.

Ex. xxxix. 21. Wir. has *ferramenta operum*. In *v.* 10 Wir. has *ferramenta*; Lugd. in both places (and Wir. elsewhere in this chapter) has *opera*.

Ex. xl. 29. Wir. has *innuuilauit in eum nebula*, but into *v.* 28 inserts what is evidently a doublet of this, *obumbrauit eum nubs*; the latter is practically what Mon. and Lugd. have in *v.* 29, both *innubilare* and *nebula* being rare in this connection.

Lev. xi. 42. Wir. apparently has *incedit ambulando*, Mon. having *ambulat* and Lugd. *incidit*; Wir. also uses each word alone in this chapter.

Lev. xix. 37. Mon. has *iustificationes*; Wir. with *iustitias* (its later equivalent) combines *mandata*. The latter is probably the true LXX, the Old Latin apparently being derived from another Greek version.

Lev. xx. 3. Wir. adds *Moloch*—possibly from Aquila, Symmachus or Theodotion.

The number of conflate readings in Lugd. is very great, the following being clear instances: Gen. xxvii. 31 *aepulas escae* (Lugd. has the former alone in *v.* 17 and the latter alone in *v.* 9); Gen. l. 22 *uniuersi omnes* (Ottob. *uniuersi*, Augustine *omnis*); Ex. iii. 15 *in generatione et in saecula* (Speculum *saecula*, Pelagius *generationes*); Ex. vi. 26 *ui et potestate*; Lev. i. 8 *partes quas diuiserunt diuisamenta*; Lev. iv. 19 *offeret et imponet* (Mon. *inponet*); Lev. v. 1 *siue intellexit siue conscius est* (Wir. and Augustine *aut conscius fuerit*); Lev. v. 5 *in eo super id ipsum* (Wir. *per ipsum*, Augustine *aduersus ipsum*); Lev. x. 6 *dissuetis scindetis*; Lev. xi. 8 *non tangetis abominamini* (a conflation of the reading of Wir. and most Greek MSS with one found only in *x* and the margins of M𝔃); Lev. xiv. 30 *de quibus inuenit secundum quod inuenit* (Mon. *sicut inuenit*—the cursives *ac* have a similar conflation); Lev. xvi. 8 *ad dimissionem pompeio* (*ad dimissionem* occurs in *v.* 10); Lev. xvi. 8 *sortem et clerum*; Lev. xxv. 29

domum fundatam domesticum; Lev.xxvi. 36 *reliquis relictis*; Num.
i. 53 *ex aduersa contra*; Num. vi. 20 *qui uouit qui orabit*; Deut.
i. 7 *tollite uos et proficiscemini* (both common for ἀπάρατε);
Deut. i. 8 *uidete ecce*; Deut. i. 30 *debellabit et expugnabit* (one
here used by Lucifer, the other by Augustine); Deut. iv. 8
uobis palam uobis (conflating, like Speculum, two Greek readings);
Deut. iv. 10 *cum quando*; Deut. iv. 13 *exponens rettulit*; Deut.
vii. 20 *reliqui qui superfuerunt*; Deut. viii. 1 *obseruabitis et custo-
dietis*; Deut. xx. 4 *ante uos uobiscum* (Augustine *uobiscum*);
Deut. xxviii. 43 *in imo deorsum* (Wir. *deorsum*, Ambrose *in
imum*); Deut. xxix. 19 *in unum pariter* (Augustine *simul*); Deut.
xxxii. 8 *nationes gentium* (Mon., Hilary, Irenaeus *gentes*); Deut.
xxxiii. 14 *conuenientibus scientibus* (Ambrose *conuenientibus*);
Deut. xxxiii. 24 *in oleo misericordia* (Ambrose *in oleo* only,
misericordia being a primitive blunder); Josh. iii. 7 *in quo in-
cipio*, if *in quo* was originally *inchoo* (Augustine *incipiam*); Josh.
ix. 10 *in dorsum asinorum* (Augustine knows both ὄνων and ὤμων
both in Greek and Latin); Josh. xxiv. 12 *reges ciuitatium* (conflating two Greek readings).

Considering the late character of Deut. in Lugd., the large
number of conflations in that book is less remarkable than the
equally large number in Lev. which has so many characteristics
of an early text. We have here another indication that this book
has a large number of later elements in spite of the primitive
character of many of its renderings.

Taking into account the small amount of Old Latin material
in Ottob. it has a remarkable number of conflate readings. Thus
we have:

Gen. xlix. 1: *conuenite et congregamini* (Aug., Amb., Ruf. *congregamini*, Lugd. *accedite*).

Gen. xlix. 21: *repromissionis quod ex defectus* (Amb., Ruf. *remissa*,
Lugd. *defectus*).

Ex. xxv. 17: *propitiatorii emeritionis*; both of these words are used
by Ottob. in this chapter, the former being usual in the Old Latin.

Ex. xxv. 29: *in faciem cumpositos* (ἐνωπίους), Lugd. having *pro-
positionis*.

Ex. xxvi. 12 and 13: Ottob. gives the greater part of these verses
twice, the first time in a form very similar to Augustine's, the second
time very much like Lugd. and Wir.

Ex. xxvi. 29: *aequales in quibus* (Aug. *in quos*), *aequales* being a
primitive mistake due to εἰς οὕς being read as ἴσους.

The Latin Fathers have more examples of doublets than of primitive blunders; a few from various texts are added here:

Gen. iii. 14. Luc. combines *quae sunt super terram* (Aug. *De Gen. ad Litt.*) with *terrae* (Cyp., Iren., Amb.); each is found in the Greek, but no Greek MS combines them.

Gen. xlix. 17. Amb. has *superbus et temerarius*; Lugd. has *audax* and Ottob. *inuidati*, and Amb. may rather represent a paraphrase than a combination of actual readings.

Ex. xxi. 18. Spec. has *pugno aut ferro* (πυγμῇ), Lugd. *ligno*. This also may be an example of an arbitrary addition.

Ex. xxii. 25. Amb. (*De Tobia* 14) has *pupillo orphano*. Wir. and Spec. have *populo* which is doubtless the earlier text. This was first corrupted to *pupillo* and then conflated with a doublet of the latter.

Lev. xxi. 17. Cyp., Aug. (*Cont. Ep. Parm.* ii. 7) and Jerome all have *macula et uitium*; the appearance of a conflation in Cyp. is particularly remarkable.

Deut. xiv. 1. Spec. has *non timebitis et non uaticinamini*; Lugd. has *non timebitis*, a primitive error due to φοιβήσετε being taken as if from φοβεῖν. Spec. has combined a correction with the original Old Latin.

Deut. xvii. 11. Luc. has *quodcumque nuntiauerint tibi, quodcumque indicauerint tibi*; Lugd. has *renuntiauerint*.

Josh. i. 4. Luc. has *fines termini*, Lugd. *fines*.

Jud. xi. 39. Amb. (*De Off.* iii. 12) combines *praeceptum* used by Aug. (*Qu.*) with *decretum*, the rendering of Lugd. and Amb. (*Ob. Val.*).

(i)   The Place of the MSS in the History of the Version

We have already attempted to estimate the place of each MS in the Old Latin version on the evidence of its vocabulary and of direct comparison with the Patristic quotations. In this way it has been shown that Mon. in the later part of Ex., in Lev. and (with a certain admixture of later elements) in Deut. xxii–xxxii represents one of the earliest forms of the Latin version; that in Num. and Deut. viii–x it gives a text almost identical with Lugd., and that in Ex. ix–xx it has a distinctly late text of an entirely different character from that of Ex. xxxi–xl. Lugd. on the other hand, though not homogeneous, is in no place 'Cyprianic' in character. Even in Lev., which is distinguished both by an earlier vocabulary and by the survival of a remarkable number of primitive mistakes, the text has many agreements with Ambrose, and appears late in character

when compared with Mon. The late character of Lugd. elsewhere is shown not only by its vocabulary and by the close
agreement with Ambrose throughout, but by the close resemblance to Lucifer in certain books and to the late Speculum
everywhere. In this section a few readings are quoted which
give further indication of the relative position of the MSS in the
history of the version, after which some of the special characteristics of the MSS in different books are collected and described.

In Lev. xi. 22 Mon. has *et ista ab eis non edetis*, representing
apparently καὶ ταῦτα ἀπ' αὐτῶν οὐ φάγεσθε though not a single
Greek MS is quoted as having this reading; οὐ is found only in
$i^a k$ Boh. Eth., though two other cursives *dp** have οὐδέ for
καί, and of all the Greek MSS only G*bwgnejsz* have the
verb after ἀπ' αὐτῶν. Lugd. also has *ab eis non*—a significant
connection with Mon.—but besides changing *ista* to *haec* and
edetis to *manducabitis* (both changes in a 'European' direction)
adds after the latter a second *ex eis* apparently to bring the order
of the words into harmony with the Greek. The reading of
Lugd. which therefore stands as *et haec ab eis non manducabitis
ex eis* evidently depends on, but is later than, that of Mon. and
shows both a desire to conform the vocabulary to later standards
and the influence of a knowledge of the Greek text.

In Lev. xv. 9 Mon. has *inscenderit* (correctly) and this could
easily give rise to the reading of Lugd., *sederit*, while it seems
unlikely that the latter is original. In Num. xxxv. 5 Mon. four
times has 2 for 2000; in Lugd. we find 2000 three times, followed by a repetition of the verse with 2 three times. There
have evidently been omission and later emendation in Lugd.
That the mistake should have been made independently in the
two MSS is quite unlikely, and it appears as if we have in Mon.
a primitive mistake which has been followed by Lugd. but
partly corrected from the Greek. We have here therefore a
parallel to the repetition of Lev. iv. 23 and 24 in Lugd., once
agreeing with Mon. and Wir. and once conformed to an inferior
Greek MS. In these places Lugd. appears to have a later text
than Mon., but occasionally there are traces of the reverse. In
Deut. xxxi. 21 Lugd. and Wir. have *obliuiscetur*, using the de-
ponent verb with passive sense; Mon. has *erit in obliuione*,
which seems to be a correction. So *secutus fueris* of Mon. seems

later than the literal *abieris post* of Lugd. and Speculum in
Deut. viii. 19. Equally noticeable is Ex. xl. 4 where *panes* of
Mon. is evidently a later corruption of *propones* of Wir. and
Lugd. It could not be derived from προθήσεις, and could not
have been the original Old Latin. In the preceding verse however a coincidence has been noticed by Prof. Burkitt with the
Samaritan Pentateuch and the Jerusalem Targum so that the
reading there (*super eam propitiatorium*) has a greater claim to
be regarded as the genuine Old Latin, Wir. and Lugd. being
conformed to the Greek.

One other reading of Mon. and Lugd. in Ex. may be noticed
here. In Ex. xxxii. 12 and 14 *malitia* is used by Mon. both for
πονηρία and κακία; Lugd. preserves a distinction having *malitia*
for the first and *malignitas* for the second. At first sight Lugd.
would seem older but the 'African' equivalents would be
nequitia and *malitia*, and *malignitas* seems European. It is
difficult to explain the reading of Lugd.; this is hardly a case
where correction to agree with the Greek would be likely to
operate, and it is not likely that *malignitas* would replace *malitia*
and at the same time *malitia* would replace *nequitia*. Perhaps
as the primitive Old Latin differed from book to book in its
vocabulary, *nequitia* never had a place in the Old Latin Ex. and
malitia was used for both words from the first. The absence
of *nequitia* from Mon. Ex. is remarkable in view of the character
of Mon. in this book; πονηρία unfortunately is not represented
in Cyprian's Ex. so that no direct evidence from him is available.

The peculiar character of Lugd. in Lev. has already been
noticed; here the text of this MS has a somewhat 'African'
appearance, but it is distinguished even more by peculiarities
which in several cases recur in no other type of Old Latin text.
Similar unusual characteristics are also found to some extent in
Num., but on the whole the distinctive features of Lugd. are
of the late or European type.

The direct influence of the Vulgate is frequently to be traced.
In Gen. we have *modo forsitam nudum* in xxxi. 42, and *uesci* in
xliii. 32, the latter word probably occurring nowhere in the true
Old Latin Heptateuch. Even in Lev. we have not only some
insertions from a later type of Greek text, but also the Vulgate
pacifica in ch. vii; in Josh. we have *conteritis* in vii. 12—Lucifer

as well as Augustine differing here, though in this book his text
is almost identical with Lugd.; in Jud. Lugd. has *uagos* for
κενούς (ix. 4), *quae ad uictum tuum* (xvii. 10) and *pacifica* (xx.
26), all apparently from the Vulgate.

Apart from actual Vulgate readings however Lugd. has in
numerous places and in most books many of the distinctive
signs of a late or European text. In Gen. *qui dixit* is used nine
times in chs. xxvii, xxxviii and xliii where the primitive Old
Latin would not introduce a relative; δέ is rendered not only
by *autem*, as regularly in early texts, but also by *uero, itaque*
and *igitur*. Gen. xxix. 7—*adhuc superest de die multum nec est
hora* etc.—seems quite idiomatic Latin when compared with
Augustine's *adhuc est dies multa, nondum est hora* etc. The
opening chapters of Ex. illustrate the same thing even more
clearly; in the first two chapters δέ is rendered *deinde, -que,
uere, itaque* and *uero* besides *autem* (contrast Tyconius who has
autem 3/3 in his quotation from ch. i); we have also *qui dixit*
four times in ch. ii and *sic et* inserted in i. 19, while in iv. 16
quae ad Dominum pertinent is used in place of Augustine's
literal *quae ad deum*. The coincidences between Lugd. and
Cassian in Ex. point in the same direction. Thus in the passage
quoted by each from ch. v we notice *otiosi sunt* and *solliciti sunt*,
and in ch. xxxii Lugd. and Cassian alone have *sin alias* for *sin
autem* of Cyprian, Mon., Wir., Augustine and Ambrose. It is
noticeable however that these European marks are not nearly
so conspicuous in the rest of the book as in the first few
chapters. It would appear as if Lugd. represents a text which a
reviser commenced systematically to improve in style but in
which the attempt at such revision was gradually discontinued
after a few chapters had been worked over.

Similar improvements are found occasionally in all books,
but Deut. is the other one in which such alterations are most
conspicuous; we may mention *ordinabo* (i. 13), the paraphrase
already noticed in i. 15, the relative *quos* for καὶ αὐτούς in ii. 20,
se facturam in iv. 13, and *particulatim* in vii. 22—words and
expressions quite unlike those found in earlier types of text.

The frequent insertion of *incipere* and *coepisse* with verbs is
also probably late, since a word for word rendering is characteristic of the earlier texts; *coepisse* is thus added by Lugd. in

Gen. xxx. 1 and 42, Ex. xxx. 15 (with Ambrose), Num. xv. 19 and xxxv. 13, Deut. vii. 1, Deut. viii. 12 and 13 (with Ambrose); it is similarly inserted by Augustine in Gen. xxi. 16 and Ex. xxviii. 31; and by Mon. in two places where the MS has a later type of text, Ex. xvii. 2 with Ottob. and Deut. ix. 4 with Lugd. and Ambrose; we find *incipere* thus added by Lugd. in Num. xv. 39 and Deut. vii. 22, and *uelle* in Num. vi. 2 and (with Augustine *Con. Faust.* xxii. 57) in Gen. xxx. 15.

The lateness of Lugd. is also suggested by the great variety of renderings for the same Greek word. Even in the earliest texts we do not always find the same Greek word rendered in the same way, but uniformity is on the whole the rule, especially in the same book or group of books of the Bible. The variety of rendering in Lugd. however is quite unusual; there are at least thirteen ways of rendering $\pi\lambda\acute{\eta}\nu$ found in the Lyons Heptateuch and though this is an exceptional case more than one Greek word could be quoted with nine different renderings. Often two or three renderings occur in the same paragraph; thus in the first paragraph of Num. xxx Augustine regularly has *definire* for $\acute{o}\rho\acute{\iota}\zeta\epsilon\iota\nu$, but Lugd. has *confirmare, terminare* and *determinare* in turn.

Perhaps direct Vulgate influence is nowhere to be found in Wir., but on the whole the text though of a different character from that of Lugd. is probably almost as late. There is no Latin Father with whom Wir. has such striking or constant agreements as Lugd. has with Ambrose or Lucifer. Frequently Wir. has decided points of contact with Augustine, but the general resemblance to the Speculum is more marked. Some of those who have designated the Speculum text as late and degenerate 'African' have noticed that this late 'African' text appears to be an offshoot of the European type, modified by 'African' influences; and if, as seems likely, Wir. may be referred to this division of the Old Latin, the undoubtedly close connection between Wir. and Lugd. becomes more explicable. The similarity between Wir. and the Speculum is seen in the fondness of each for insertions, paraphrases and alterations made independently of any reference to the Greek—the kind of corruption which is described by the expression 'a degenerate text.'

There are several alterations and paraphrases in Wir. which

seem rather due to a desire to explain the meaning than to a failure to understand it: such are *somnii* Gen. xl. 12, *super uinum in officio tuo* Gen. xl. 13, *ad locum ut uideat* Ex. xxii. 13, and the insertion of *rei* after *dominus* Ex. xxii. 15; *quoniam* on the other hand in Ex. xxii. 9 seems due to failure to understand ὅτι οὖν ἂν ᾖ. It is not easy to see why in Gen. xl. 20 *qui a uenis* (*uinis*) is used, while just after and before *qui erat super pistores* occurs in a similar phrase; perhaps the former is a rough primitive rendering and the latter a later improvement.

It will be noticed that most of these examples are from Gen. and Ex. xxii, and it is in fact in these portions of Wir. that such signs of paraphrase are most frequently found; they are however not altogether wanting elsewhere. Thus in Ex. xxxii. 18 we have *ludentium* inserted, in xxxii. 25 *ut essent* (with Lugd.); in xxxiv. 18 *in ipso* avoids the repetition of *in mense nouorum* which we find in Lugd. as in the Greek. A suggestion may here be added with regard to Gen. xl. 16; the editor of Wir. proposed *hagere* (or *habere*) *et olera* (χονδριτῶν αἴρειν) for what now appears as *ha....etolera*. The use of *et* seems unaccountable and it is more likely that *halicae tollere* may be intended. Augustine uses *alicae* in this connection and *tollere* is quite the rendering of αἴρειν which would be expected.

The general primitive character of Mon. has already been illustrated in detail, but even where its text is very old it has occasionally (at least in the concluding chapters of Deut.) received modifications which are clearly of later date. *Recentesque* in Deut. xxxii. 17 is probably derived from the Vulgate, for except in Ex. ix–xx -*que* is nowhere else used in the MS, and is extremely rare in the Old Latin as a whole; *cunctae* in Deut. xxviii. 10 can hardly be a genuine Old Latin rendering, for even in the late texts it is very rare indeed; it is noticeable that Lugd. in both these cases differs, though most of the European elements in these chapters of Mon. bring it into harmony with Lugd.

In Ex. ix–xx however Mon. represents a version of an entirely different character. The vocabulary of this section has already been shown to be distinctly late, but the peculiar nature of Mon. here is seen not so much in the actual vocabulary as in the general character of the renderings. The Latin here is considerably better and shows more smoothness and variety of expression than is usual in the version; grammatical blunders are rare and the rendering suffers much less than usual from the attempt to follow the Greek literally. In general character in fact the version is very similar to the Vulgate, the influence of which seems clear in some places. *Quod cum uidissent* (xvi. 15), *ingredi debeant* (xviii. 20), and *tonitrua* (ix. 23) have almost certainly found their way into Mon. from Jerome's version, but in most cases the expressions though more like Vulgate expressions than those generally found in the Old Latin are not actually derived from that version.

In this section there is much more variety in the pronouns and conjunctions employed; we have for example *qualis, quanta, quidquam, quidquid, ne quis, uel una, deinde, mox, mox autem, siue* and *uero*. There is also more freedom of translation in these chapters; scarcely two or three consecutive verses could be found without some departures from the original text, and these are evidently frequently intended to express the sense more naturally or correctly. In places we have additions to the text; e.g. *si non cito exierint* is added in xii. 33, *et imposuerunt* in the next verse and *gauisus* in xviii. 2; λευκόν (xvi. 31) is expanded into *tenue et album ut gelu*, and *grex magnus* added before *coturnicum* (xvi. 13). In xiii. 17 we have *demonstrauit eis uiam* where Augustine, literally following the Greek, has *deduxit eos uiam*. In xvii. 3 we have *huc coegisti nos uenire* where *eduxisti nos*, which is given by Ottob., represents the Greek more closely. *De seruis* (ix. 20) is better than the genitive which Augustine retains fom the Greek; this however may be an example of Vulgate influence. Examples of this kind are very numerous and while many of them improve the version, very few in any way spoil it. Even when the words do not represent the original the sense is not generally destroyed, e.g. *induras* (ix. 17) for ἐντοιῇ τοῦ λαοῦ μου has no resemblance to the unintelligent blunders which are so often met with in the Old Latin MSS. Προστιθέναι, which occurs twice, is translated neither by *adponere* as in Num. nor by *adicere* as usually in the Old Latin; in ix. 28 Mon. gives *amplius non eritis hic* and in ix. 34 *magis magisque coepit peccare*; each seems due to an effort to improve the usual rendering rather than to ignorance of it. On the whole these chapters, in remarkable contrast to the following parts of Mon., seem to give us the Old Latin version in its latest and most thoroughly revised form.

(j) Connections between the Latin Authorities

The close relation between Lugd. and the texts used by Ambrose, Lucifer and Speculum has been illustrated in ch. ii; but in addition to this the texts of the MSS themselves are almost as closely related. We have seen that throughout Num. and in Deut. viii–x Lugd. and Mon. are unusually close; the two MSS in fact here represent practically the same text agreeing not only in their general character and vocabulary but in details and blunders. In Num. xxxi. 15 ζωγρεῖν is rendered in both *uiduas* (doubtless for *uiuas*) *capere* and in *v.* 18 *custodire*, Augustine in each place having *uiuificare*. In Num. xxxiii. 49 Lugd. has *et promouerunt ab Iordanen de medio in terra Etimot*, Mon. agreeing except in having *e* for *de* and *Esimoth*; the Greek is καὶ παρενέβαλον παρὰ τὸν Ἰορδάνην ἀνὰ μέσον Αἰσιμώθ, there being no variants which give any support to the Latin rendering; *promouerunt* however throughout this chapter is used to represent ἀπῆραν, παρενέβαλον being rendered *deuerterunt*. So in Deut. ix and x we have in both MSS *minutatim* for καταλέσας σφόδρα (probably influenced by Ex. xxxii), *paruit* (*apparuit*) for ἐγνώσθη (ix. 24), and *duc te et* for βάδιζε (x. 11).

In Ex. we have a connection not quite so remarkable, but maintained throughout, between Lugd. and Wir. which again extends to points of detail; e.g. *animo* for *animae*, *quibus quod dabat* for ὧν ἔφερεν (xxxv. 21) and numerous common insertions and omissions (xxv. 32, 33, 37, xxvi. 10, 12). The unity of the version however can only be established by examining the authorities where they differ most widely and seeing whether their coincidences in these places are numerous or remarkable enough to demand the hypothesis of a common Latin original. In the first chapter a connection between the vocabularies of Mon. and Lugd. has been shown to exist even in Ex. and Lev. where these MSS differ most widely, and this connection seems too remarkable to be accidental. A selection of further coincidences of various kinds will strengthen our belief that even in those places where the variations between the MSS are most marked we seem to be dealing not with separate versions of the LXX but with different recensions of a single version.

In Lev. xi where the three MSS coexist over a passage of considerable length, they are comparatively widely separated from each other, but there are numerous agreements which indicate that the three go back to a common source; e.g. in v. 33 all have *confringetis* though with the exception of three cursives (*gnx*) all Greek MSS have a passive; Augustine differs from them here, but in the same verse agrees with them in having *eis* though only four cursives (*fior*) have αὐτῶν for τούτων. All three MSS omit τοῦτο (v. 39), καὶ and ὑμῖν (v. 42), though these omissions are supported, the first only by the Ethiopic version, the second by *g* and the Armenian, and the third by *b₂* and the obelus of G. In Ex. xxxii, xxxix and xl where again the three MSS coexist over considerable passages, there is obviously a very close relation between Lugd. and Wir., but Mon. differs from them as widely as any Old Latin text differs from any other; yet here again we have numerous connections between the MSS which are sufficient to prove an underlying unity between the three; in xxxii. 15 all three have *testamenti* (Augustine *testimonii* with the Greek), in xxxii. 19 all insert *populi* with no other authority, in xxxii. 29 the three MSS with Lucifer all omit ὑμῶν with no support except that of Philo; all three omit *Aaron* in xxxix. 13 and *eius* in xl. 4 and have *stolam sanctam* for the plural in xl. 11, in each case agreeing in a text with practically no Greek support. So in Deut. xxxi, the only other chapter in which direct comparison between the three MSS is possible, we notice that all depend on a false reading in v. 20, and insert *hunc* in v. 26 with the support of Cyril and the Ethiopic but of no Greek MS whatever. In the same passage we have several noticeable coincidences between Lugd. and Mon., e.g. *et erit* in v. 19 and *in testimonio* v. 21 (Wir., *ut fiat* and *testificans*, following the Greek more closely), which are all the more remarkable because in the general character of their vocabulary Wir. comes between the other two MSS., being nearer to each than they are to each other, and also because Lugd. and Wir. are in this chapter the closest of the three in regard to the Greek text followed.

More numerous and more striking connections between the

two surviving MSS could be quoted from places where the third is not extant; thus there is no doubt that in Ex. xxxi–xl Mon. and Lugd. are as dissimilar as any two Old Latin versions of any passage of the Heptateuch—probably of the Bible. Yet sufficient evidence can be collected to show that the two MSS do not represent independent versions of the Greek; both MSS omit οἱ βλαστοί xxxviii. 15, both insert *et misit in ignem* xxxii. 4 and transpose *zosteribus* (Mon. *gestatoris*) xxxviii. 10, though in each case they oppose all Greek MSS in doing so.

Such close connections however are found not only between the three MSS, but also between the MSS and Fathers or the texts of different Fathers. In the following list is given a selection of significant coincidences between authorities which represent on the whole widely differing forms of the version:

Gen. i. 14 *De Pasc. Comp.*, Aug., Niceta have *ut luceant* following E*n* only.

Gen. i. 26 Cyp., Nov., Hil., Tert., Spec., Aug., Iren. all transpose *nostram* and have *ad* for κατά.

Gen. iii. 17 Cyp., Aug., Amb. omit three words which are in all Greek MSS.

Gen. iv. 5 Luc., Aug., Amb. represent ἐλυπήθη with one cursive and Clement of Rome.

Gen. vii. 4 Spec., Aug. have *diluuium aquae*, though, as Aug. says, the Greek = *pluuia*.

Gen. ix. 5 Tert., Amb., Jer., Aug., Iren. omit two words with two Greek cursives only.

Gen. xix. 23 Lugd., Spec., Tyc. have *(ex)ortus est* for ἐξῆλθον.

Gen. xxviii. 2 Lugd., Aug., Amb. have *uade*, though, as Aug. notes, the Greek = *fuge*.

Gen. xxxvii. 36 Lugd., Aug., Amb. have *praepositus coquorum*.

Ex. iii. 2 Cyp., Lugd., Hil., Aug., Amb. have *flamma ignis*, though πυρὶ φλογός has better Greek support.

Ex. xii. 5 Cyp., *De Pasc. Comp.*, Amb., Niceta, Jer. follow a few cursives which add ἄμωμον.

Ex. xxii. 27 Wir., Spec., Amb. have *quodsi* for ἐὰν οὖν.

Ex. xxiii. 21 Cyp., Tert., *Adu. Iud.*, Ottob. read αὐτῷ for σεαυτῷ.

Ex. xxiii. 24 Spec., Aug. have *simulacra* for στήλας.

Ex. xxvi. 10 Wir., Lugd., Aug., Ottob. add *uelum* with no Greek authority, and all have *commissuram* though this word is otherwise represented elsewhere.

Ex. xxviii. 39 Cyp., Lugd., Aug., Amb., Jer. have καί for ἤ with two Greek MSS only.

Ex. xxxii. 2 and 3 Mon., Lugd. and Amb. insert *anulos uestros*.

Ex. xxxiv. 12 Spec., Wir., Lugd. have future tense with the rare future participle: the Greek has the present.

Lev. v. 1 Wir., Lugd., Aug. have *conscius esse* for σύνοιδεν.

Lev. xx. 27 Wir., Aug. have *si forte* for ὃς ἄν.

Lev. xxi. 11 Aug., Tert., Jer., Or.-Lat. have *et* for οὐδέ with two Greek cursives (*bw*) only.

Lev. xxi. 17 Cyp., Aug. (Parmenian), Jer. have *macula et uitium* for μῶμος.

Num. xvi. 26 Cyp., Spec., Aug., Jer. have a superlative which is not given by the Greek.

Num. xxxiii. 1 Lugd., Mon., Jer. (*Ep.* 78) have *qui* for ὡς—one cursive having a participle.

Deut. i. 17 Lugd., Luc., Spec. have comparatives (*maior* and *minor*): the Greek has positives.

Deut. viii. 3 Lugd., Spec., Iren., Or.-Lat. have *uiuit* for future— the Gospels also having ζήσεται.

Deut. viii. 19 Mon., Lugd., Spec. insert *ecce* and in *v.* 20 have *si* for ἀνθ᾽ ὧν.

Deut. xxxii. 6 Lugd., Spec., Luc., Iren. have *retribuistis* in place of the present tense.

Deut. xxxii. 14 Lugd., Mon., Luc., Hil. have *bibit* with six Greek MSS, and attach it, as Clem. Rom., to *v.* 15 instead of *v.* 14.

Deut. xxxiii. 9 Cyp., Spec., Lugd., Aug., Amb., Iren. all have *noui* for ἑόρακα.

Josh. i. 8 Cyp., Lugd., Luc. with a few Greek cursives adopt the reading of Aquila, Symm. and Theod. for that of the LXX.

Examples like these—and the above list is by no means exhaustive—strongly suggest that all our Latin authorities represent recensions of one Latin version. The strongest evidence on the other side is provided by Augustine; but though the difference between the Greek text underlying his version and that of the other Latin authorities is so marked, yet the connection between his version and theirs has been shown to be very close—too close indeed to be accidental. The theory that Augustine corrected the Latin text from a Greek MS which he evidently had before him and consulted when writing such treatises as *Qu.* and *Loc.* and probably *De Gen. ad Litt.*, seems best to suit the facts. His more casual quotations are generally given in a form which reminds us very much of the version of Cyprian and often links them up with Speculum and the Old Latin MSS. Such a verse as Ex. xxxiii. 13 is particularly instructive on this point; here Lugd., Hilary, Tertullian, Or.-Lat. and Augustine, both in *De Trin.* and *De Ciu. Dei*, insert *ut* with one cursive, the Armenian and the Sahidic; Augustine also inserts it in *Qu. Deut.*, but in *Qu. Ex.* he omits it with the Greek. It has moreover been shown in the first chapter that Augustine's vocabulary, when examined as a whole, has a fundamental relation with that of the MSS; this and the remarkable coincidences of rendering collected in ch. II make it clear that, in spite of revision from the Greek, his version really is one with that underlying the MSS and the other Old Latin Fathers. Even between the most dissimilar passages there is nothing like the divergence which would exist between independent translations of the original, such *e.g.* as exists between the Vulgate and Beza's version.

If however Augustine does not represent a separate version it is certain that neither any other of the Fathers nor the Speculum can. The close agreement between Ambrose, Lucifer and Lugd. is not in itself surprising if we accept Lugd. as a European text, but such agreements of the 'African' Mon. as those with Lugd. and Ambrose in Ex. xxxii. 2, with Lugd. and Lucifer in Ex. xxxiii. 5, with Lugd., Lucifer and Ambrose in Ex. xxxii. 26 and with Lucifer in Deut. xxxi. afford clear evidence of the unity of the 'African' and 'European' forms of the version. In spite of its eccentric readings and many peculiarities, Speculum also has evident connections with each MS, with Wir. in Ex. xxii. and Lev. xix. and xx, with Mon. in Deut. viii and with Lugd. everywhere; Wir., Cyprian, Speculum, Augustine and Ambrose in Ex. xxii are another group of Latin authorities whose versions are all linked up together.

Revision of the Latin version from the Greek however has been made clear several times. Augustine's differences in text (being chiefly in *Qu.* and *Loc.*) could perhaps be explained as alterations or corrections made by him from Greek MSS which he himself knew and used, and a knowledge of Greek texts or authorities may account for some of the differences in underlying text presupposed by Tertullian and Ambrose; but there are other cases of dependence on different Greek readings which cannot be thus explained. Even in Cyprian we have found an example of the correction of a primitive error (Num. xxiv. 8) and there are several such examples in the later MSS and Fathers. Lugd. and Lucifer also show at times an assimilation of their text to distinctly later and inferior Greek MSS.

An improvement in the Latinity of the Version is seen already in Novatian, and it seems to have gone on continuously, side by side with the revision from the Greek. The Latin text was perhaps at no period regarded as being in itself unalterable or authoritative in the sense that the LXX was; hence changes were made continuously and repeatedly, and hence in spite of an underlying unity, the forms varied so much in later times that it seemed no great exaggeration to say that the forms of the Latin Version were as numerous as the MSS of it.

SOME NOTEWORTHY WORDS IN THE
OLD LATIN HEPTATEUCH

Accidere is primitive in Ex. xxxii (Mon., Cyp.) where Wir., Lugd.,
Aug. have *factum esse*; it is not used by Aug. or Lugd. though
Amb. has it Lev. x. 19. *Contingere* is used in most texts; Cyp.
uses all three words.

adaquare, see *potare*.

adgrauescere, see *ingrauari*.

adhaerere, see *adiungere*.

adhuc and iam (ἔτι) are both early as Cyp. uses each frequently. Wir.,
Ottob., Spec. use *adhuc*, Nov. *iam*, Hil. both equally. *Amplius*
and *ultra* seem later, the former being frequent in Luc., the latter
in Jer. In Aug. *adhuc* prevails in all books, *amplius*, *ultra* and *iam*
being rare. In Lugd. *adhuc* is used almost exclusively in Gen.,
Lev., Jud. and often in Num.; elsewhere *iam* is usual, *amplius*
being found occasionally, *ultra* once or twice in Josh. Mon. has
adhuc six times, *iam* twice (Num.), *amplius* three times (Ex. ix),
ultra Deut. xxxi. 2. Amb. uses *adhuc* in Gen. and Jud., *amplius*
in Deut.

adicere, see *adponere*.

adiungere and adhaerere (προσκολλᾶν) are both frequent in Lugd.;
Mon. and Aug. also use both words. *Adhaerere* is used by Wir.,
Amb., Spec. (which also has *herere*); and by Tert. Deut. xiii. 17.
The primitive rendering was evidently *adglutinari* or *conglutinari*,
often changed in Cyp. A text to *adhaerere* or *coniungere*; *adglu-
tinari* is used by Tert. (Gen. ii. 24, Deut. vi. 13), *conglutinari* by
Aug. (Gen. ii. 24).

adponere (προστίθεσθαι) is used about fifty times in Lugd., *adicere*
about ten, half of which are in Jud.; Aug. has *adponere* regularly
in Ex. and Deut., *adicere* in Num. *Adicere* is the earlier, being
used almost regularly by Cyp., Nov. and *Ad. Nov.*—cf. Is. xxx. 1,
Cyp., *Ad. Nov. adicere*; Spec., Wir. *adponere*. Wir., Tert. have
adicere, Spec., Jer., Amb. use both. Mon. has *adponere* four times
(all in Num.) but *adiectio* (πρόσθεμα) Lev. xix. 25. Lugd. uses
(*ad*)*augere* five times in Lev. (chs. xxvi and xxvii) and five in
Deut.; so Amb. Gen. iv. 12.

For προσκείμενος *adpositus* is usual, but we also have *adiunctus*
(Lugd. Lev. xvi and xvii), and *applicitus* (Aug. Lev. xxv. 6 and
a few times in Lugd.).

aduena (προσήλυτος) Mon. Ex. xii and xviii, but *proselytus* in Lev.
Aug. and Lugd. use *aduena* in Deut., but *proselytus* in Lev. and
Num. (so Lugd. Josh.). Amb. uses *proselytus* (Lev.) and Wir.
prefers it (4/6); but Spec. has *aduena* 11/13 (in Ex. and Deut. 8/8).

adulescens and adulescentula, see *iuuencula*.

aemulari, see *zelari*.

aequalis, aequitates and **aequus**, see *iustificatio* and *par*.

aes (χαλκός) Mon. Ex. xxxix, as in *k*; *aeramentum* is usual in all other texts, but Aug. uses both words.

aeternus (αἰώνιος) regularly in Cyp. and generally elsewhere. Lugd. in Ex. usually has *sempiternus*, which is found in Mon. Ex. xxxi. 17, Spec. Ex. iii. 15, and occasionally in Amb. Nov. has *sempiternus* once, *aeternus* three times. Lugd. has *aeternalis* in Lev. vii.

For εἰς τὸν αἰῶνα Cyp., Tyc. use both *in aeternum* and *in saeculum*, Tert., Nov. and Amb. generally the former. Lugd., Aug. use both these and also *in sempiternum*. The latter is used twice in Mon., and once in Wir. Ex.; a tendency to use *sempiternus* in Ex. seems clear. *In aeuum* is used by Mon. Ex. xix. 9 and Deut. xxiii. 3; it is not found in Aug., but occurs a few times in Lugd. (Ex. and Deut.) and in Tert. (Gen.). *In perpetuum* is not used in the Old Latin Heptateuch.

For ἡ διὰ παντός *sempiternus* is usual in Mon. and Lugd. Num. Elsewhere Lugd. generally has *semper*, but *per omnia* in Lev. xxv and Deut. xxxiii. 10. Aug. uses *semper* and *sempiternus*.

aeuum, see *aeternus*.

agnoscere, see *scire*.

alere (τρέφειν) Mon., Luc., Deut. xxxii. 18; Lugd. has *alere* once in Josh., but *nutrire* is usual in Lugd. and Aug. *Alere* is 'African,' being used by Cyp. (3/3) and changed by A text, Hil. and Spec. in Matt. vi. 26 to *pascere*. *Pascere* is found a dozen times in Gen. in various texts.

ales, see *uolucer*.

altare (θυσιαστήριον) always in Mon. (sixteen times) except in Ex. xxxii. 5 where *ara* is used of Aaron's idolatrous altar. *Altare*, used always by Cyp. (except in Apoc.), is evidently early. Aug. uses *ara* in Gen., elsewhere *altare*. Wir. has *altare* (or *altarium*) a dozen times (7/7 in Lev.), but in Ex. *ara* is more common. Amb. nearly always uses *ara* (cf. Ex. xxviii. 43 Cyp., Parm.-apud-Aug. *altare*; Lugd., Amb. *ara*), Ottob. *altare* and *altarium*. Lugd. has *altare* regularly in Lev., *altarium* in Josh. and Jud.; in Ex. and Num. both of these and *ara* are common. In Deut. Lugd. has *sacrificium* (ch. xii) and *sacrarium* (six times, all after ch. xv); the latter is much used by Luc. in Kings. Hil. in Gen. xxxv. 1 uses *altarium* and *sacrificium* (var. lec. *sacrarium*); Lugd. has *sacrificatorium* Num. iii. 31.

For βωμός *ara* is usual in all texts, but Lugd. has *altarium* in Josh.

amare is not common in the version. Mon. has it Lev. xix. 34; Cyp. uses it six times, Luc., Amb., Lugd. occasionally; in Gen. xxxiv. 3 Aug. has *adamare*.

Amb. has *amabilis* Deut. xxi, and *amantissimus* Gen. xxii. Aug. also uses the latter occasionally for the more common *dilectus*.

amaritudo, see *pigrida*.

ambulare (πορεύεσθαι) Mon. Lev. xi and xix. Cyp. has *ambulare* seventeen times (eight in Is., three in Ps.), *uadere* six (generally imperative), *ire* four, and *pergere* once. *Ambulare* is evidently 'African' (cf. Ps. cxxv. 5 Cyp. *ambulantes ambulabant*; A text, Spec., Luc. *euntes ibant*), and becomes less common in later texts, where *ire* and *abire* become more frequent and *incedere* is also used. In Lugd. *ire* and *abire* are found in most books, the latter especially in Jud.; *ambulare* is common only in the early part of Deut.; *incedere* is rare except in Lev.; *uadere* is used several times in Jud.; *proficisci* often in Ex., and also in Num. In Aug. *ambulare* is characteristic of Lev., though it also occurs a few times in Ex.; elsewhere *ire* is generally used (*abire* in Jud. as in Lugd.), but *pergere* and *uadere* occur a few times, *incedere* and *proficisci* at least once each. Amb. also has several renderings, but *ambulare* only three times early in Deut. (cf. Lugd. above); Hil. also has *ambulare* in Deut. x. 12 and xiii. 4. Spec. has several renderings including *iter facere* in Gen. xxviii. 20 and (with Lugd.) Deut. vi. 7.

Pergere may be another early rendering—cf. Ex. iv. 12 Cyp. *perge*; Lugd., Aug., Amb. *uade*. It does not occur in Lugd., but is found in Mon. Ex. xxxiii. 1, Spec. Deut. xiii. 4, and Jer. (*Adu. Pelag.*) Gen. xxviii. 20. The use of *pergere* by Philo-Lat. in Gen. xxv–xxviii has already been noticed; it is also used by Mon. and Wir. for ἴτω Ex. xxxii. 26, and by Wir. for βάδιζε Ex. xxxii. 34. All texts tend to use *uade* for the imperatives πορεύου and βάδιζε.

ampliare, see *latificare* and *plenitudo*.

amplius, see *adhuc*.

animatio, animositas and animus, see *ira* and *sensus*.

apotheca, see *repositio*.

apparere and parere are used by Lugd. fourteen times in Ex. and Deut.; *uideri* is seldom used in these books, but almost regularly elsewhere. Aug. has *uideri* in Lev. (3/3), Ex. (3/7); *apparere* or *parere* in Ex. (4/7), Gen., Qu., Loc., *De Ciu. Dei* (8/8), though he has *uideri* in Gen. quotations in other works (*e.g.* three in *De Trin.*). Cyp. has *apparere* Gen. xxxv. 1 and Ex. iii. 2, *uideri* Gen. xlviii. 17, but the preference for *uideri* in Lev. suggests that it is 'African.' Spec. has *uideri* 4/5 (*paruit* only Gen. xviii. 1), and so Nov. 2/2; Hil. uses *apparere* except in one quotation of Gen. xxxv. 1, and so generally Jer. Amb. has *parere* or *apparere* (6/9), especially in Gen. (5/6), and Ottob. generally *parere*; so that *uideri* does tend to disappear from later European texts. Mon. has *parere* Ex. xiii and xvi, *uideri* Lev. xiv. 35; Wir. has *apparere* four times, *uideri* Ex. xxxiii. 23.

applicare (προσάγειν) Wir. Lev. viii. 13, and Mon. three times (two in Lev.). *Adducere* and *offerre* are usual, but *applicare* is found a dozen times in Lugd., of which half are in Lev. See also *adponere*, *appropinquare* and *deuertere*.

appropinquare (ἐγγίζειν) is as common as *accedere* in Lugd., but elsewhere is rather rare; in Mon. and Wir. it only occurs Ex. xxxii. 19. *Adpropiare* is found a few times in Lugd. (with Amb. Gen.

xxxvii. 18) and three times in Aug. (Deut.). Lugd., Amb., Ottob.
have *applicare* in Gen. xlviii. 13.

ara, see *altare*.

arula, see *foculus*.

aspectus, see *facies*.

atrium (αὐλή) regularly, except that in Lev. Lugd. uses *aula* (ch. viii)
and *regia* (ch. vi). Wir., Lugd., Ottob. also use *atrium* for αὐλαία
but Mon. distinguishes the two, using *aulaea* (*aulea*) for the latter
Ex. xxxvii. and xl; Aug. notices that the two are confused in some
MSS, and approves of the distinction made in Mon. Ottob. occasionally uses *ianua*, another reading which Aug. knows and con-
demns. Since Cyp. distinguishes the words (*atrium* Ps., *aulaea* Is.)
the assimilation may have been made later when the original
Greek was lost sight of.

augere, see *adponere*.

aulaea, see *atrium*.

Balteus (στεφάνη) Mon. Deut. xxii. 8; otherwise *corona* regularly.

bracae, see *cruralia*.

breui, see *celeriter*.

Cacumen (κορυφή) Mon. three times (all Ex.); so Cyp. and, generally,
Aug. *Uertex* is used by Lugd. (except Num. xiv. 40), Amb. (5/5),
Jer., Ruf., Hil., Spec., Ottob., and occasionally by Aug.

For ἄκρον Mon. has *summum* (Ex. xxxviii. 16), Wir. *cacumen*
(Ex. xxxiv. 2); Aug. has the former in Deut. and Jud., the latter
in Gen. Lugd. generally has *cacumen*, but also uses *summum*
(Jud., Lev.), *extremum*, *extrema pars* and *extremalia* (Ex., Deut.).
Tert. uses *summum*.

caedes (φόνος) Mon. Ex. xvii. 13, Cyp. Deut. xiii. 15. Aug. uses *nex*,
Lugd. generally *occisio*.

caliga (ὑπόδημα) Cyp. *De Pasc. Comp.* Ex. xii, but elsewhere Cyp. has
the usual *calciamentum*.

candidus (λευκός) often in Lugd. (*e.g.* Lev. xiii) but on the whole rare,
and its use by eight authorities in Gen. xlix. 12 is noticeable.
Mon., Cyp., Tert., Aug. generally use *albus*.

capere, see *sumere*.

castificare, see *sancire*.

(ne) casu (μή ποτε) Mon. Ex. xiii and xix; so Spec. Ex. xxxiv, but
otherwise rarely or never in the Old Latin. The primitive rendering was *ne forte* (Cyp. 7/7), and this is usual in Lugd. and Aug.,
except in Lugd. Ex. and Jud., and Aug. Ex. and Deut., where
ne quando is more common. *Ne quando* is found in Mon. Ex.
xxxii. 12, and twice in Wir. Ex. xxxiv. Spec. has *ne forte* twice
in the Heptateuch, but sometimes (*e.g.* Ps. ii. 12 with Cyp. A
text) replaces Cyprian's *ne forte* by *ne quando*.

causa for *propter* is evidently African; it is used in *k*, and twice in
Cyp., being replaced by *propter* each time in the A text, Spec. or
Luc. (Matt. v. 10 and Rom. viii. 36). It occurs in Mon. and Lugd.

Num. xii. 1 (ἕνεκεν) and Num. xxxi. 16 (τοῦ and inf.) and occasionally elsewhere in Lugd.

celeriter and **cito** (with and without *quam*) are used by Lugd. about equally. The latter is used by Cyp. (5/6), Amb. and Luc., the former by Mon. (Deut. ix) and Aug. Lugd. has *uelociter* Ex. xxxii. 7, and *uelocius* twice in Josh.; the former is used by Luc., the latter once by Cyp. (*in loco* Mon. Deut. xxviii. 20 may be a corruption of one of these). Mon. in Ex. xxxii. 7 has *mature* (*maturius* is found in Luc.). Luc. has *in breui* Deut. xxviii. 20; this is found in Spec. and the A text of Cyp. (*e.g.* Ps. ii. 12 for *cito*) and is evidently late.

cellarium (ταμεῖον) Mon. Deut. xxviii. 8. The Cyprianic *cubiculum* is used by Lugd. (Gen. and Jud.) and Aug. (Jud.). *Promptuarium* occurs Mon. Deut. xxxii. 25, Amb. Gen. xliii. 30, and in Lugd. and Aug.

ceruix (τράχηλος) Mon. Deut. xxxi; Wir., Lugd. *collum*. Cyp. uses *collum* (2/2) *e.g.* in Is. lviii. 5 where Spec. and Luc. have *ceruix*; so that though *ceruix* seems 'African' in Deut. it is not so elsewhere. Amb. uses *collum* in Gen. xlv. 14 and (with Philo-Lat.) in Gen. xxvii. Lugd. has *collum* seven times, *ceruix* four; Hil., Aug., Luc. also use both.

For σκληροτράχηλος Mon. has *ceruicatus* Ex. xxxiii, *ceruicosus* (with Lugd.) Deut. ix. Wir., Aug., Amb. use *dura ceruice*, Lugd., Luc., Iren., Jer. *durae ceruicis* (Lugd. *duri colli* Ex. xxxiii. 3).

cessare, see *desinere*.

ceteri, see *residuus*.

cibare and **cibus**, see *esca*.

cito, see *celeriter*.

clamare, see *uociferari*.

claritas (δόξα) Wir. Ex. xxxiii. 18 and 19, a well-known 'Africanism'; Wir. also uses *gloria* twice. *Claritas* is used by Iren. Ex. xxxiii. 22, Lugd. Num. xxiii. 22, and occasionally by Aug. (*e.g.* Ex. xxxiii. 18 and Num. xii. 8 *De Gen. ad Litt.*) but not in *Qu.* or *Loc.* *Gloria* is the usual rendering; *honor* is used almost regularly in Lugd. Gen., Num. and Josh., with Spec. and Mon. in Num. xii. 8, and Prisc. in Num. xxiv. 8; Mon. also has it in Ex. xxxiii. 5. *Maiestas* occurs in Lugd. Deut. v. 24, and is used by Aug. a few times in Ex. (*De Trin.* and *Ser.*), and by Amb. and Ottob. Ex. xxiv. 17. Nov. altogether uses *claritas* three times, *gloria* three times, *honor* (and *honorificare*) five times, and *maiestas* once. Spec., Luc. and even Nov. generally replace Cyprian's *claritas* by *gloria* or (as in Is. lviii. 8) by *maiestas*; and like Mon., Wir. and Lugd. replace *clarificare* by *glorificare*, *honorificare* and *magnificare*. Hil. retains Cyprian's *claritas* and *clarificare* a dozen times, but more often has *gloria*, *honor*, *glorificare* and *honorificare*.

clibanus, see *furnus*.

coepisse, see *inchoare*.

colligere is used a dozen times in Mon., *concolligere* three times in Num. xi, but Mon. does not use *congregare*. *Colligere* is usual in *k, e,* Tyc. (except Ezek.) and Cyp., and since the A text and Spec. sometimes replace it by *congregare,* it seems 'African.' Aug. and Luc. generally use *congregare,* but Lugd. retains *colligere* (and *concolligere*) frequently, not only in Num. but also in Ex., Deut. and Jud. (cf. Deut. xxxiii. 5, Lugd. *colligere,* Aug. *congregare*). Spec. uses *colligere* (3/3); so do Tert. and, generally, Ottob. Amb. has *congregare* rather more than *colligere.* Lugd. has other renderings also, such as *congerere.*

Both συναγωγή and ἐκκλησία are frequently transliterated, but various renderings also occur in Aug. and Lugd., and Aug. tends to use *congregatio* for each, even where Lugd. (as in Gen. xxviii. 3, xlviii. 4, and Deut. xxxiii. 4) has *synagoga* or *ecclesia.* In Lev. xi. 36 it would seem that *collectio* of Mon. (συναγωγή) is earlier than *congregatio* of Wir. and Lugd.

collum, see *ceruix.*

color (χρώς) Mon. and Tert. Lev. xiii; so Aug. (6/8) and Lugd. occasionally. Mon. has *corpus* Lev. xv. 7; this is usual in Lugd. and found twice in Aug.

commorari, see *morari.*

confirmare, see *fortitudo.*

conflatile, see *fundere.*

confortare, see *fortitudo.*

congregare and congregatio, see *colligere.*

coniux (γυνή) Mon. Ex. xxxii. 2, Deut. xxii (four times) and xxviii. 30, changed by Lugd. to *mulier* in Ex. and *uxor* in Deut. Cyp. has *coniux* Ex. xxii. 24 where A text, Spec., Wir. have *uxor*; it is therefore primitive, but strangely enough in one passage in Matt. the A text of Cyp. has substituted *coniux* for *uxor* of LMB. *Coniux* is very common in the inscriptions.

consecrare, see *sancire.*

considerare and consideratio, see *uisitatio.*

consolari, see *rogare.*

conspectus, see *facies.*

constituere, see *deuertere* and *praeceptum.*

consummare and consummatio, see *perficere* and *finis.*

contaminare, see *profanare.*

contingere, see *accidere.*

cooperire, see *operire.*

corium, see *pellis.*

corpus, see *color.*

crastinus and hodiernus in Mon. are used without *dies* four times, and seven times with it, but five of the latter are in Ex. x–xvii. The omission of *dies* is usual in *k* and Cyp. Aug. and Ottob. generally insert it, so does Amb. in Ex. viii. 10. Lugd. always adds *dies* in Deut., but rarely in other books.

cremare (κατακαίειν) evidently 'African,' being used by Cyp. (4/5), *e.g.* in Ex. iii. 2 where Lugd. and Aug. have *comburere.* It occurs in Mon. Ex. xxxii. 20, Lev. iv. 21, and in Spec. Deut. vii. 5 and 25, Lugd. in all four places having *comburere. Cremare* is seldom

used in Aug. or Luc., but occurs in each of them with Lugd. in
Josh. vii. 15, and is found twice in Lugd. Lev. *Concremare* is
used by Tert. Deut. xii. 3, and Aug. Ex. xii. 10; Aug. has *exurere*
three times in Num.

cruralia (περισκελῆ) Mon. Ex. xxxvi.36; Lugd. *bracae*, as Lugd., Amb.,
Spec. Ex. xxviii. 38. In Lev. Lugd. has '*curare*' (vi. 10), and
peristolum (xvi. 4); Aug. uses *femoralia*.

cubiculum, see *cellarium*.

cultus (κόσμος) Mon., Aug. Ex. xxxiii. 5 and 6; it occurs once in Cyp.,
but Cyp. also uses *ornamentum* once. Lugd. and Luc. use *ornamentum* and *ornatus*, Aug. (except in Ex. xxxiii. 5) *ornatus*.

curare (ἰᾶσθαι) used in *Ad Nov.* (Is. lvii. 18) and in *k*, and clearly
'African.' Cyp. uses *curare* and *sanare* each three times, but he
uses *curatio* (with *De Pasc. Comp.*) for the later *sanitas*, and in
Ps. cvi. 20 the A text replaces *curare* by *sanare*. Mon. has *curare*
Lev. xiv. 48 and Deut. xxviii. 27, but *sanare* Num. xii. Lugd.
always uses *sanare*.

custodire, see *obseruare*.

cutis, see *pellis*.

Declinare, see *deuertere*.

defendere and defensio (ἐκδικεῖν and ἐκδίκησις) Lugd. four times in
Num. and once or twice in Deut. and Jud.; Lugd. however
more often has *uindicare* and *uindicta* which are used regularly in
other texts.

delictum and delinquere (ἁμαρτία) Mon. regularly Ex. xxxii, Lev. xii-
xix (except xix. 22), and as frequently as *peccatum* and *peccare* in
Lev. iii–iv. Wir. generally has *delictum* in Lev. iv–vii, but not
elsewhere. Lugd. uses *delictum* almost exclusively in Lev., but
rarely elsewhere. *Delictum* and *delinquere* appear only occasionally
in Aug., Luc., Amb., Spec. That they had a place in the primitive
Ex. is shown not only by their occurrence in Mon. and Cyp. in
ch. xxxii, but by Ex. xxviii. 43 where Cyp. and Parmenian (*apud*
Aug.) have *delictum*, but Lugd. and Amb. *peccatum*. Tert. uses
delictum in Ex., Lev. and Deut. See also p. 39.

  Delictum is also used in Mon. Lev. xix. 22 and Wir. Lev. vii. 27
for πλημμέλεια; so regularly in Aug. and twice in Lugd. Num.
Elsewhere Mon. and Wir. use *negligentia* and *negligere*, and these
are usual in Lugd. and were known to Aug. Lugd. in Lev. also
uses *indiligentia* and *indiligens esse*.

demptio (ἀφαίρεμα) Wir. Ex. xxxv. and xxxix, apparently a late word.
It is used in Ex. always by Aug. and generally by Lugd.; but
ablatio (*oblatio*) is used always by Mon., and, except in Ex.,
generally by Aug., Lugd., Spec., Amb. Lugd. also has *exceptio*
and *abscisio* in Lev., and *decerptio* in Num.

  So for ἀφαιρεῖν or περιαιρεῖν *demere* is used by Aug., Lugd.,
Wir. Ex. xxxii. 24, and Lugd. Deut. iv. 2. *Tollere* is used by
Mon. Ex. x. 17, xiii. 12 (with Amb.) and xxxii. 24, and by Amb.
Ex. xxxiii. 23; *deponere* by Lugd. and Aug. especially in Gen.,

and by Amb. Ex. xxxii. 2 and Luc. Ex. xxxiii. 5; *auferre* however (or *offerre*) is frequent in all texts.

denudare, see *operire*.

deponere, see *demptio*.

depraecari, see *exorare*, *rogare* and *uotum*.

deprimere, see *pressura*.

derelinquere, see *relinquere*.

desertum, see *eremus*.

deseruire, see *ministrare*.

desiderium (ἐπιθυμία) Lugd., Amb., Ottob. Gen. xlix. 26, Aug. (*Con. Adim.* xiv. 1) Deut. xii. 15, Jer. Gen. xlix. 6. This appears late since Spec. substitutes it for Cyprian's *concupiscentia* (*e.g.* in Eph. iv. 22). *Cupiditas* is used by Amb. and Ruf. in Gen. xlix. 6, and *cupere* by Aug. in Deut., but *concupiscentia* and *concupiscere* are found in Ottob. and Tert. Gen. xlix. 6, and are usual in Aug. and Lugd.

desinere Mon. Ex. ix (four times) and Ex. xxxii. 12, but *cessare* in Ex. xxxi. 18 with Lugd. and Aug. Aug. uses both in Gen., but *desinere* does not occur in Lugd. It is not clear whether either is distinctly 'African,' for though Cyp. has *desinere* in Num. xvii. 10 where Lugd. has *cessare*, he has *cessare* in Is. i. 16 where Hil. and Luc. have *desinere*. In Num. xxv. 11 Lugd., Amb. have *sedauit*, Luc. *compescuit*, both here only in the Heptateuch. In all these places the Greek has either παύειν or καταπαύειν. For ἀναπαύειν *requiescere* is always used by Cyp., and generally by Lugd., but Lugd. has *refrigerare* (or *refrigerium*) in Gen. xxix. 2, Num. x. 33 and (with Prisc.) xxiv. 9, and Deut. xxviii. 65. These words are also used occasionally for ἀναψύχειν, καταψύχειν, ψυγμός and καταλύειν.

In Ex. xxxi. 17 Mon. has *refrigerare*, Lugd. *requiescere*; since these words do not seem to be used for καταπαύειν, it is just possible that the Old Latin here is founded on Aquila's ἀνέψυξεν.

deuertere (παρεμβάλλειν) Mon., Lugd. Num. xxxiii (often); but *castra constituere* Num. iii (often) and, without *castra*, Num. xxxi. 19, xxxiii. 7. Amb. (Num.) uses *constituere* both with and without *castra*; Aug. *castra collocare* and *in castris esse*, but *adplicuit* in Gen. xxxiii. 18 and Ex. xix. 2. Jer. generally has *castrametari*, but sometimes *deuertere*. Lugd. uses *mittere* (*inmittere, committere*) in Gen. xxxii. 1, Deut. xxiii. 9 (with Spec.), and several times in Jud. (with Luc., Jud. vi. 3).

For ἐκκλίνειν Lugd. has *deuertere* and *declinare* each a dozen times, *deuertere* is also used by Hil., Aug. (*De Trin.*) Gen. xix. 2, Spec. Ex. xxiii. 2, and Amb. Num. xx. 17, but Aug. and Amb. often use *declinare*. Since Cyp. does not use *deuertere*, this word may be late (cf. Prov. ix. 4 Cyp. *declinare*, Amb. *deuertere*).

dilatare, see *latificare*.

dimidium is generally a noun in Mon., but it is used adjectivally with *pars* in Ex. xxxix. 2 and in Num. 4/9. In Cyp. it is a noun, but in Wir., Lugd., Aug., Amb. generally an adjective.

dirigere (εὐοδοῦν) Mon. Deut. xxviii. 29 and generally in Lugd. and Amb.; but Lugd. has *suffragare* Deut. xxviii. 29, and *prosperam facere* Jud. xviii. 5. Aug. regularly uses *prosperare*.

disperdere, see *exterminare*.

dispergere (διασκεδάζειν and διασκορπίζειν) Mon. Ex. xxxii. 25; but *dissipare* Deut. xxxi. 16 and 20, as Wir. in each place. Aug. has *dispergere* in Num., and so Lugd., Spec. Num. x. 35, but Aug. and Lugd. generally use *dissipare*. As *dispergere* of Cyp. is once replaced by *dissipare* in the A text, Mon. seems the earlier in Ex. xxxii. 25.

Dispergere is more frequent for διασπείρειν in all texts, but Nov. and Jer. have *disseminare* Deut. xxxii. 8; in Deut. xxviii. 25 Lugd. has *disseminatio*, Mon. and Jer. *dispersio*.

dissipare, see *dispergere*.

dolum, see *insidiose*.

domesticus, see *famulus* and *propinquus*.

donec, see *quoadusque*.

donum (δῶρον) Mon. in Lev., but *munus* in Num.; both are used by Wir. in Lev. Each occurs four times in Cyp., but *donum* is used in *k* and seems more primitive, the change from *donum* to *munus* being more intelligible than the converse. Aug. generally uses *donum*, Lugd. nearly always *munus*, though *donum* remains five times in Lev. i. 2–14, *munus* being used just previously (Lev. i. 2) and regularly after i. 14. Amb. has *donum* Num. xxviii. 2 but *munus* in Gen.; Spec. has *donum* in Lev. (2/2) and *munus* in Ex. and Deut. (3/3).

Ecclesia, see *colligere*.

edere and manducare are found in all texts but their relative frequency varies considerably. *Edere* is very common in Cyp., but in five cases the A text, and in five others Spec., replace it by *manducare*, the converse change never occurring (cf. Ex. xii. 7 and 8 Cyp., *De Pasc. Comp. edere*; Aug., Amb. *manducare*). Evidently the later texts tend to replace *edere* by *manducare*. *Edere* is similarly found twelve times in Mon. or Wir. or both where Lugd. has *manducare*, but the converse never happens. In Lev. xi Mon. has *edere* eight times, Lugd. having *manducare* each time, Wir. and Aug. the two words equally. Altogether in Mon. we have *edere* fifteen times, *manducare* eight (three in Ex. xvi and xviii); in Wir. we have *edere* eight times, *manducare* thirteen. Lugd. has ten occurrences of *manducare* for each one of *edere*. In Lev. and Num. Aug. shows as much preference for *edere* as Mon., but elsewhere *manducare* is more common. *Edere* is rare in Amb., Ottob. and Spec. and comparatively so in Luc., but more frequent in Tert. *Comedere* is used eight times in Mon., six in Wir., two in Spec. and two in Tert.

egens (πτωχός) Mon. Lev. xix. 10, otherwise *pauper* is used in Mon. both for πτωχός and πένης. *Egens* is 'African,' occurring six times in Cyp., but being twice replaced by *pauper* in the A text. *Egens* and *egenus* however are found at times in Lugd., Spec., Aug. for ἐνδεής. Tert. and Cyp. seem to prefer *indigens*, which is once changed to *egens* in the A text of Cyp.

egredi (ἐξέρχεσθαι and ἐκπορεύεσθαι) is rare in all texts, *exire* being the common rendering. It is used twice by Cyp., in Deut. xxiii. 23 where Lugd. and Spec. have *exire*, and in Ps. xviii. 6 where the A text substitutes *procedere*. On the other hand the A text introduces *egredi* in Ps. lxvii. 9 where Cyp. has *prodire*. *Egredi* is found four times in Mon. and once in Wir.; it is often used by Jer., but only occasionally in Aug. and Lugd. Nov. has it in Ps. xviii. 6 only; Spec. and Hil. only once each in the Heptateuch, Amb. not at all.

Procedere occurs once in Nov. and seven times in Cyp. (replaced by *exire* in Lugd. and Amb. Num. xxiv. 7). Spec. has it in Lev. x. 2, Lugd. and Aug. once or twice in Num.; Amb. has it in Gen. ii. 10.

Prodire, which occurs three times in Nov. and four in Cyp., is used by Aug. in Josh. vi. 1 and (*De Gen. con. Man.*) Gen. ii. 10. Lugd. has it several times in Jud., and occasionally in other books.

Proficisci seems later; it occurs once in Cyp. and once in Nov., but is common in Lugd. especially in Num. and Josh. Mon. has it in Ex. xviii and five times in Num.

eicere (ἐξάγειν) Mon. Deut. xxii. 21, and five times in Ex. xxxii and xxxiii. It is evidently 'African,' being used by Cyp. and *Adu. Iud.* in Ex. xxxii and in *Ad Nov.*; cf. Jud. ii. 12 Cyp. *eicere*, Lugd. *educere*. *Eicere* is found in Spec. Gen. xix. 17 and Deut. iv. 20, in Aug. Num. xix. 3 and Gen. i. 20 and 21 (*De Gen. con. Man.* and *De Gen. Impf.*—*De Gen. ad Litt.* has *educere*), in Hil. Gen. i. 20, but two or three times only in Lugd. *Educere* is the usual rendering, but *producere* is found in Mon. Deut. xxii. 24, four times in Cyp., three times in Aug. Deut., and occasionally in Lugd. The A text of Cyp. once replaces it by *educere*, but it is not so clearly 'African' as *eicere*.

For ἐπάγειν Mon. has *inmittere* and *importare* Ex. xxxii and xxxiii; Spec. has the latter Ex. xv. 26, otherwise *inducere* or *adducere* is regularly used.

For βάλλειν and its compounds *mittere* and *iacere* (and compounds) are both used widely. Mon. and Cyp. tend to use *mittere*, and so does Lugd. in Gen. *Ponere* is rarer, but Cyp. has *imponere* Gen. xxii. 12 and *ponere* Gen. xlviii. 17, the former being changed by Hil., Aug., Spec., Amb. to *inicere*, the latter by Lugd. to *mittere*. Lugd., Amb. have *imponere* Gen. xlviii. 14, and Aug. has *superponere* Num. xix. 2 (Lugd. *inicere*). In Ex. xxxiii. 2 Mon. has *excludere* (Lugd., Aug. *eicere*), in Num. xxx. 10 Aug. has *expellere* (Lugd. *eicere*); Lugd. has *expellere* Num. xxi. 32, Jud. xi. 7, *excludere* in Jud. ii. 3 (Aug. *eicere*); the last however represents ἐξωθεῖν.

For ῥίπτειν *abicere* is used by Cyp., but *proicere* usually in the

MSS. *Mittere* is so rare that its use by Wir., Lugd., Aug., Amb. in Ex. xxxii. 24 (Mon. *proicere*) is a noticeable agreement.

For ἀναβιβάζειν compounds of *ducere* are usual, but *eicere* is used by Mon. Ex. xxxii. 9, and Lugd. Gen. xxxvii. 28. *Imponere* Lugd. and Cyp. Num. xx. 25 is a connection between two very different texts.

For φέρειν see *portare*.

eliberatio, see *redimere*.

emeritio, see *manuale* and *placatorium*.

epulari, see *iucunditas*.

eradicare, see *exterminare*.

eremus (ἐρῆμος) Mon. five times Ex. xvi–xix, but *desertum* three times Ex. xiii–xvi; the latter is used by Wir. in Gen. xxxvi. 24 and frequently by Mon. in Num. and Deut. Cyp. uses *eremus* only three times but it is natural to regard it as primitive, especially as each time either the A text or Luc. replaces it by *desertum*; Cyp. however uses *desertum* a dozen times (Matt. and Is.) and *solitudo* three times. Aug. uses *eremus* and *desertum* equally but always the former in Num. (3/3), the latter in Deut. (3/3). Lugd. has *solitudo* a few times in Deut. and Jud., *eremia* five times in Num., *eremus* nine times (Ex., Lev., Deut.), but *desertum* in all books. Ottob. has *eremus* twice, but generally *desertum*.

eruere, see *redimere*.

esca (βρῶμα and βρῶσις) Mon. Deut. xxxii. 24, Wir. Lev. xi. 39; both however have *cibus* Lev. xi. 34. *Cibus* is used in Cyp. (6/7), Tyc., *k* and Nov. (*Adu. Iud.* Gen. ix. 3); *esca* replaces it once in Cyp. A text, and we have in Deut. xxiii. 19 *cibus* Cyp., but *esca* Lugd., Spec., Amb., so that *cibus* is clearly 'African.' Aug. has *cibus* in Num., *esca* in Gen., both in Lev.; Lugd., Amb., Hil., Ottob. have *esca* practically always, Spec. has *esca* twice, *cibus* once (Jud.). Tert. uses *esca* (Gen. i. 29 and ix. 3), Ruf. has *cibus* Gen. xlix. 27.

Cibare is used by Amb. Num. xi. 4 (Tert., Jer. *uesci*), and Mon. Deut. xxxii. 13; Lugd. uses *cibare*, *escare*, *adescare* and *escam dare*.

excelsus (ὑψηλός) Mon. 4/4 (Ex. xxxii, Num. xxxiii, Deut. ix and xxxii), Wir. Deut. xxviii. 52. In spite of its use in Mon. it seems a later word; *e.g.* we have Gen. xxii. 2 Cyp. *altus*, Aug., Amb. *excelsus*; and *excelsus* replaces Cyprian's *altus* in the A text Is. xxvi. 11, and in Hil. Is. xlv. 14. Lugd., Luc., Amb. use both words; Tyc. *altus* in Is., *excelsus* in Ezek.

excludere, see *eicere*.

execratio (βδέλυγμα) is early, being used by Cyp., Tyc., *k*, *De Pasc. Comp.* and *Adu. Iud.* Mon. has it three times in Lev. xviii, Lugd. uses it in these three places and twice elsewhere in Lev. but in no other book. *Abominatio*, the usual rendering, is found in Cyp. and Tyc.; *abominanda* and *abominata* also occur. We have also *spurcitia* Spec., Lugd. Deut. vii. 26, *aspernamentum* Tert. Deut. xxvii. 15. For the verb we have *inodiare* Lugd. Ex. v. 21, *execrabilem facere* Aug. (twice), but elsewhere *abominare* or *abominari*.

eximere (ἐξαιρεῖν) Mon. Lev. xiv. 43, seems early as it is used by
Cyp. in Ps. xlix. 14 and replaced by *eripere* in the A text.

exorare (ἐξιλάσκεσθαι) Mon., Wir. Lev.; so Luc. (Num. xxv. 13) and
Aug. (who also knows *depropitiare*). Lugd. almost regularly uses
exorare in Ex., *propitiare* in Lev., and *depraecari* in Num.; the
exceptions are interesting—Ex. xxxii. 30 where Lugd., Wir., Mon.
all have *depraecari*, and Num. xxix. 11 where Lugd. and Mon.
have *propitiare*. In Lev. iv. 31 Wir. has *expiare*; this word is
often used by Jer., but was not unknown earlier as it is found in
De Pasc. Comp. Lugd. and Aug. both have *placare* in Gen. xxxii.
20. For ἐξίλασις Mon., Lugd. have *depraecatio* Num. xxix. 11 (so
Cyp. in 1 Jn.); Aug. uses *depropitiatio*. See also *placatorium*.

expellere, see *eicere*.

expiare, see *exorare*.

exterminare (ἐξολεθρεύειν) Wir. Lev. xvii and Deut. xxviii; Mon.
Lev. xviii and Deut. xxxi. It is used by Cyp., Tyc. and Aug.,
but the A text of Cyp. replaces it by *disperdere*, which is used by
Amb., Luc. and occasionally Lugd. Lugd. uses *extirpare* almost
exclusively in Lev. and the first half of Deut. (so Mon. in Deut.
ix and x), but in the latter part of Deut. and in Josh. *exterminare*
as regularly. *Eradicare* is found a few times in Lugd., in Cyp.,
Spec., Aug. Ex. xxii. 20, and in Spec. Deut. xviii. 12.

exterus, see *extraneus*.

extirpare, see *exterminare*.

extraneus (ἀλλότριος) Lugd. occasionally (Gen., Deut.); Aug. has *exterus* twice in Ex.

extremus, see *cacumen*.

Facies is the usual rendering of πρόσωπον, but we have *persona* in Mon.,
Spec., Luc. Lev. xix. 15, Cyp. (not Wir., Spec., Luc.) Lev. xix. 32,
and two or three times in Lugd. *Vultus* is used by Cyp., Amb.,
Iren. and Aug. *De Gen. con. Man.* (not *De Gen. ad Litt.*) Gen.
iii. 19, by Luc. and Tert. (not Aug.) Gen. iv, by Wir. and Spec.
Lev. xx, and once each in Ottob. and Aug. (Gen.). *Aspectus* occurs
once or twice in Lugd. and Aug. (Ex.); *conspectus* occasionally in
Mon., Lugd., Aug., Amb. in the phrase ἀπὸ or πρὸ προσώπου,
most of the occurrences being in Deut.

For ὄψις Mon., Aug., Tert. have *aspectus* in Lev. xiii and xiv,
but *facies* is usual.

Aspectus is more common for εἶδος, but we have *species* in Mon.,
Lugd., Aug., Spec., Tert. Num. xii. 8, and once or twice in Lugd.,
Aug., Amb., Ottob. *Forma* also occurs occasionally. In Gen.
xxxii. 30 Aug. has *aspectus*, Lugd. *facies*, Spec., Nov., Amb.
uisio—the last apparently a correction.

For ὅρασις we have *aspectus* Aug., Amb. Gen. ii. 9, but *uisus*
is usual.

famulus (θεράπων) Mon. Num., but *seruus* Ex. ix–xii and Deut.
ix. 27 (with Lugd.). *Famulus* is usual in Lugd. except in Josh.;

seruus is more common in Aug.; Lugd. and Luc. have *minister*
Ex. xxxiii. 11.

For οἰκέτης Lugd. generally has *seruus*, but in Ex. xxxii. 13
agrees with Mon. in having *famulus*. Lugd. uses *domesticus* often
in Gen. and occasionally elsewhere, *inquilinus* a few times in
Deut.

femoralia, see *cruralia*.

ferire, see *interficere*.

festus dies (ἑορτή) Mon. Ex. xxxii, Num. xxix, Deut. xxxi; so Cyp.
In Ex. x. 9 and xiii. 6 Mon. has *dies solemnis*, which is used by
Wir. Ex. xxxiv (three times) and is doubtless later (in 1 Cor. v. 8
Spec. substitutes *solemnitas* for Cyprian's *festa*). Lugd. uses
solemnis in Ex. (4/4), elsewhere *festus*. Aug. uses *solemnis* in Lev.,
but *festus* in Num. and Deut. Ottob. generally has *solemnis*; Amb.
uses *festus* in Num., but in Ex. xii. 14 combines the two.

fieri is rare in Mon. except in Num. and Ex. ix–xix, *esse* being used
five times where Lugd. and Wir. have *fieri*. See also *accidere*.

finis (τέλος) Mon., Wir. Deut. xxxi. 24; Lugd. always has *consummatio*
in Deut. and Gen., but *finis* in Josh. and Jud. *Finis* is used in
Cyp. (7/8) and in *De Pasc. Comp.*, and is evidently early, though
Cyp. uses *consummatio* for συντέλεια. Aug. has *finis* Gen. xlvi. 4.
For *fines* = ὅρια, see *termini*.

firmus, see *solidus*.

flere and fletus, see *plorare*.

foculus (πυρεῖον) Mon. Ex. xxxviii. Lugd. has several renderings,
arula Num. xvi and Lev. xvi. 12, *ara* Lev. x. 1, *uatillum* Ex. xxxviii
and Num. iv. 14. Ottob. has *uatillum* (Ex. xxvii), Amb. *arula*
(Num. xvi), Aug. *turibulum* (Num. xvi).

foedare, see *humilis*.

foenum, see *pabulum*.

fornax, see *furnus*.

(ne) forte, see *casu*.

fortitudo (ἰσχύς) Mon. Deut. xxxii. 13, a recognised 'Africanism' (cf.
Is. xi. 2 and lviii. 1 Cyp. *fortitudo*; Nov., Spec., Luc. *uirtus*) used
occasionally by Aug. and Lugd., and frequently by Jer. for the
common *uirtus*. *Uires* is found once or twice in Lugd. and Amb.
(Deut. and Jud.). The adjective *fortis* is much more common
than *fortitudo*, being usual in Mon., Lugd., Aug., Amb.; *ualidus*
and *potens* however are occasionally found in Lugd., Aug. and
Amb. For ἰσχύειν and its compounds *ualere* and its derivatives
are usual in Lugd., Ottob., Amb.; *confirmare* occurs in Mon.
Ex. xviii. 23 and occasionally in Lugd. (Deut. and Josh.); Aug.
prefers *confortare* which is also used by Cyp., Hil., Ruf. and by
Lugd. in Josh. and Jud. In Jud. Lugd. also uses *conroborare*.
For δύναμις and κραταιός see *uirtus*.

fragrantia, see *suauiolentia*.

fructus, see *hostia*.

frumentum, see *triticum*.

fucatus (κίβδηλος) Mon. Lev. xix. 19, Deut. xxii. 11. In the former
place Spec. has *execrabilis*, in the latter Lugd. has *monstruosus*.
fundere (χωνεύειν) Mon. Ex. xxxviii. 3 (Lugd. *conflare*); so Mon. has
fusilia (or *deos fusiles*) Lev. xix. 4, Num. xxxiii. 52, but *conflatile*
Deut. ix. 12 and 16. Wir. has *deos conflatiles* (Ex. xxxiv. 17) and
conflatio (Ex. xxxix. 4); Ottob. *fundere* (Ex. xxvi. 37). Spec. has
each form twice; Aug. *fusilia* but *conflare*; Tert. *fusile*; Jer. *conflatile*. Lugd. has *fusilia* in Num. but *conflatilia* in Ex., Deut., Jud.,
so that *fusilia* appears to be the earlier, though Cyp. has *conflare*
twice.
furnus (κλίβανος) Lugd. Lev. ii. 4. In Gen. xv. 17 Amb. and Aug.
(*De Ciu. Dei*) have *fornax*, but *clibanus* is used by Lugd. in Lev.
and Aug. in Ex.
furor, see *ira*.

Gallina and gallinula (ὀρνίθιον) Mon. Lev. xiv; Lugd. *pullus*.
generatio, see *natio*.
gloria and glorificare, see *claritas*.
glutinare and compounds, see *adiungere*.
grandis (μέγας) Mon. Ex. xxxii; evidently 'African,' being used by
Cyp. here and in Ex. iii. 3 (Lugd., Aug., Amb. *magnus*) and by *k.*
It is found half a dozen times in Lugd.; Jer. has it Gen. l. 9, Jer.
and Spec. with Lugd. Deut. xxv. 13 and 14. Lugd. occasionally
has *ingens*.
gremium (κόλπος) Luc., Tert. Deut. xiii. 6; Cyp., Lugd. have *sinus*,
the word used by Tert. in Ex. iv, and by Wir., Aug., Amb. For
δράγμα, see *manipulus*.
gyrus (κύκλος) Mon. Ex. xxxvi–xl in the expressions *in gyrum* and
in gyro. The word occurs nowhere else in the Heptateuch, but
it is found in Cyp. Wisdom xiii. 2, and the present phrase in
Hil. 2 Kgs. vi. 17, Luc. 1 Kgs. xviii. 32, Wir. Ezek. xxxvii. 21.
The usual *in circuitu* is used by Mon. Ex. xix. 12, Lev. xiv. 41,
and often in Num.

Haedus (χίμαρος) Mon. regularly, and Wir. Lev. iv. 24; so Lugd. in
Num. *Hircus* is used by Amb., Aug., Jer. and (except in Num.)
by Lugd., but in Lev. x Lugd. has *primitiuus hircus*, and in ch. ix
primitiuus alone.
hereditare (κληρονομεῖν) and *possidere* are both used by Cyp. In Lugd.
possidere prevails in each book (except the early part of Deut.),
but *hereditatem capere* is used four times in Num., and in Deut.
we have *possidere hereditatem* twelve times (chiefly early), *heres
esse* nine times (chs. ix–xvi) and *hereditare* ten times; the last also
occurs eight times in Jud. Mon. generally uses *possidere* but has
hereditare in Deut. xxxi. 7, and in Deut. ix and x has *heres esse*
six times with Lugd. *Heres esse* is also used by Lugd. twice in
Jud., and by Aug. four times in Gen. (*Qu.* and *De Ciu. Dei*);
Ottob. has it Ex. xxiii. 30, Amb. in Gen. xxi and (with Vindob.)

in Gen. xv. Aug. shows a preference for *hereditare*, even in those books where it is not used by Lugd. He also uses *hereditate possidere*, as do Luc. and Tert. (*e.g.* Deut. xii. 2). *Possidere* is usual in Amb., Jer., Spec. Κληρονομία is rendered *hereditas* by Cyp., Mon., Lugd. except that in Josh. Lugd. generally has *possessio*. Elsewhere *possessio* is regularly used for κατάσχεσις and κτῆσις.

hircus, see *haedus*.

hodiernus, see *crastinus*.

holocaustum is used by Lugd. almost exclusively in Lev. and Num., *holocaustoma* in Ex. Aug. generally uses *holocaustoma* except in Lev., where the two occur equally. Amb., Jer., Tyc. use *holocaustum*; so does Wir. except in Lev. v–vii, and Mon. except in Ex. xviii. 12. Cyp. however uses both. In Deut. Lugd. has *adolitio*.

honor and honorificare, see *claritas*.

horrere, see *ingrauari*.

hostia (κάρπωμα and κάρπωσις) Wir. Lev. xxii. 27; so Aug. in Lev., and Lugd. in Lev. and Josh. *Fructus* or *fruges* is used by Wir. in Ex., by Lugd. in Ex., Num. and Deut., and by Mon. in Ex., Lev. and Num. Wir. also has *sacrificium* and *offeritiuum* (Lev. vii). For θυσία, see *immolare*.

humilis (ταπεινός) Mon., Aug., Tert. Lev. xiii and xiv. Lugd. here has *infirmus*, but *humilis* elsewhere. For ταπεινοῦν *humiliare* is almost always used, but Mon. has *foedare* Deut. xxii. 24, and Cyp. *deprimere* Ex. i. 12.

Iacere and compounds, see *eicere*.

iam, see *adhuc*.

ianua, see *ostium*.

ignorare, see *scire*.

illic Mon. Deut. xxx. 18 and (*illoc*) 16. *Illic* and *illuc* are doubtless 'African' (cf. Gen. xxxv. 1 Cyp. *illic*, Hil., Spec., Aug., Amb. *ibi*; Num. xx. 26 Cyp. *illic*, Lugd. *ibi*), but they are occasionally found in Luc. (Deut. i. 28), Aug. and Lugd. (especially in Num. and Gen.). Nov. has *illic* 4/6 (three in Gen.); Amb. has *illuc* Gen. xxii. 5, *illo* Gen. xxiv. 6 and xlii. 2; Aug. also uses *illo* twice.

immaculatus (ἄμωμος) Wir. Lev. xxii. 21; Mon. has *sine macula* Lev. iv. 3, otherwise Mon. and Wir. have *sine uitio* regularly. In Ex. xii. 5 Cyp. has *sine uitio*, Amb. *sine macula*, Nic., Jer. and *De Pasc. Comp. immaculatus*; but Cyp. sometimes uses *immaculatus* and Tyc. *sine macula*, so that though *sine uitio* seems most distinctively primitive, each form has early testimony. Aug. and Lugd. use *sine uitio* regularly in Num., elsewhere Aug. has *sine macula* and Lugd. *immaculatus*. For μῶμος *uitium* is usual; Wir. has *macula* Lev. xxii. 20, and Lugd. *repraehensio* Num. xix. 2; Cyp., Aug., Jer. have *uitium et macula* in Lev. xxi. 17.

immolare (θύειν, θυσιάζειν) is found in the A text of Cyp. (in Cyp. only once in 1 Cor.), in Luc. often, in Amb. 4/6, and therefore seems late. Wir. has it in Ex. xxii. 20 (Cyp., Spec., Aug. *sacrifi-*

care), Ottob. in Ex. xxiii and xxiv, Aug. in Ex. and Deut., and Lugd. in Ex. and Gen. Mon. and Spec. use *sacrificare*, and so does Lugd. in Lev. For θυσία Wir., Ottob., Lugd., Aug. sometimes use *immolatio*, but practically only in Ex.; this seems a late usage as Cyp. only uses *sacrificium* and *hostia*. *Sacrificium* is generally used by Mon., Wir., Spec., by Lugd. in Lev. and Jud., and by Aug. in Lev., Num. and Jud. *Hostia* is used by Lugd. and Aug. generally in other books, and occasionally by Mon., Wir. and Ottob.

    For σφάζειν, see *interficere*.

imperare and imperium, see *praecipere*.

imponere (ἀναφέρειν) Mon. Lev. xiv. 20; Wir., Lugd. Lev. iv. 31. It is used by Cyp., *e.g.* in Gen. xxii. 2, where Aug. and Amb. have the usual *offerre*, and so may be early.

importare, see *eicere*.

imprudenter, see *inuitus*.

inanis (κενός) Aug. regularly (found also in *k* and Cyp.), but *uacuus* is usual in other authorities. *Vanus* more often represents μάταιος.

incedere, see *ambulare*.

incensare (θυμιᾶν) Lugd. Ex. xxx, Wir., Lugd. Ex. xl may be a late word; Mon. has *incendere*.

inchoare Aug. Gen. ii. 3 (*De Gen. ad Litt.*), Gen. xi. 6 (*De Ciu. Dei*) and once in Deut.; it is seldom found elsewhere except six times in Lugd. Deut. *Incipere* is used rather more frequently by Aug. and Lugd. (especially in Josh. and Jud.). *Coepisse* is much more common in all texts.

incipere, see *inchoare*.

incola and incolare, see *morari*.

indicare (ἀναγγέλλειν), fourteen times in Lugd. Jud., and occasionally in Gen. in various texts. One occurrence in Aug. Jud. is noticeable as another link with Lugd. It is probably a late word, as Cyp. uses *nuntiare* (or *adnuntiare*) always (12/12). Lugd. also uses *referre* occasionally.

indigens, see *egens*.

indignari and indignatio, see *irasci* and *ira*.

indiligens and indiligentia, see *delictum*.

induere (ἐνδύειν) Mon. 3/3. Lugd., Luc., Wir., Aug. use both *induere* and *uestire*. *Induere* is evidently early, being used by Tyc. and Cyp. (except twice in Apoc.). In Num. xx. 26 Cyp., Amb. have *induere*, Lugd. *uestire*; Amb., Spec. and Lugd. all have *induere* in Deut. xxii. 5.

    For ἐκδύειν Cyp. has *exuere* Num. xx. 26; Lugd. here and in Lev. has *expoliare*, but *exuere* in Gen. xxxvii. 23.

infirmus, see *humilis*.

infra Tert. Gen. i. 7 and Ex. xx. 4, all other texts (except Aug. occasionally in the former) using *sub* or *subtus*. *Infra* may therefore be early especially as it is used by Mon. in Deut. xxviii. 13, where Lugd., Luc. have *subtus*, Amb. *subter*.

ingrauari and adgrauescere (προσοχθίζειν) both in Mon. Lev. xviii; Wir. and Aug. have (ex)horrere. Lugd. has six renderings (offendere more than once) but none of the above.

ingredi, see intrare.

initiari, see perficere.

initium (ἀρχή) Lugd., Amb. frequently (especially in Deut.). It is also used by Lugd. and Wir. Ex. xxxiv. 22, and Vindob. Gen. xiii. 4, but is not exclusively European, for De Pasc. Comp. has it with Amb. and Niceta in Ex. xii. 2, and with Tyc. in Gen. i. 16.

For ἀπαρχαί Spec., Amb., Lugd., Ottob. all use initia in Ex.; so Lugd. Deut. In Num. Spec. and Amb. use primitiae, but Lugd. uses decerptiones as well as both initia and primitiae. Aug. has primitiae in both books.

iniuriam facere (ἀδικεῖν) Mon. Lev. xix. 13; used by Cyp. and at times by Aug. and Lugd. Nocere which becomes more frequent in Aug., Lugd., Luc., Spec. (e.g. Lev. xix. 13) is found in Cyp. only Apoc. xxii. 11. For the passive iniuriam accipere is used by Mon. Deut. xxviii. 29 (Lugd. noceri) and Amb. Gen. xvi. 5; Cyp. uses iniuriam pati. Lugd. in Lev. uses laedere and, for ἀδικία, laesio and laesura, renderings which seem to occur nowhere else.

innotescere, see scire.

inquinare (μιαίνειν) regularly in Mon. (a dozen times) where we never find the compound coinquinare. Lugd. generally has the compound except in Lev. Polluere is found only rarely, e.g. Aug. Num. xix. 13, Amb., Ruf. Gen. xlix. 4.

insidiose (δόλῳ) Mon. Lev. xix. 16, where Spec. has subdole, Luc. in dolo. Lugd. uses dolo (alone or with in, cum or per); this is evidently late, being used in the A text for Cyprian's subdole and insidiose (Ps. xxiii. 4 and xxxiii. 14). Spec. has in dolo (Deut. xxvii. 24).

integer, see totus.

interficere is everywhere rarer than occidere in the Old Latin. In Ex. xxxii Mon. uses ferire and perimere; the last at least is primitive, being used by Cyp. Ex. xxii. 24, but replaced in the A text, Spec., Wir. by occidere. So interimere Cyp., Hil. Deut. xxxii. 39 is replaced by occidere in Spec., Lugd., Aug. Perimere is used by Lugd. Josh. x. 30 for φονεύειν.

Occidere is also the usual rendering of σφάζειν. Lugd. has interficere occasionally (with Mon. Num. xi. 22). Mon. has a remarkable variety of renderings for this word; besides occidere and interficere it has iugulare (Lev. iv), laniare (Lev. iv and xiv), immolare (Lev. xiv) and mactare (Deut. xxviii). Wir. in Lev. iv uses laniare and uictimare. Of these words laniare is used by Jer. (Lev. iv), mactare by Cyp. (Prov. ix. 1), uictimare is supported by the noun uictima in Cyp. and Hil. Is. liii. 7, and Cyp. Rom. viii. 36 (where it is replaced by occisio in Spec., Luc. and the A text); iugulare is used by Or.-Lat. in Lev., and Nov. has iugulatio in Is. liii. 7. This evidence suggests that some of these renderings may be primitive.

Some of these words are found occasionally for other Greek words; *ferire* is used by Aug. and Lugd. for τύπτειν and πατάσσειν, and the latter is twice represented in Lugd. Josh. by *mactare*. Lugd. has *mactare* in Num. xxii. 40, and *uictimare* and *uictima* several times (Gen., Deut.) for θύειν and θυσία.

intrare (εἰσπορεύεσθαι and εἰσέρχεσθαι) is more common than *introire* in Wir. (3 to 1), in Lugd. Ex., Deut., Jud. (82 to 23) and Aug. Gen., Ex., Deut., Jud. (28 to 3–32 to 3 including De Ciu. Dei and De Trin.); it does not occur in Cyp. and is evidently late, or, since it occurs in Italian inscriptions from about 100 A.D., perhaps rather European. *Introire* is used regularly by Cyp. and prevails in Mon. (22 to 16), in Lugd. Gen., Lev., Num., Josh. (60 to 28), and in Aug. Lev., Num., Josh. (11 to 2). *Intrare* prevails in Amb. (6/8), Ottob. (5/7), Iren., Hil., Jer. and Luc., but does not occur in Tert., though he sometimes uses *ingredi*. Spec. uses the two about equally. *Ingredi* is found twice in Mon. and once in Wir., and occasionally in Lugd., Aug., Amb., Jer. It is used twice by Cyp., and so is not exclusively late.

inuitare, see *uociferari*.

inuitus (ἀκουσίως) Wir. Lev. (twice). Mon. has *nolens* Lev. iv. 2 and *nolenter* Lev. iv. 23. *Nolens* is usual in Aug., though he uses also *nolenter*, *non sponte* and *inuita*. Lugd. always has *imprudenter* in Lev.; elsewhere *nolens* is usual, but *inuitus* and *non sponte* also occur. Amb. has *inuitus* Num. xxxv. 11 (with Lugd.).

inuolare (κλέπτειν) Mon. Lev. xix. 11, Wir. Ex. xxii. 12, Spec. Ex. xxii. 1, and once or twice in Lugd. and Luc. Amb. has it Gen. xl. 15, where Wir. has *abripere*. Elsewhere *furari* and *furtum facere* are usual.

ira (ὀργή) almost uniformly in Mon. (4/6), Cyp., Tyc., Aug., Lugd., etc. Mon. has *animus* Ex. xxxii. 10 and 11 (but *ira v.* 12). In Ex. iv. 14 Lugd. and Aug. agree in using *iracundia*, which elsewhere is found not at all in Aug. and once only in Lugd. θυμός is more variously rendered. *Animositas* is used by Mon. Ex. xxxii. 12, and elsewhere perhaps only by Cyp. in Gal. v. 19; *animatio* by Aug. (4/7), by Hil. (Num. xxv. 11) and once by Cyp.; *animus* by Cyp., Spec., Wir. Ex. xxii. 24, by Lugd , Mon., Wir. Ex. xxxii. 19 and by Mon., Lugd. Num. xii. 9. These all seem primitive, and it is noticeable that *animus*, though it does not seem to occur elsewhere, is used by several authorities in each of these places. *Indignatio* is generally regarded as the 'African' equivalent, being found four times in Cyp.; it is used in Spec. Num. xii. 9, and once or twice in Tert. and Aug., but it does not occur in Mon. or Wir. and is rare in Lugd. *Iracundia* is also rare, but is used by Amb. Ex. xv. 8, Ottob. Ex. xi. 8, and once in Lugd. *Furor* is particularly common in Lugd. (about 25/40); it is also frequently used in Amb. and Jer. and is evidently European. It is not used in Cyp., but occurs five times in Mon. (Num. xxxii and Deut. xxxi and xxxii), being one of the clearest evidences of a European strain in this MS towards the end of Deut. *Ira* occurs in most texts even if not frequently.

irasci is usual for both θυμοῦσθαι and ὀργίζεσθαι. *Indignari* is found in Tert. in Ex. xxxii. 10 and Deut. vi. 15, and is considered 'African' from its occurrences in Tyc. and *k*. It is generally used by Lugd. for θυμοῦσθαι (*e.g.* Num. xi. 33 with Mon.) except in Ex. and Deut., but only two or three times for ὀργίζεσθαι. In Jud. ix. 30 Lugd. has *furiari*.

ire and abire, see *ambulare*.

iter (ὁδός) Mon. four times (Ex. and Deut.), but *uia* is also used several times. In Lugd. *iter* is used occasionally in Josh. and Jud., in Aug. only Josh. v. 7 (*uia* occurring fifteen times). Cyp. uses *iter* in Ex. (2/2), *Adu. Iud.* agreeing in Ex. xxiii. 20; it is used by Amb. Deut vi. 7, and occasionally by Hil. and Luc., but may probably be regarded as 'African' in the Pentateuch. See also p. 40.

Iter facere is found in Mon. Ex. xiv. 2 (στρατοπεδεύειν) and a few times for πορεύεσθαι (see under *ambulare*).

iucunditas (εὐφροσύνη) Wir., Lugd. Deut. xxviii. 47; so Lugd. in Gen. and Jud., but in Num. x. 10 Lugd. and Amb. have *laetitia*. *Iucunditas* seems earlier since the A text of Cyp. changes *iucundari* often to *laetari* and once to *epulari*, and apparently *iucunditas* to *laetitia* in Ps. lxvii. 4. For the verb *epulari* is usual in Aug. and Lugd.; but *laetari* is used by Aug. twice in Deut.; and by Lugd. in Jud., once or twice for εὐφραίνεσθαι, but more often for ἀγαθύνεσθαι. Hil. quotes Deut. xxxii. 43 with both *iucundari* and *laetari*.

iugulare, see *interficere*.

iustificatio (δικαίωμα) Mon. Lev. xix. 37, Num. xxxi. 21; but Mon. also has *iustitia* twice. *Iustificatio* is evidently primitive being used twice in Cyp. and replaced by *iustitia* in the A text in Ps. xlix. 16. It is used also by Hil. (Deut. x. 13), Iren. (Deut. iv. 14), Philo-Lat. (Gen. xxvi. 5) and generally by Aug. Spec., Amb., Wir., Ottob. use *iustitia* regularly; Lugd. has *iustificatio* in Num. (5/6), *aequitates* in Deut. iv. 6, but elsewhere *iustitia*. For δίκαιος in Lev. xix. 36 Wir. has *aequus* three times, Spec. *aequalis* once and *iustus* twice; Mon. *iustus* each time. *Aequus* is rare and probably late.

It seems probable that *iustus* was also the early rendering of ὅσιος, for Cyp. has it several times, though the A text usually changes it to *sanctus*. Aug., Lugd., Amb. use *sanctus*, though *iustus* also occurs in Lugd.

iuuencula (νεᾶνις) Lugd., Amb. Deut. xxii; Mon., Aug. *adolescentula*. A preference for *iuuencula* is found elsewhere in Lugd.; Lugd. and Amb. however use *adulescens* and *adulescentior* in Gen. for the commoner *iuuenis* and *iunior*.

Laetari and laetitia, see *iucunditas*.

laniare, see *interficere*.

latificare (πλατύνειν) Aug. and Amb. (*Ep.* not *Noe.*) Gen. ix. 27.
Ampliare and *adampliare* occur in Lugd. and Amb. Deut. once
or twice, but *dilatare* is more usual in Aug., Amb., Lugd. (with
Wir. in Ex. xxxiv. 24).
latus, see *pars*.
lenire and lenitio Wir. eleven times, *unguere* and *unctio* five. Mon.
always uses *unguere* and *unctio*, and these are evidently the early
renderings as they are used by Cyp. Aug. has *lenire* and *lenitio*
each once in Ex., Lugd. frequently has them in Ex., but elsewhere
always keeps the earlier words. It is noticeable that the later
words appear in Wir. Lev. but not in Lugd. Lev.
lenis, see *mansuetus*.
lepra and leprosus, see *uarius*.
libare and libatio, see *litare*.
liberare, see *redimere*.
litare and litatio (σπονδεῖον) are regularly used by Lugd. in Num.,
but elsewhere only Deut. xxxii. 38. Mon. has *litatio* in Num.
xxix, but *libare* and *libatorium* in ch. iv; the latter, with *libatio*,
are regularly used from Cyp. and *De Pasc. Comp.* onwards. Mon.
has *profusorium* in Ex. xxxviii. 12.
logium, see *manuale*.
longanimis, see *miserator*.
lucifer (ὄρθρος) Nov. Gen. xxxii. 26; Lugd. and Spec. (*Cod. Sess.*)
have *oriens*, Aug. *aurora*.
lugere, see *plangere*.
lustrare, see *sancire* and *purgare*.

Mactare, see *interficere*.
macula, see *immaculatus*.
magnanimis, see *miserator*.
magnificare and maiestas, see *claritas*.
maior natu, see *presbyter*.
malignus (πονηρός) usual in Lugd. (except Num.) and Aug., occurring
also in Mon. (Deut. xxii) Spec. and Vindob.; Cyp. uses it only
twice in Jud. *Malus* occurs three times in Spec. and four in Mon.,
but is not common. For the noun *malitia* is usual, *malignitas*
occurring in Lugd. Jud. *Nequam* and *nequitia* are 'African,' being
used by Cyp., Tyc. and *Ad Nov.* Mon. has *nequam* Deut. xxii. 22,
Mon., Lugd. and Wir. *nequitia* Deut. xxxi. 21; in Aug. and Lugd.
these words survive two or three times in Num., and in Lugd.
and Ottob. Gen. 1. 20. Luc. has *nequam* and *nequitia* fairly often,
but he has other examples of distinctly Cyprianic words. Amb.
has *saeuus* three times in Gen., and Lugd. has it a few times in
Gen. and Deut.; Vindob. has *saeuissimus* and in Gen. xxxvii
Lugd. and Amb. have *insaeuire*; these words do not occur elsewhere and form a striking link between these three texts.
manare, see *trahere*.
mandare and mandatum, see *praeceptum*.

manducare, see *edere*.

manifestare and manifestatio, see *ostensio*.

manipulus (δράγμα) almost regularly Aug., Lugd., Amb., Spec. Aug. in Lev. xxiii. 15 has *gremium*; this is primitive being used by Cyp. in Ps. cxxv. 5 and changed to *manipulus* in Spec., Luc. and A text.

mansuetus (πραΰς) Mon., Lugd., Spec., Jer. Num. xii. 3; Cyp., Aug. *lenis*. Elsewhere Cyp. uses *mitis*, which is also replaced by *mansuetus* in Hil. Zach. ix. 9, and Spec. Matt. xi. 29. Cyp. uses both *lenitas* (twice) and *mansuetudo* (once) for the noun.

manuale (λογεῖον) Mon. Ex. xxxvi, and Wir. Ex. xxxv; Wir. in Lev. viii and Iren. use *logium*. Aug. and Amb. use *rationale*; Lugd. has *emeritio* five times in Ex. xxviii and xxix, but elsewhere *logium*.

mature, see *celeriter*.

mens, see *sensus*.

ministrare (λειτουργεῖν) Mon. Ex. xxxix; used by Cyp. and apparently primitive. It survives only three or four times in Lugd., but is used by Aug., with the nouns *ministerium* and *administratio*, in Num. and Deut. (7/7). Mon. has *deseruire* and *deseruitio* in Num. iv, and *seruire* in Deut. x. *Deseruire* is much the commonest rendering in Lugd., and it is used by Aug. in Ex., *ministrare* in Ex. xxviii. 43 being doubtless due to Augustine's use of the words of Parmenian. Wir. uses *ministrare* and *deseruire* in Ex. xxxix, but *sacrificare* Ex. xxxv. 18; the last is used by Lugd. a few times in Ex., and also by Amb. in Ex. xxviii. 43. Amb. has *ministrare* and *ministerium* in Num., even when Lugd. has (de)seruire and *seruitus*. The corresponding adjective is rendered *sacerdotalis* by Mon. Ex. xxxix. 13 (Wir., Lugd. *deseruitionis*); and *religionis* by Lugd. in Num. iv.

miserator (οἰκτείρμων) Wir., Lugd., Jer. Ex. xxxiv. 6; Iren. has *misericors* as Lugd. in Deut. iv. 31. *Pius* is found in Cyp., Luc. (Joel ii. 13) and *Ad Nov.* (Ecclus. ii. 11) but Cyp. also uses such words as *misericors* and *miseratio* for the same root.

For πολυέλεος (Ex. xxxiv. 6) Wir. has *multa misericordia*; Lugd. has *multum misericors*, and so Spec. in Joel; Cyp., Luc., Iren. and *Ad Nov.* have *multae* (Iren. *magnae*) *miserationis*. (For ἔλεος Cyp. uses *misericordia* eight times and *miseratio* twice.) Ἐλεήμων is rendered *misericors* Wir., Lugd., Jer. Ex. xxxiv. 6, Spec., Wir., Amb. Ex. xxii. 27, and Cyp., Luc., Spec. Joel ii. 13.

In Ex. xxxiv. 6 and Joel ii. 13 to these is added μακρόθυμος. Wir. represents this by *longanimis*, which is also used by Jer. (*Adu. Pel.*) in Num. Lugd. in Ex. has *magnanimis*, but in Num. *patiens*, which is used by Luc. (Joel), Cyp. (four times) and Jer. (Ex. xxxiv). Cyp. however also uses *magnanimus* (1 Cor.); Spec. has *patiens* in 1 Cor., and in Joel has apparently conflated *magnanimus* and *patiens*.

mittere and compounds, see *eicere*.

monstrare and demonstrare are rarely used for δεικνύναι in the Old Latin, *ostendere* being everywhere usual; Cyp. uses *ostendere*

always except in Matt. viii. 4. *Monstrare* is used in Mon. Ex.
xxxiii. 5, Wir. Ex. xxxiii. 18 and once each in Aug., Amb., Tert.;
demonstrare in Aug. (*De Ciu. Dei*) Gen. xii. 1, Mon. Ex. xiii. 21,
Wir. Ex. xxv. 40 and two or three times in Amb. and Lugd.
   Demonstrare is occasionally used for Greek words other than
δεικνύναι. It is found in Mon. and Aug. Ex. xviii. 20 for σημαίνειν,
in Mon. Ex. xiii. 17 for ὁδηγεῖν (elsewhere rendered by *ducere* or
a compound), in Ottob. Ex. xxiii. 23 for ἡγεῖσθαι, and in Spec.
and Amb. Deut. vi. 7 for προβιβάζειν (Lugd. *producere*).
   For δηλοῦν, see *ostensio*.

morari and **commorari** (in place of *habitare* and *inhabitare*) occur in
Lugd. twenty times in Gen. (chiefly *morari*), twenty in Josh.
(chiefly *commorari*) and half a dozen in Deut. They occur occasionally in Luc. and Ottob. but are not found in Cyp., and are
possibly late. In the Heptateuch they are almost entirely limited
to Gen. and Josh. Aug. uses them in Josh. only, and they are
found in Gen. in Vindob. (xiii. 12), Amb. (xx. 3) and Wir. (xxxvi.
20). So *commoratio* is used for *habitatio* by Lugd. in Gen. xxvii.
39, *moratio* by Mon. in Lev. iii. 17, the latter a noticeable occurrence as being the only one in Mon. and also the only one in Lev.
Aug. also uses *incolare, incola esse* and *incolatus*; these occur in
most books but more often for παροικεῖν than for κατοικεῖν; Lugd.
however also has *incola esse* for the latter in Lev. xviii. 3.

mortariolum, see *patera*.

morticinum (θνησιμαῖον) Wir. and Aug.; Mon. uses *mortuum* or *sibi
mortuum*; Lugd. has both in Lev., but *morticinum* in Deut.

mox (ἡνίκα or ὡς) Mon. Ex. ix. 29, xvi. 21 and xxxi. 18. It occurs once
in Cyp. (2 Cor. iii. 16) but is used again in the A text in Is. lv. 6,
where Cyp. has *cum*. Mon. generally has *cum* in the older portions; Aug. uses *cum, postquam* and *statim ut, mox ut* only once in
Gen. (*De Ciu. Dei*). Lugd. has a variety of renderings, *mox* occurring five times (all in Ex. and Deut.), *statim ut* more frequently
in Josh. and Jud. *Mox* and *mox ut* both occur in Luc. (*e.g.* Ex.
xxxiii. 9, *mox* Luc., *cum* Lugd.); evidently they were more frequently used in the later forms of the version, but are already
found in Nov.

multiplicare and **multitudo**, see *plenitudo*.

mundare and **mundus**, see *purgare* and *purus*.

munus, see *donum*.

Natio (ἔθνος) Mon. Deut. xxviii. 12. It is used ten times in Cyp. (*e.g.*
Matt. vi. 32, where Spec. has *gens*), frequently in Tert. and also
in *De Pasc. Comp.* (Gen. xxii. 18), Tyc., *k* and Nov., and is clearly
early. It occurs only once in Lugd.—conflated with *gens*—but is
often found in Luc. in certain books (*e.g.* Wisdom) and occasionally in Amb. (Num. xxiv. 20, Deut. xxxii. 21) and Aug. (once in
Gen. in *De Ciu. Dei*).
   For γενεά *natio* occurs Mon. Num. xxxii. 13, Deut. xxiii. 3 and

xxxii. 7, but *progenies* is used by Mon. six times in Ex. (chiefly early), *proles* in Ex. xxxi. 16, and *generatio* in Deut. xxxii. 20. Wir. has *progenies* (2/2). Cyp. has *progenies* (once) and *natiuitas* (twice), the latter being replaced by *generatio* in the A text in Ps. xxiii. 6. Tyc. has *generatio* and *saeculum*, *k* has *natio* and *saeculum*, Tert. *natiuitas* in the second commandment. *Natio*, *natiuitas* and *saeculum* are therefore all early, and in Aug., Amb. and Jer. are nearly always replaced by *progenies* and *generatio*. Lugd. generally has *progenies*, but preserves *natio* in a dozen places (seven in Num.); it has *natiuitas* once (Deut. xxix. 22), *generatio* more often (especially in Lev. and Jud.). Luc. has *natio* Deut. xxxii. 5; in Gen. xxxi. 3 Lugd. and Amb. have *gens*, in Ex. iii. 15 Spec. has *saeculum* (conflated in Lugd. with *generatio*).

For γένεσις Lugd. has *natio* twice (Gen.); Nov. has *natiuitas* Gen. xxxi. 13, and so Aug. twice. Aug. also has *procreatura* (Gen. xxxvii. 2) but usually *generatio*.

negligentia and **negligere**, see *delictum*.

nequam and **nequitia**, see *malignus*.

nex, see *caedes*.

nimis (σφόδρα) Mon. six times, but *ualde* Ex. ix. 24, Deut. ix. 20, *uehementer* Ex. x. 14, *nimium* Num. xii. 3. *Nimis* is certainly 'African,' being used exclusively in Cyp., Tyc. and *k*, though Nov. uses *ualde*. In Lugd. *uehementer* is characteristic of Gen., and *nimis* of Num. and Josh., but *ualde* is very common. Aug. uses *ualde* regularly in *Qu.* and *Loc.*, but he occasionally uses *nimis* in his more casual quotations and remarks on its frequent use in the Old Latin. Luc. generally uses *ualde*, and so do Amb. (except Gen. xli. 31), Vindob., Hil., Ottob. and Tert.; Jer. on the other hand uses *nimis* very often. In addition to the occurrences noticed above, *uehementer* is found in Lugd., Spec. Josh. xxiii. 6, Lugd., Ottob. Gen. l. 10, Lugd. Ex. i. 7, Aug. (*De Trin.*) Ex. xix. 18, Philo-Lat. Gen. xxvii. 33, and five times in Jer. (four in Gen.). Lugd. has *diligenter* Deut. iv. 15.

nocere (κακοῦν) Spec. three times Ex. xxii. 21–23, Wir. having *nocere* once and *uexare* twice. *Vexare* is used by Cyp. (Ex. xxii and elsewhere) and Tyc., and is certainly the earlier. Lugd. has nine renderings, *uexare* three times in Num. and two in Josh. (Spec. also using *uexare* in Josh.). Aug. and Amb. generally use *nocere* or *affligere*.

nolens and **nolenter**, see *inuitus*.

noscere and compounds, see *scire*.

nouellare (φυτεύειν) Mon. Lev. xix. 23, Deut. xxviii. 30; characteristic of *k*, and evidently 'African.' Lugd., Aug., Amb. use *plantare*, but Aug. has *pastinare* in Deut. xx. 6.

nutrire, see *alere*.

Obseruare (φυλάσσειν) Mon. Ex. xxxi. 16, six times in Lev. xviii and xix, and twice in Deut., *custodire* being used in Ex. xix. 5 and in

Num. Wir. has *seruare* Ex. xxii. 10, *conseruare* Lev. xix. 37, but *custodire* four times. *Seruare* and its compounds are evidently 'African'; Cyp. uses these words ten times, *custodire* only four, and the latter often replaces the former in the A text (*e.g.* Ps. lxxxviii. 32) and in Luc., Lugd. and Spec. (*e.g.* Deut. xiii. 18, xxiii. 23, Josh. i. 8). In Lugd. *seruare* (or *obseruare*) is used in Ex. (3/4), Lev. (except ch. xxvi) and in the early part of Deut. (twenty times); elsewhere *custodire*. Luc., Amb., Spec. generally use *custodire*, and so does Tert. in Ex. xxiii. 20 and Deut. xiii. 4. For the corresponding noun Mon. and Lugd. have *custodia* and *custodienda* in Num., but Lugd. has *obseruatio* in Num. ix. 19 and 23. Aug. in Num. uses *custodiae*, but knows also a rendering *excubiae*.

For διατηρεῖν *seruare* and its compounds are used in all texts.

obtinere, see *sumere*.

obuiam and obuiare, see *occurrere*.

occidere and occisio, see *interficere* and *caedes*.

occurrere (συναντᾶν) Mon. Deut. xxiii. 4; so Jer. and Amb. regularly. Lugd. and Aug. always use *occurrere* in Num., though on the whole they use *obuiare* as frequently. *Occursus* is very rare except for four occurrences in Lugd. Num.

odio habere Mon., Spec., Aug. Lev. xix. 17 (Luc., Tert. *odire*), but in Deut. xxii. 16, where Aug. has *odio habens*, Mon. with Lugd. has *odiens*. *Odio habere* is found five times in Cyp. but in two places the A text substitutes *odisse* with the sense of a past tense. This latter occurs a dozen times in Cyp. (especially in Psalms and St John) and the new verb *odire* half a dozen times. Luc. often uses *odio habere* (*e.g.* in Matt. xxiv. 9 where Cyp. has *odire*) but Lugd. never uses it. Lugd., Luc. and Spec. all at times use *odisse* with present sense, but they also use *odire*, with a perfect *odiui* or *odii* and a participle *odiens*. Aug. uses the classical *odisse* and the compound *odio habere*. The new verb *odire* however occurs in Tert.

operire and cooperire (for καλύπτειν and σκεπάζειν) occur five times in Mon., *tegere* and *contegere* three. Wir. has the former once, the latter three times. Cyp. has a preference for *tegere*, and since this is occasionally replaced by *cooperire* in later texts, it appears to be more primitive. Aug. and Amb. have the two about equally, but in Lugd. *tegere* is used only four times (out of about 50). Ottob. generally has *tegere*, and so has Tert. in Lev. xiii (neither Latin word seems to go more than the other with either of the Greek words). For ἀποκαλύπτειν Mon. has *reuelare* in Lev. xviii, but *denudare* in Deut. xxii. 30. Cyp. and Aug. use *reuelare*; *denudare* is most common in Lugd., but Lugd. and Wir. both have five different renderings. So for the corresponding nouns *tegumentum* and *tegumen* occur, but *operimentum* is more common, especially in the later texts. Thus it replaces the *tegumen* of Mon. in Ex. xl. 5, and the *tegumentum* of Mon. in Deut. xxii. 30 and of Cyp.

in 1 Tim. vi. 8, in Lugd., Wir. or Spec. *Velum* and *uelamen* also occur in Mon., Wir. and Lugd. at times in Ex., *protectio* in Lugd. and Aug. in Jud.

orare and oratio, see *rogare* and *uotum.*

orfanus Wir., Spec., Cyp. Ex. xxii. 24; Cyp., Aug., Luc. use both *orfanus* and *pupillus*, but the latter does not occur in Lugd. or Spec.

ostensio (δήλωσις) Wir. Lev. viii. 8; Lugd. has *manifestatio*, Aug. *demonstratio.* For δηλοῦν Lugd. and Aug. have *demonstrare* Ex. xxxiii. 12; Lugd., Amb. *manifestare* Deut. xxxiii. 10. See also *monstrare.*

ostium (θύρα) Mon. eleven times, *porta* being used twice and *ianua* four times. Cyp. uses *porta* (Is.) and *ostium* (Josh. and St John), *ianua* taking the place of the latter in Lugd. Josh. ii. 19, and in Hil., Luc. and A text Jn. x. 9. *Ianua* is evidently late, not occurring at all in Cyp. Luc. uses it, but Nov., Hil. and even Amb. (6/6) retain the earlier *ostium.* Lugd. uses the two about equally, but *ostium* prevails in Gen., Ex., Num., *ianua* in Lev., Deut., Josh.; Aug. uses *ostium* in Gen., Ex., Lev., but *ianua* in Deut. and Jud.; Spec. has *ostium* in Gen. and Lev., *ianua* in Deut.; Wir. has *ostium* in Lev. and five times in Ex., *ianua* in Deut. and twice in Ex.

Πύλη is regularly rendered *porta* in Mon., Wir., and Cyp. Lugd. has *ianua* half a dozen times, with Spec. and Amb. in Deut. vi. 9; Aug. has it once in Deut.

Pabulum (χόρτος) seems primitive in Gen. iii. 18, being used by Cyp. and Aug. *De Gen. con. Man.*, Aug. using *foenum* in his other quotations of the verse. In Gen. i Aug. generally uses *pabulum*, but Tert. *foenum*; Amb. uses each word frequently. In Gen. ix. 3 Amb. and Nov. use *pabulum*, Tert. and Luc. *foenum*; in Deut. xxxii. 2 Spec., Lugd., Hil., Amb. all use *foenum.* That the latter is not altogether late is shown not only by its use in Tert., but also by its appearance in Cyprian's Isaiah.

pallium, see *uestis.*

par Mon. Ex. xxxviii. 15, Lugd. *aequans. Par* seems the earlier being used in Cyp. and *k*, but Cyp. has *aequalis* in Deut. xiii. 6, where Luc. and Tert. have *par. Aequalis* is used by Mon. in Num., and generally by Aug., Lugd. and Ottob.

parere, see *apparere.*

pars (μερίς and μέρος) Mon., Wir., Aug. and Cyp. regularly. *Portio* is found in Lugd. Gen. and Josh., in Spec. (2/2), in Iren. (Deut. xxxii. 9); Hil. and Amb. use both words.

For κλίτος Mon. has *pars* seven times, and so Lugd. regularly in Num., but *latus* is more usual in Lugd. Ex. Wir. uses both, and Aug. knows both renderings.

pascere, see *alere.*

pastinare, see *nouellare.*

patera (θυίσκη) Lugd. in Ex., Ottob. having *thyisca*. In Num., Lugd. and Mon. have *mortariolum* (ch. iv) and *turabulum* (ch. vii).

patiens, see *miserator*.

pellis (δέρμα) Wir. Ex. (2/2), but *pellicula* Lev. xi. 32. Mon. has *corium* Lev. xi. 32, Num. iv. 6, but *cutis* in Lev. xiii. In Lugd. *corium* is generally used in Lev. and Num., *pellicula* in Gen., but *pellis* elsewhere. Aug. has *cutis* with Mon. and Tert. in Lev. xiii, and once uses *corium*, but generally *pellis*. Ottob. has *pellis*.

　　See also *uelum*.

perficere (συντελεῖν and τελειοῦν) Mon. Lev. xix. 9, but in Ex. xl. 27 and three times in Deut. xxxi and xxxii Mon. has *consummare*; Wir. has *consummare* (2/2). *Perficere* is doubtless primitive; it is used by Tyc. and by Cyp. (5/6), *consummare* being substituted for it in the A text in 2 Tim. iv. 6. Aug. uses *perficere* in Lev. (except xxi. 10) but elsewhere *consummare*; Lugd. has *perficere* in Lev. and occasionally in Num., *initiari* three times in Num., but elsewhere *consummare*. Tert. has *initiari* Num. xxv. 3 (a significant connection with Lugd.), *perficere* Gen. xlix. 5, *consummare* Gen. xviii. 21. Rufinus has *perficere* Gen. xlix. 5; Hil. sometimes has *perficere* in St John, but otherwise Amb., Jer., Spec. and Hil. use *consummare* regularly. For the corresponding nouns Lugd. regularly has *perfectio* in Lev. (ten times) but *consummatio* in Ex. and Deut. Aug. however uses *consummatio* in Lev. also (3/3); so does Spec. (viii. 33). Amb. has *consummatus* Ex. xii. 5; so Spec. and Lugd. Deut. xviii. 13; Cyp. and *De Pasc. Comp.* in the former place, and Aug. in both, have *perfectus*.

pergere, see *ambulare*.

perimere, see *interficere*.

persona, see *facies*.

pigrida Cyp., *De Pasc. Comp.* (one MS) and Aug. Ex. xii. 8, and so Lugd. in Num.; Nic., Tert. and Amb. however with two MSS of Cyp. and one of *De Pasc. Comp.* have *amaritudo*.

pius, see *miserator*.

placatorium (ἱλαστήριον) Mon. Ex. xxxviii, but *propitiatorium* chs. xxxvii and xl. Lugd. has *propitiatorium* in Ex., *propitiatio* in Lev., *praecatorium* in Num. *Propitiatorium* occurs in Aug., Amb., Iren. Ex. xxv. 16, but Aug. on Lev. xvi. 16 notices *exoratorium* as another rendering. Ottob. in Ex. xxv uses *emeritio* as well as *propitiatorium*. Mon. has *placatus* Ex. xxxii. 14 (ἱλάσθη), Lugd. *propitius*, Aug. *propitiatus*.

plangere (καταπενθεῖν) Mon. Ex. xxxiii. 4, Lugd. *lugere*. Tyc. and Cyp. use both words, but *plangere* is primitive in Matt. v. 4 (Cyp., *k*—A text, Spec. *lugere*). Lugd., Aug., Amb., Ottob., Philo-Lat. use *lugere* and *luctus* regularly.

　　Plangere however is used for κόπτεσθαι by Aug. Gen. xxiii. 2, and by Lugd., Aug., Jer., Ottob. Gen. l. 10. From Matt. xxiv. 30 however we should conclude that *lamentare* was the primitive rendering of κόπτεσθαι, for there Spec. and Tyc. change Cyprian's *lamentare* to *plangere*.

plebs (λαός) Mon. Deut. xxxi. 7, Wir. Deut. xxxi. 12, Ottob. Gen. xlix. 33, a somewhat rare word. Aug. has it only in Ex. xx. 18 (*Serm.*) and Gen. xxiii. 7 (*Con. Max.*, not *Qu.*). Spec. has it in Deut. (4/5), and it is common in Luc.; in Cyp. it occurs three times outside Isaiah, but is sometimes substituted for *populus* by the A text, as by Lugd. in Num. xxiii. 24. In Isaiah however Cyp. uses *plebs* five times, and it is removed twice by Luc. and Spec. in ch. lviii. In Lugd. *plebs* is common in the latter half of Deut., and in Gen. It occurs seven times in Josh., but four of these are in what seems a late insertion in v. 4–6.

Plebs is used for δῆμος in Mon. and Lugd. Num., as in Lugd. Josh. and Jud., but Aug. uses *populus* for this word as well as for λαός.

plenitudo (πλῆθος) is used occasionally in Lugd. Deut. for the more usual *abundantia*. Cyp., Tert., *De Pasc. Comp.* have *uulgus* Ex. xii. 6; in this sense *multitudo* is usual in all texts.

For πληθύνειν *replere* is much used in Lugd. Deut.; this seems late, being used in Gen. iii. 16 and Deut. xiii. 17 by later authorities where Cyp. has the usual *multiplicare. Complere, ampliare* and *adampliare* also occur occasionally.

plorare (κλαίειν) Mon. and Lugd. Num. xi. 20. *Plorare* occurs only twice in Cyp., *flere* three times, but the former is doubtless 'African'; e.g. Ps. cxxv. 6 Cyp. *plorare*, A text, Spec., Luc. *flere*. Cyp. also has *ploratio* Matt. viii. 11 (A text *fletus*), but in Joel ii. 12 he has *fletus* with Spec. and Luc., while *Ad Nov.* has the earlier *ploratio. Plorare* however often survives in later texts. Aug., Luc. and Ottob. use both words; Lugd. generally has *plorare* (25/32), but Amb. nearly always *flere* and *fletus*. Lugd. uses *ploratio* and *fletus* each twice (in Jud. ii. 5 the former is retained as a place name).

polluere, see *inquinare*.

porta, see *ostium*.

portare (φέρειν) Mon. Ex. xxxii. 2 and 3, Lugd. *adferre*; so in Lev. xiv. 45 Mon. has *exportare* and Lugd. *proferre* for ἐκφέρειν. Both words occur in most authorities, but these examples suggest that *ferre* was preferred to *portare* in later times. *Eicere* is used in Mon. Deut. xxii. 15 (Lugd. *proferre*), Cyp. Ex. xii. 46 (Mon. *efferre*), Spec. Lev. xiv. 45. Lugd. sometimes uses *ducere* and compounds.

For αἴρειν, see *tollere*.

portentum (τέρας) Lugd. and Aug. occasionally in Ex., but *prodigium* is more usual; in Deut. iv. 34 Lugd. has *monstrum*.

portio, see *pars*.

possessio and possidere, see *hereditare*.

potare (ποτίζειν) Wir., Lugd. Ex. xxxii. 20; *dare bibere* Mon., Aug., Amb. *Potare* is clearly primitive, being used six times in Cyp.

and in Tyc., Nov. and *k*. Cyp. uses *adaquare* once, but never *dare bibere*. Lugd. has *adaquare* nine times, *potare* four times, *dare bibere* once. Aug. and Amb. use *adaquare* and *dare bibere*.

potens, see *fortitudo* and *uirtus*.

praecatorium, see *placatorium*; and for **praecari**, see *rogare* and *uotum*.

praeceptum and **praecipere** are alternative renderings to *mandare* and *mandatum* for ἐντολή and ἐντέλλειν both in early and late texts. The former predominate in Cyp., but later there is evidently a tendency to use *mandatum* and *mandare* instead, as is shown by their introduction into Lugd. in Deut. xiii. 18 and xviii. 18, and into the A text in Ps. lxxxviii. 32, where Cyp. has *praecipere*. So Mon. has *praeceptum* (and *praecipere*) ten times in Deut. xxviii and xxxi, but Wir., Lugd., Luc., Aug., Amb. replace them by *mandare* and *mandatum* wherever these authorities are extant. The latter in fact only appear in Mon. in Lev. iv. 13, Deut. xxxi. 10 and a few times in Num. In Aug. the earlier words prevail in Ex. and Lev. (9/11) but the later in Deut. (9/9) and Jud. (4/5). In Lugd. the earlier are almost regularly used in Gen., Lev., Josh. and the first half of Deut. (about 95/110), but the later in Num. and the latter half of Deut. (also about 95/110). In Ex. and Jud. they occur about equally. Luc. and Jer. show a decided preference for *mandare* and *mandatum*, Tert. for *praecipere* and *praeceptum*: Spec., Amb., Nov. and Hil. use both freely.

If however *praecipere* tends to disappear as a rendering of ἐντέλλειν, it reappears for τάσσειν and its compounds. These are regularly represented in Cyp. by *imperare*, and this is used by Mon. and Tert. Lev. xiv. 36 and 40, but does not appear at all in Lugd.; we have *e.g.* Josh. v. 14 Cyp. *imperare*, Lugd., Aug. *praecipere* (cf. Ps. ii. 7 Cyp. *imperium*, A text *praeceptum*). In Ex. xvi. 16 and 34, and generally in Num., Mon. has *constituere*, which is used nearly as much as *praecipere* by Aug., but less frequently in Lugd. (fourteen times of which nine are in Num.). Amb. has it Ex. viii. 9, Ottob. Ex. xvi. 34. A fourth rendering *condicere* appears in Mon. Ex. xxxvi. 14 and Wir. Ex. xxxix. 11 (where Mon. has *dicere*). Spec. and Lugd. have *praedicere* Deut. iv. 23 (Aug. *constituere*). In Ex. xxxvii. 19 Mon. had *constitutio* (σύν-ταξις); Lugd. here has *dispositio*, but uses *constitutio* in Num. *Constitutio* also occurs in Lugd. Gen. for πρόσταγμα. *Mandare* and *mandatum* occur once or twice in Wir. and Lugd., but these seem to be subsequent alterations, since these words are never used in the early texts for derivatives of τάσσειν.

praecordia, see *sensus*.

prehendere, see *sumere*.

presbyter (πρεσβύτερος) Mon. Num. xi and Deut. xxxi. 9, but *senior* occurs seven times (Ex., Lev., Deut.). Cyp. has *presbyter* (with Wir., Luc., Spec.) Lev. xix. 32 only, *senior* seven times, *maior natu* four times. *Maior natu* is found in *k*, but except in a literal sense (as five times in Lugd. Gen.) seems to have disappeared early; it survives in Ottob. Ex. xvii. 5, though elsewhere this MS has both *senior* and *presbyter*. Aug. and Amb. use *senior*; so does Lugd. generally except in Num. and Deut., where *presbyter* is nearly always used.

For γερουσία Mon., Lugd. and Luc. have *seniores* in Deut. xxii; Aug. has *seniores*, *senes* and *senatus*; Lugd. *seniores*, *maiores natu* and, in Josh., *curia*.

pressura (the regular word for θλῖψις in *k* and Cyp.) and deprimere are found in Lugd. Ex. iii. 9, *comprimere* in Lugd. and Aug. Num. xxii. 25, but *tribulatio* and *tribulare* are elsewhere used for θλίβειν, etc.

primitiae, see *initium*.

primitiuus is used by Lugd. in Deut., *primogenitus* in Lev., Num., Josh. and Jud.; both are used in Gen. and Ex. Mon. has *primogenitus* in Num., but *primitiuus* in Ex. xii and xiii; Wir. uses the latter. *Primogenitus* is usual in Cyp. (3/4), Jer. and Aug., though in Gen. xlviii. 18 Cyp., Lugd., Aug., Amb. have *primitiuus*. Amb. generally uses *primitiuus* (9/12).

procedere and prodire, see *egredi*.

prodigium, see *portentum*.

producere, see *eicere*.

profanare (βεβηλοῦν) Mon. (5/5); doubtless the primitive rendering— occurring in Cyp. (3/3), *k* and Tyc. (Zeph.). In Lev. xviii. 21 Wir. has *contaminare*, the later equivalent, used in Tyc. (Ezek.), Luc., Spec., Jer. (cf. Zeph. iii. 4 *profanare* Tyc.; *contaminare* Spec., Luc.). Aug. and Spec. use both words, Lugd. has a variety of renderings.

For βέβηλος Lugd. and Donatists (*apud* Aug.) in Lev. x. 10 use *profanus*, but Aug. *contaminatus*.

proficisci, see *egredi* and *promouere*.

profusorium, see *litatio*.

progenies and proles, see *natio*.

promouere (ἀπαίρειν and ἐξαίρειν—in the sense of journey) Mon., Aug., Lugd., Amb. regularly in Num. It is doubtless early being used by Cyp. (Ex. xiv. 19); Mon. also has it in Deut. x (three times) and Ex. xii. 37, Ottob. in Ex. xvii. 1. *Proficisci* is used by Jer., in *XLII Mansiones*, and Vindob. (Gen. xiii. 11), and is apparently late. It is used by Mon. Ex. xvii and xix, by Aug. once in Josh., by Lugd. once in Gen. and often in Josh. and Jud. Generally in Deut. and occasionally elsewhere Lugd. has *tollere* (and *sustulisse*); Aug. uses the latter in Ex. xii. 37.

promptuarium, see *cellarium*.

propinquus (πλησίος) is rare, *proximus* occurring *e.g.* regularly in Aug. (20/20 in *Qu.*, *Loc.*, *De Ciu. Dei*). *Propinquus* is used by Amb. Ex. xxii. 26, Niceta Ex. xii. 4, Wir., Lugd., Luc. Ex. xxxii. 27, and half a dozen times in Lugd., and so may be late.

For οἰκεῖος *propinquus* is used once by Aug. and twice by Wir. (Lev. xviii and xxi). Lugd. has *domesticus* throughout Lev. xviii, and once in Num.

propitiare and derivatives, see *exorare* and *placatorium*.

proselytus, see *aduena*.

prosperare, see *dirigere*.

pupillus, see *orfanus*.

purgare (καθαρίζειν and καθαίρειν) and purgatio thirteen times by Mon. in Lev., but *mundare* in Num. and twice in Lev. *Purgare* is evidently 'African' (cf. Prov. xvi. 6, *purgare* Cyp., *mundare* Spec.), but Cyp. uses *mundare* or *emundare* almost as frequently as *purgare*, so that *mundare* is not distinctively late; Cyp. however never uses *purificare* and *purificatio*. Aug. uses *purgare* and *purgatio* in Lev. (6/6), *mundare* and *emundare* in Num. (3/3), *purificare* and *purificatio* in Ex. (2/2). In Lugd. *purgare* and *purgatio* occur seven times (Lev., Num., Josh.), *mundare* over forty times, *purificare* and *purificatio* nine times (five in Ex.). Nov. has *purgare*, Spec. in Deut. xviii. 10 *lustrare*.

purificare, see *purgare* and *sancire*.

purus (καθαρός) Mon., Wir., Ottob. Ex., but only in a physical sense (*e.g.* pure gold), *mundus* being used (except in Wir. Ex. xxxix. 16) only in a moral or ritual sense. The same distinction is generally found in Aug., but Lugd. and Amb. occasionally use *purus* in a moral sense (*e.g.* Gen. xx. 6, Aug. *mundus*, Amb. *purus* with *cor*); this seems late for in Matt. v. 8 we have Cyp. *mundus*, A text *purus*. Cyp. always uses *mundus* but only in a ceremonial or moral sense. Aug. however (with Amb.) has *purus a iuramento* in Gen. xxiv. 8.

(ne) Quando, see *casu*.

quoadusque (ἕως and ἕως ἄν) eight times in Mon., *donec* three times, *usquedum* not at all. Wir. does not use *quoadusque*, and has *donec* twice, *usquedum* four times. *Quoadusque* is certainly early, and *usquedum* late; the former is found seven times in *k*, and Cyp. uses it as often as *donec*, but *usquedum* is found neither in Cyp., nor *k*, nor Tyc. Hil. uses *quoadusque* occasionally, but Nov. has *donec* only. In Lugd. *donec* and *usquedum* are common in most books, but *quoadusque* only occurs a dozen times and half of these are in Num., in which book *usquedum* is used twice only. In Lev. Lugd. always uses *quoad*, which seems to occur elsewhere in the version only once in Cyp. (Dan.). *Usquedum* is used by Ottob. and is frequent in Luc., but Aug. prefers *donec* and the earlier *quoadusque*, *usquedum* not occurring in his Heptateuch. Amb. has *quoadusque* Num. xx. 17, but *usquedum* Gen. xiii. 10. *Usque* is used by Vindob. (Gen. xiii. 10), Mon. (Lev. xii. 4), and once in Ottob.

Racemare (τρυγᾶν) Spec. Lev. xix. 10; Mon. (here and Deut. xxviii. 30), Lugd. and Aug. use *uindemiare*.

rationale, see *manuale*.

recte esse (ὑγιαίνειν) Lugd., Amb. Gen. xxxvii. 14 and xliii. 27; Aug. *saluus esse*.

redimere (λυτροῦν) Mon., Tert. Lev. xix. 20; so Lugd. Lev. and Num. (20/20), and Cyp. and Tyc. regularly; it therefore appears to be early. In other books Lugd. uses *redimere*, *liberare* and *eruere* (with Mon. Deut. ix). Aug. always uses *redimere* and *redemptio* in *Qu.* and *Loc.*, but Amb., Spec., Wir. use *liberare* also. In Num. iii where Lugd. and Amb. have *redemptio*, Mon. has *eliberium* and *eliberatio.*

For ῥύεσθαι, *liberare* is almost always used; so Cyp. 8/8 (altered in Ps. xxi. 21 to *eripere* and *eruere*). *Eruere*, which would seem later, is found in Hil. Gen. xlviii. 16, and once or twice in Lugd. and Amb. Ex.

refrigerare, see *desinere.*

relinquere and derelinquere are usual in all texts for καταλείπειν. For the passive *remanere* is found in Mon. Lev. xix. 6, Mon. and Wir. Ex. xxxix. 13, and three times in Aug.; it may be early as it is found in Cyp. and Tyc., and of its fourteen occurrences in Lugd. half are in Lev., certainly the most 'African' book in that MS. *Superare* is found in Mon. Lev. xiv. 29; it is rare in Lugd. and is not found in Cyp. or Tyc., but is relatively more frequent in Aug.—cf. Ex. xii. 10, where Aug. has it for *derelinqui* of Cyp. and *De Pasc. Comp. Superesse* occurs in Mon. Lev. xiv. 18, twice in Wir. (Lev.), and a few times in Lugd.; Amb. uses it in Lev. x. 16. It is twice used by Cyp. and the change to *reliquum est* in Spec. and the A text in 1 Cor. vii. 29 suggests that it is early.

Superare occurs in Wir., Lugd., Ottob., Aug. Ex. xxvi. 12, and *superesse* in Mon. Ex. xvi. 23 for πλεονάζειν, but *abundare* is usual. For λοιπός, see *residuus.*

remanere, see *relinquere.*

repens, see *serpens.*

reperire Mon. Deut. xxii. 14, Lugd. *inuenire*; elsewhere Mon. has the usual *inuenire*. In Apoc. v. 4 Cyp. has *reperire*, A text *inuenire.*

repositio (ἀποθήκη) Mon., Ottob. Ex. xvi. 32; in Deut. xxviii. 5 Mon., Lugd. have *apotheca.*

reptile, see *serpens.*

residuus (λοιπός) Mon. Ex. xxxix twice, Wir. and Lugd. having *reliquus*. *Residuus* does not occur in Cyp., but it is found in *De Pasc. Comp.* and *De Rebapt.* and is therefore early. It occurs only once in Lugd., and once in Aug. (in each case in Lev.). *Ceter(us)* is more common; it is found half a dozen times in Cyp., and in Lugd. and Aug. is almost as frequent as *reliquus*. Mon. and Spec. have it Deut. viii. 20, Wir. Ex. xxxix. 21.

retro is used in most MSS of Spec. in Gen. xix. 17, *Cod. Sess.* alone having *post te*. Since the A text of Cyp. once in Psalms replaces *retro* by *post te, Cod. Sess.* here may possibly be inferior. A prepositional use of *retro* is found in Aug. only in Ex. xxvi. 22; it is seldom found in Lugd., but appears in Gen. xix. 17, Lev. xvii. 7, Num. xv. 39, Deut. xix. 6 and in Josh. viii. In Lev. xx. 6 Spec. has *sectando* in this sense.

reuelare, see *operire*.

rogare (δεῖσθαι) Lugd., Mon. Num. xii. 11 and 13, and occasionally elsewhere in Lugd. (chiefly in Gen.); in Gen. xix. 18 Aug. has *rogare* in *De Trin.*, but *orare* in *Qu., De Ciu. Dei* and *Con. Max. Rogare* may be early as it is used in Cyp.; the usual rendering is *praecari*, but in Deut. ix. 18 Mon. and Lugd. have *depraecari*.

Rogari may have been the early rendering of παρακαλεῖσθαι, for Cyp. has it in Lk. xvi. 25 and there it is changed to *consolari* in Spec. and the A text. Lugd. has *rogare* in Gen. l. 21, and *conrogari* in Deut. xxxii. 36; the other authorities in both places, as Lugd. elsewhere, have *consolari*.

Sacerdotari (ἱερατεύειν) Mon. Ex. xl. 11 and 13, Wir. *sacerdotare*, Lugd. *sacrificare*. Mon. and Lugd. have *sacrificare* in Deut. x. 6, but this verb only occurs five times in all in Lugd., *sacerdotium agere* being used six times in Ex., and *sacerdotio fungi* three times in Num.; the last is used by Amb. Num. xvi. 10, and regularly by Aug. For the corresponding noun *sacerdotium* is used by Aug., Amb., Luc., Mon., Wir. and by Lugd. in Num.; Lugd. however uses *sacrificium* in Ex.

For λειτουργεῖν, see *ministrare*.

sacrificare and sacrificium, see *sacerdotari* (ἱερατεύειν), *ministrare* (λειτουργεῖν), *immolare* (θύειν); and for *sacrarium* (θυσιαστήριον), see *altare*.

saeculum, see *aeternus* and *natio*.

saeuire and saeuus, see *malignus*.

saluare (σώζειν and διασώζειν) is evidently early; it is found in Cyp. twenty times, and is replaced several times in the A text and Luc. by *saluum facere* and (passive) *saluus esse* or *fieri*, though these forms also occur in Cyp. Both forms are used by Lugd. and Aug. in various books; the close connection between Lugd. and Amb. is shown by their use of *liberationem habere* in Num. x. 9, and *sanare* in Gen. xlvii. 25.

sanare and sanitas, see *curare*.

sancire (ἁγιάζειν) Mon. Ex. xl (three times), a rare if not unique word in Biblical quotations. Wir. has *consecrare* Lev. viii. 9, but Mon. and Wir. both use *sanctificare* several times. *Purificare* in Mon. Ex. xix. 14 and 22 may be influenced by *v.* 10 where it correctly represents ἁγνίζειν.

Ἁγνίζειν is represented by *purificare* (and *purificatio*) in Cyp. (7/7 in Num.) and Aug. (regularly); Cyp. however has *sanctificare* Ex. xix. 10, the only occurrence in Cyp. outside Num. Lugd. in Num. has *purificare, sanctificare, lustrare* (with Mon. ch. xxxi) and *castificare*. Lugd. in other books and Mon. in Lev. xiv use *purificare*.

satiari (ἐμπίμπλεσθαι) occasionally in Mon., Lugd., Luc., Spec., Aug., all in Deut. *Saturari* is used by Wir. Deut. xxxi. 20 and Aug. Deut. xiv. 28; Lugd. has *eritis saturi* Lev. xxvi. 26, but *impleri* and *repleri* are usual in all texts.

scire Mon. almost regularly for εἰδέναι and nine times for γιγνώσκειν
(all however in Ex. ix–xiii, Num., Deut. ix–x); in fact the only
exceptions to the use of scire are nouerunt (ᾔδεισαν—so Lugd.)
Deut. xxxii. 17, noui (ἐπίσταμαι—Lugd. scio) Deut. xxxi. 27,
agnoscar (γνωσθήσομαι—so Lugd.) Num. xii. 6, and agnitum fuerit
(γνωσθῇ—Lugd. cognitum fuerit) Lev. iv. 14. In Cyp. scire is
generally used for εἰδέναι, but not often (only 11/50) for γιγνώσκειν,
the latter being generally represented by cognoscere or other compounds of noscere. Wir. preserves this distinction except in Ex.
xxxiii. 13, where (with Lugd.) scire is used for γιγνώσκειν. A preference for scire certainly seems later (cf. Ezek. xxxvii. 14 Cyp.
cognoscere, Tyc., Spec. scire; Ps. lxxxi. 5 Cyp. non cognoscere,
A text nescire; Gen. xviii. 21 Tert. agnoscere, Aug., Amb., Hil.
scire); it is seen in just those parts of Mon. which are least primitive, and is general in Lugd. except in Lev., where alone the distinction seen in Cyp. is preserved. Innotescere (γιγνώσκεσθαι) is
used by Aug. and Lugd. in Ex. ii. 25 and xxx. 36, but by neither
elsewhere. It is used by Ottob. and Amb. Ex. xxv. 21, and by
Spec. Num. xii. 6. Ignorare is found three times in Aug. Gen.,
a few times in Lugd. (Deut. and Jud.) and in Tyc. Ex. i. 8. It
is used twice in Cyp.
secernere is used by Tert. (Lev. xiv), and once by Lugd. (Num.);
Lugd. also uses secretio in Lev. x. These words are rare and may
be 'African,' for in Prov. viii. 27 secernere of Cyp. is replaced in
Spec. and Hil. by segregare. In Lev. Lugd. uses separare and Aug.
segregare for both ἀφορίζειν and χωρίζειν; elsewhere however they
use both freely. Cyp. also uses both these words as well as
secernere.
sectando, see retro.
sempiternus, see aeternus.
senior, see presbyter.
sensus (διάνοια) regularly in Wir., usually in Mon. and Lugd., and
occasionally in Aug. Cyp. uses sensus once (Jer.) but animus three
times (Is.); the latter may be 'African' as Tyc. also uses it, and
in Lev. xix. 17 Mon., Aug., Spec., Tert. have animus, but Luc.
sensus. Mens seems later, being generally used by Amb. and Jer.;
Aug. uses it frequently, but it does not occur in Lugd. The A text
of Cyp. twice replaces sensus by mens, but in each case the Greek
has νοῦς.
    For καρδία Mon. has sensus four times Ex. ix–xiv; so Lugd.
in various books. Lugd. has praecordia three times for καρδία,
once for διάνοια, and once (Gen. xlix. 6) for ἧπαρ.
sermo (λόγος) Mon. five times, uerbum also being used five times.
Sermo appears frequently in Luc., but there can be no doubt
that it is a primitive mark. It is often found in Tert., Tyc. and
k, and in Cyp. is more frequently used than uerbum, often (as in
Jn. i. 1) where the A text, Nov., Hil. and Spec. have uerbum.
In Lugd. sermo is found only ten times in all (cf. Deut. xxii. 20
Lugd. uerbum, Mon. sermo); Nov. has it only once (Jn. xiv. 23)

and Spec. only once in the Heptateuch. Amb. has *uerbum* Num.
xi. 23, where Mon. and Lugd. both have *sermo*.
    From the first (*e.g.* in Cyp.) ῥῆμα seems to have been more
regularly rendered *uerbum*. In the few places where Cyp. uses
sermo (*e.g.* Eph. vi. 17) Spec. and Luc. show the same tendency
to replace it by *uerbum*. Mon. and Spec. have *uerbum* regularly,
but Lugd. has *sermo* a few times in Gen.
serpens (ἑρπετόν) Mon. regularly; so Cyp. (Hosea iv. 3), but Lugd.
    has *repens* regularly. *Serpens*, *repens* and *reptile* are all used by
    Wir. in Lev. xi, and by Aug. and Amb. in Gen. i–vii; in Lev.
    Aug. has *serpens* and *repens*. Tert. uses *serpens* and *repens*, but
    Ad Nov. has *reptile* in Gen. vi. 7; Spec. has *serpens* in Deut. iv. 18.
seruare, see *obseruare*.
seruire, see *ministrare*.
seruus, see *famulus*.
simila (σεμίδαλις) Mon. and Aug. Lev.; in Num. both have *similago*,
    the word used in Lugd., Wir. and Amb.
singuli (ἕκαστος) *De Pasc. Comp.*, Cyp., Aug. (not Niceta) Ex. xii. 3.
    The word here appears to be 'African,' though it only occurs three
    times altogether in Cyp.; *Ad Nov.* has it Apoc. xx. 13. It is used
    only three times in Aug. and six in Lugd.; it is also found in
    Mon. Ex. xxxix. 2, Wir. Ex. xxxii. 29, Amb. (and Lugd.) Ex.
    xxx. 12. The distributive use of *singuli* (for κατά) is more common.
sinus, see *gremium*.
solarium (δῶμα) Aug. Deut. xxii. 8; Mon., Lugd. *tectum*. Lugd. uses
    solarium in Jud.
solemnis, see *festus*.
solidus (στερεός) Mon. Ex. xxxviii. 14, but *firmus* Deut. xxxii. 13;
    Lugd. agrees in both places and has *solidus* twice again in Num.
    Solidus seems primitive, for Cyp. uses both it and the verb
    solidare, and in Ps. xxxii. 6 the latter is replaced in the A text
    and Spec. by *firmare*. *Solidamentum* (*De Pasc. Comp.* and Nov.)
    also seems the primitive rendering of στερέωμα in Gen. i. 15.
solitudo, see *eremus*.
species, see *facies*.
sponte, see *uoluntarium* and *inuitus*.
statim, see *mox*.
suauiolentia (εὐωδία) regularly in Lugd. Lev., but elsewhere Lugd.
    has *suauitas*, as Wir., Mon., Cyp., Aug., Spec. In Gen. viii. 21
    Nov. and Jer. have *bona fragrantia*, Amb. *suauitas*.
subdole, see *insidiose*.
sumere (λαμβάνειν) Mon. Deut. ix. 21, and three times in Ex. xiii–xviii.
    Sumere is found only four times in Cyp., once in Nov. (Gen.
    xxi. 18) and not at all in Tyc. and is evidently late or European
    (cf. Ex. xii. 5 and 7 Cyp., *De Pasc. Comp. accipere*; Amb., Nic.
    sumere). It is noticeable that all the occurrences in Mon. are in
    the portions where the text is of a later type. Wir., Lugd., Luc.
    often have *sumere* where Mon. has *accipere* (Deut. ix. 17 and often

Ex. xxxii–xl). Tert. shows a decided fondness for *sumere*, *e.g.* in Lev. xix. 17 (Mon., Spec., Aug. *accipere*) and Deut. xxiv. 1 and xxx. 13 (Lugd. *accipere*), but it is not certain that his usage always represents that of the Latin version of his time. *Sumere* is frequent in Amb. and Ottob.; Spec. has it five times, *accipere* nine. Lugd. shows a different usage in different books, *sumere* being used practically always in Ex., frequently in Jud. and the early part of Deut., but seldom in Gen. and never in Lev. and Num. In Aug. *sumere* never occurs in Lev., Num. and Josh., and only seldom in Deut. and Jud.; it is however more common than *accipere* in Ex. (13/24), but most conspicuous in Gen., where it is used ten times in *Qu.* and *Loc.* and ten times in *De Ciu. Dei*, as well as in *De Trin.*, *De Gen. con. Man.* and *De Gen. ad Litt.*

Other renderings of λαμβάνειν occur; *capere* is used a dozen times in Josh. and Jud. in Lugd. and the occurrence of this word in Aug. in the same books is a significant agreement. *Adsumere* is found occasionally (three times in Aug.); Lugd. uses *tollere* four times in Josh., and *obtinere* three times (with Mon.) in Num. xxxii. Cyp. has *prehendere* Num. xx. 25 (Lugd. *accipere*), and this word and its compounds are used for compounds of λαμβάνειν in Cyp. and Lugd. Gen. xlviii. 17, in Spec. Ex. xxii. 4, three or four times in Mon., and a dozen times in Lugd.

summum, see *cacumen*.
superare and **superesse,** see *relinquere*.
synagoga, see *colligere*.

Tegere and derivatives, see *operire* and *solarium*.
termini (ὅρια) Mon. and Lugd. Num. xxxii–xxxiv several times, but in Ex. xxxiv. 8 both have *fines*. Only in Num. is *termini* frequently used by Lugd., and that is the only book in which Aug. uses it at all. It is found in Ruf. and Iren. Deut. xxxii. 8, and in Amb. Num. xx. 17 and Deut. xix. 14. *Fines* is usual in all three MSS, and occurs also in Amb. (Deut. xxxiii. 13), Spec., Hil., Nov. (Deut. xxxii. 8), and in *XLII Mans.* in Num. Cyp. uses *termini* in Psalms, and though this is a rendering of πέρατα, the change to *fines* in the A text in one place may indicate that *termini* is the more primitive.
thyisca, see *patera*.
tollere (αἴρειν) Mon., Wir., Ottob., Lugd. and Aug. *Portare* does not occur in Mon., Wir. or Ottob., but is found occasionally in Aug. and Amb. and ten times in Lugd. (seven in Josh.). Cyp. uses both words as well as *auferre*, so that none of them seems distinctively late, especially as the changes made in Cyprian's text by Spec., Luc. and the A text are not all in the same direction; *e.g.* if *portare* is substituted for *tollere* by Spec., Luc. and A text in Ps. cxxv. 6, Cyprian's *portare* is replaced by *tollere* in Spec. in 1 Cor. vi. 20.

See also *demptio*, *promouere* and *sumere*.

totus (πᾶς) twenty-six times in Mon., nearly half of these being in Ex. ix–xiii and Num., where primitive marks are rare in Mon.; it occurs ten times in Wir., but twice in Lev. xi Wir. and Lugd. have *omnis* where Mon. has *totus*. *Totus* is common in *k*, and though in Cyp. it is comparatively rare, his *totus* is replaced by *omnis* once in Nov., and in Josh. ii. 18 by Lugd., so that the word is probably correctly regarded as 'African.' Lugd. has *totus* about twenty times; Aug. has it only once in *Qu.* (Num.), but a few times in *De Ciu. Dei* (Gen.). *Uniuersus* occurs neither in Mon. nor Wir., but is common in Luc. and in Lugd. Josh., and occurs three times in Aug. It is generally considered European (cf. Josh. i. 8 Cyp. *omnis*; Lugd., Luc. *uniuersus*) but it is found three times in Cyp. Amb. does not use *uniuersus*, but shows a clear tendency to use *totus*, especially in Gen.; he has *totus*, *e.g.* in Gen. xiii. 9 and 10 (Vindob. *omnis*), and in Ex. xii. 6 (Cyp., *De Pasc. Comp.*, Tert. *omnis*). Ottob. uses *totus* four times, *uniuersus* twice; Tert. has *totus* in Lev. xiii, but *uniuersus* in Gen. ix. 3.

Mon. has *cunctus* Deut. xxviii. 10, but this is not likely to be a genuine Old Latin reading.

Ὅλος is more generally rendered *totus*, but in Ex. xxv. 36 Wir. has *integer*. Aug. and Lugd. use *integer* for ὁλόκληρος.

trahere (ῥεῖν) Mon. Ex. xxxiii. 3, Lev. xv. 3, Lugd. and Aug. having the usual *fluere*. Tert. and Jer. sometimes have *manare* in such places as Ex. iii. 8.

triticum is used in Mon., Wir., Spec. (twice in each) for πυρός or σῖτος; so Cyp. and Aug. generally. Amb. however uses *frumentum* (4/4); and, except in Deut., Lugd. seems to prefer *frumentum*.

turabulum and turibulum, see *patera* and *foculus*.

Vadere, see *ambulare*.
ualde, see *nimis*.
ualere and ualidus, see *fortitudo* and *uirtus*.
uarius (λεπρός) Mon. Num. v. 2, doubtless primitive, being used in *Ad Nov.*; Lugd. and Aug. always use *leprosus*, which Mon. has in Num. xii. 10. For the noun Mon. has *uarietas* in Lev. xiii and xiv; Lugd. and Aug. use *lepra*, Tert. both words. In Lev. xiv. 57 Mon. uses *uitiligo*.
uatillum, see *foculus*.
uehementer, see *nimis*.
uelamen, see *uelum*.
uelociter and uelocius, see *celeriter*.
uelum (καταπέτασμα) Mon. Ex. and Lev. (six times), but *uelamen* in Num. Lugd. uses *uelamen* in Ex., Lev., Num., but in each book *uelum* more frequently (13/18 in all); as a rule Aug. has *uelamen*, Wir. *uelum*. Cyp. (2 Cor.) uses *uelamentum*, which is found once in Lugd. Lev.

For δέρρις Wir. has *uelum* Ex. xxvi; so Lugd. and Aug. in Ex.,

but both have *pellis* in Jud.; in Num. iv. 25 Lugd. has *sagestrum*.
For κάλυμμα, see *operire*.

uerbum, see *sermo*.

uertex, see *cacumen*.

uestimentum, see *uestis*.

uestire, see *induere*.

uestis (ἱμάτιον) Mon., Lugd. in Num. occasionally, and once each in
Aug., Amb. and Spec. It occurs four times in Cyp., but three of
these are in Apoc. *Pallium* is used by Aug. and Tert. once each
in Deut., and in Lev. Lugd. uses *uestitum* and *tunica*, but *uestimentum* is usual in all texts. *Vestis* however is the usual rendering
of ἱματισμός in Cyp. (3/3), Mon., Aug., Amb. and Lugd.

uexare, see *nocere*.

uia, see *iter*.

uictima and uictimare, see *interficere*.

uideri, see *apparere*.

uindicta and uindicare, see *defendere*.

uirtus (δύναμις) almost regularly. *Vires* is found in Spec. Deut. xvi. 17,
and in Tert., Hil. Deut. vi. 5; *potentia* and *fortitudo* occur only
rarely. *Potens* however is almost always used for the corresponding adjectives, *fortis* occurring a few times in Aug. and Lugd.
Josh. and Jud. In Jud. vi. 34 Aug. has *confortare* (ἐνδυναμοῦν).

For κράτος *potentia* is generally used; κραταιός is rendered
potens in Mon. Ex. xiii, and by Lugd. in Ex., but *ualidus* is more
usual both in Aug. and Lugd.

uisitatio (ἐπίσκεψις and ἐπισκοπή) Mon., Wir., Aug., Lugd. regularly
in Ex.; so *uisitare* Mon., Lugd. Ex. xxxix. 2, Hil. Gen. xxi. 1
and Cyp. (3/3). In Num. iii and iv Mon. and Lugd. have *consideratio* and *considerare*, or *numerus* and *numerare*. Aug. has *re-
cognitio* in Num.; Lugd. has *deliberare* in Lev. xiii. 36, and *epi-
scopia* (and *episcopus*) in Num. iv. 16.

uitiligo, see *uarius*.

uitium, see *immaculatus*.

ultra, see *adhuc*.

umbo, see *umerale*.

umerale (ἐπωμίς) Mon., Aug. Ex. xxxvi. Ottob. and Wir. have *umbo*,
which Lugd. uses in Ex., though it has *fibula* in Lev. viii. *Super-
humerale* is used by Jer., and by Aug. in Jud.

unctio and unguere, see *lenire*.

uniuersus, see *totus*.

uociferari Mon. Deut. xxii. 27, Cyp. Ex. xxii. 23, and Lugd. Num.
xiv. 1; but *clamare* and its compounds generally represent both
βοᾶν and κράζειν. For καλεῖν we have *clamare* Mon. Ex. xix. 3
and Aug. Ex. iii. 4, *inuitare* Wir., Lugd., Spec. Ex. xxxiv. 15 and
Tert. Num. xxv. 2, but generally *uocare*.

uolatile, see *uolucer*.

uolens, see *uoluntarium*.

uolucer (πετεινόν) Mon. five times in Lev. xi, Wir. Lugd., Aug. all using *uolatile*; Aug. and Wir. use *uolucer* in Lev. xx, but Lugd. never has it. *Volatile* is used by *k* in Matt. xiii, where *e* has *uolucer*, whence Sanday concluded that *uolatile* was 'African,' but Cyprian's usage suggests the opposite conclusion. He uses *uolatile* only in Matt. vi. 26, but *uolucer* several times, and for it the A text has substituted *uolatile* in Hosea iv. 3. In the early chapters of Gen. Aug., Amb., Tert. and *Ad Nov.* all use *uolatile*; Mon. in Deut. xxviii. 26 has *alites*.

uoluntarium (ἑκούσιον) Wir., Aug. Lev. vii. 6; Lugd. *uolens*. In Num. xxix. 39 Mon. and (practically) Lugd. have *quae sponte facitis*. In Ex. xxxvi. 2 Aug. has *sponte*, Lugd. *uolumptariae* (ἑκουσίως).

uotum (εὐχή) Wir. (3/3); Cyp. always uses *uotum* and *uouere*, and so Aug. except where they are evidently unsuitable; Lugd. has *oratio* and *orare* more frequently, sometimes (as in Num. vi. 20, xxix. 39 and xxx. 3) conflating or confusing the two. In Deut. ix Mon. and Lugd. have *praecari* and *depraecari*. For the compounds with πρός *oratio* and *orare* are more frequent from Cyp. onwards.

usquedum, see *quoadusque*.

uulgus, see *plenitudo*.

uultus, see *facies*.

Zelari and aemulari are both used by Cyp., but we twice find Cyp. *zelus*, Spec. *aemulatio*, which shows the tendency of later times. *Zelari* however remains usual in all texts.

INDEX OF PRINCIPAL BIBLICAL TEXTS

INDEX OF SUBJECTS

Vulgate influence in MSS of the Old Latin, 62, 63–64, 174–175, 176, 177, 178

Würzburg Palimpsest:
    Intermediate position of vocabulary between Mon. and Lugd., 35–36
    Mixed character of vocabulary, 36–38
    Differences from other MSS in Greek text implied, 95–97, 100–102
    Primitive errors, 161–163; cf. 165–166
    Greek words, 167–168
    Hexaplaric element in its text, 124–125; cf. 130
    General character of its version, 176–177
    Relation of its version to Cyprian, 41–43, 45
        to Lucifer, 47–49, 51; cf. 136
        to Ambrose, 52–53
        to Speculum, 59; cf. 176
        to Augustine, 65
        to Ottobonian MS, 71

For EU product safety concerns, contact us at Calle de José Abascal, 56–1°, 28003 Madrid, Spain or eugpsr@cambridge.org.

www.ingramcontent.com/pod-product-compliance
Ingram Content Group UK Ltd.
Pitfield, Milton Keynes, MK11 3LW, UK
UKHW040616240426
470322UK00010B/158